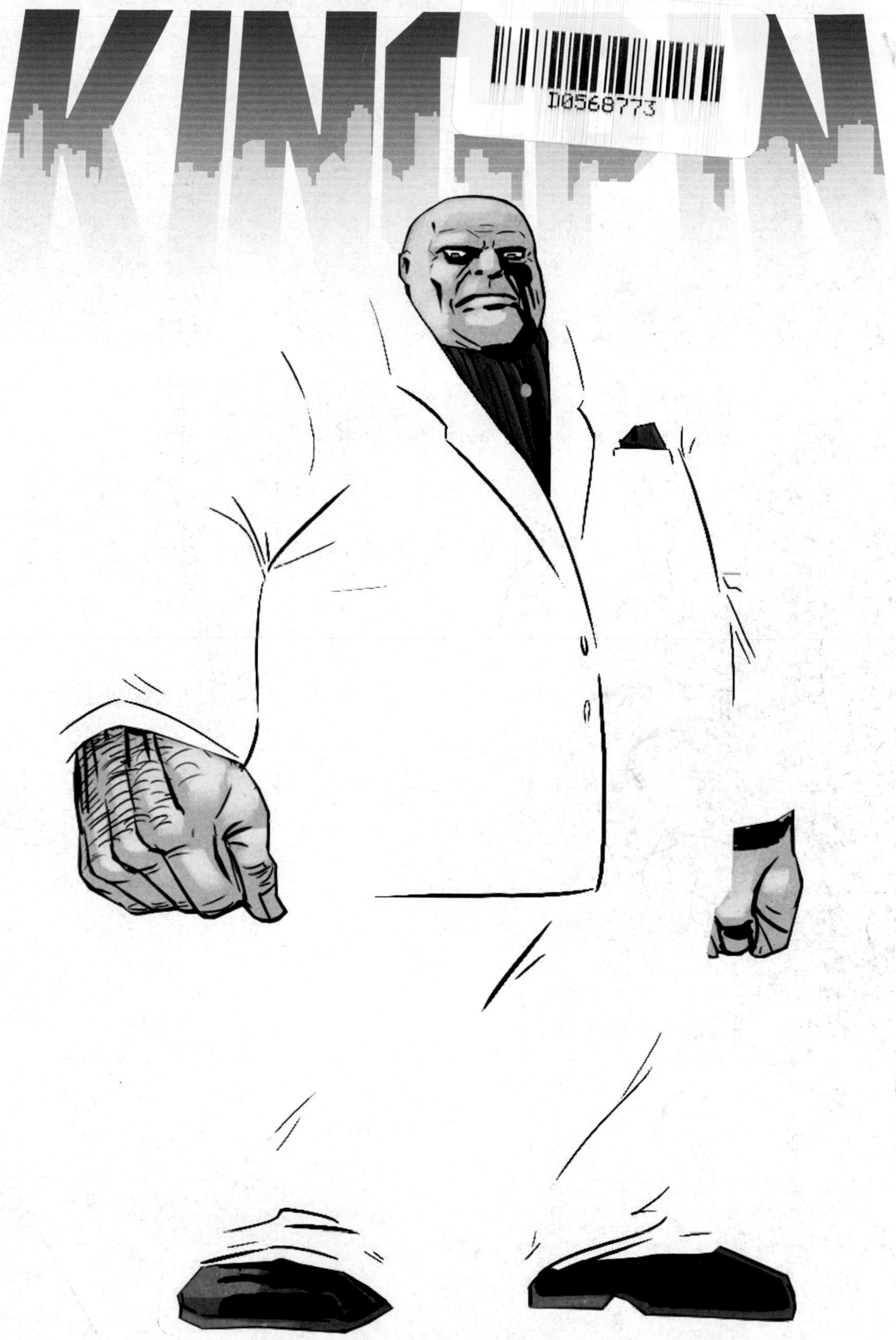

In his time, **WILSON FISK** has done deplorable things. He has blackmailed rivals. He has twisted the law. He has killed. He allowed no one, not even his hated foes Daredevil and Spider-Man, to stand in his way. For years, he was the head of organized crime in his hometown of New York City, but he has new plans. He may be down, but never count him out. He is the...

KINGPIN
BORN AGAINST

MATTHEW ROSENBERG
WRITER

ISSUES #1-3 & #5

BEN TORRES
ARTIST

MARC LAMING
LAYOUT ARTIST, #3

ISSUE #4

MIGUEL SEPULVEDA
PENCILER

WALDEN WONG WITH DON HO
INKERS

JORDAN BOYD
COLOR ARTIST

VC's TRAVIS LANHAM
LETTERER

JEFF DEKAL
COVER ART

MARK BASSO
EDITOR

MARK PANICCIA
SENIOR EDITOR

COLLECTION EDITOR JENNIFER GRÜNWALD
ASSISTANT EDITOR CAITLIN O'CONNELL
ASSOCIATE MANAGING EDITOR KATERI WOODY
EDITOR, SPECIAL PROJECTS MARK D. BEAZLEY
VP PRODUCTION & SPECIAL PROJECTS JEFF YOUNGQUIST
SVP PRINT, SALES & MARKETING DAVID GABRIEL
BOOK DESIGNER ADAM DEL RE

EDITOR IN CHIEF AXEL ALONSO
CHIEF CREATIVE OFFICER JOE QUESADA
PRESIDENT DAN BUCKLEY
EXECUTIVE PRODUCER ALAN FINE

KINGPIN: BORN AGAINST. Contains material originally published in magazine form as KINGPIN #1-5. First printing 2017. ISBN# 978-1-302-90570-5. Published by MARVEL WORLDWIDE, INC., a subsidiary of MARVEL ENTERTAINMENT, LLC. OFFICE OF PUBLICATION: 135 West 50th Street, New York, NY 10020. Copyright © 2017 MARVEL No similarity between any of the names, characters, persons, and/or institutions in this magazine with those of any living or dead person or institution is intended, and any such similarity which may exist is purely coincidental. **Printed in the U.S.A.** DAN BUCKLEY, President, Marvel Entertainment; JOE QUESADA, Chief Creative Officer; TOM BREVOORT, SVP of Publishing; DAVID BOGART, SVP of Business Affairs & Operations, Publishing & Partnership; C.B. CEBULSKI, VP of Brand Management & Development, Asia; DAVID GABRIEL, SVP of Sales & Marketing, Publishing; JEFF YOUNGQUIST, VP of Production & Special Projects; DAN CARR, Executive Director of Publishing Technology; ALEX MORALES, Director of Publishing Operations; SUSAN CRESPI, Production Manager; STAN LEE, Chairman Emeritus. For information regarding advertising in Marvel Comics or on Marvel.com, please contact Vit DeBellis, Integrated Sales Manager, at vdebellis@marvel.com. For Marvel subscription inquiries, please call 888-511-5480. **Manufactured between 7/21/2017 and 8/21/2017 by QUAD/GRAPHICS WASECA, WASECA, MN, USA.**

10 9 8 7 6 5 4 3 2 1

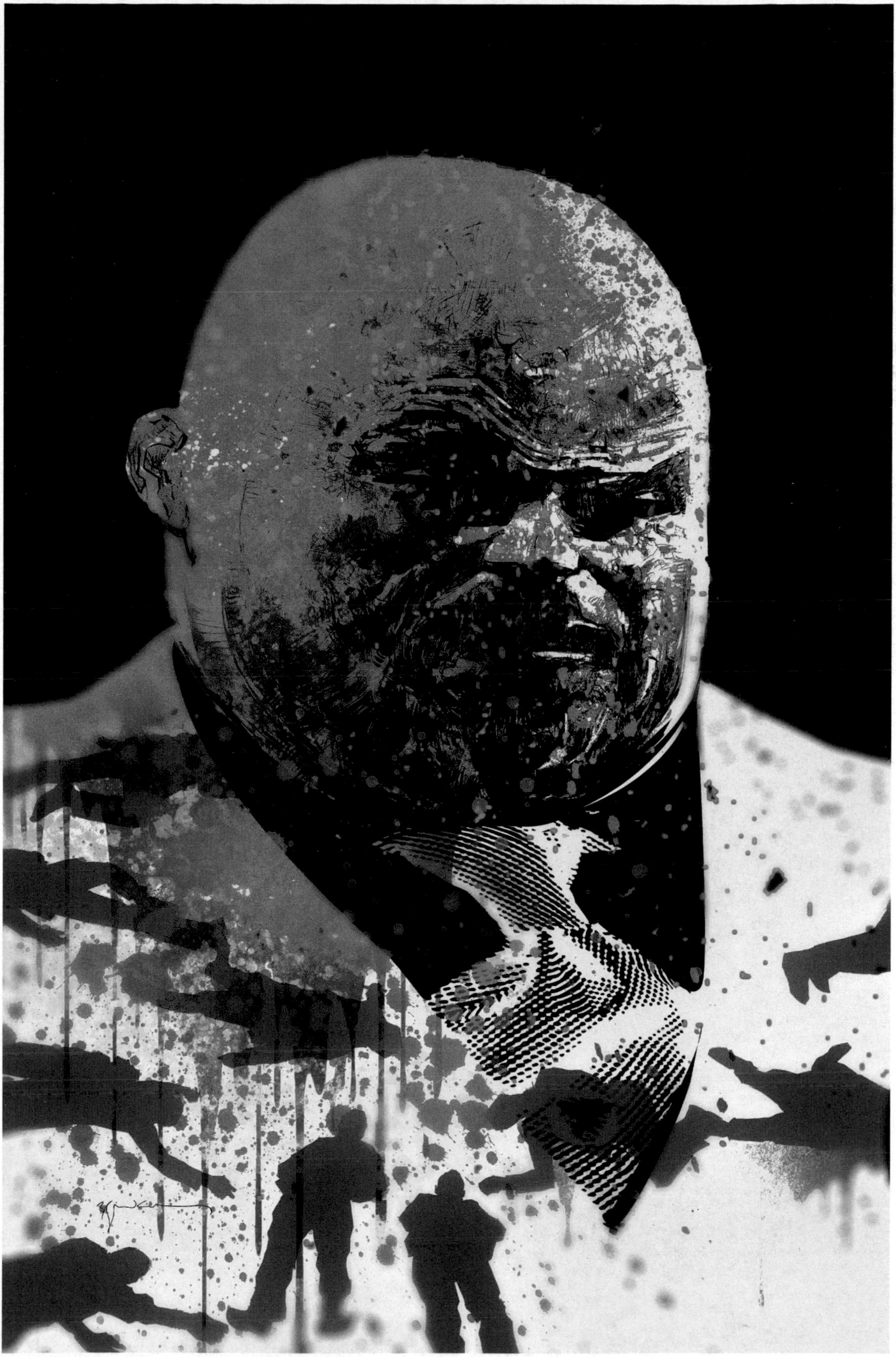

BILL SIENKIEWICZ
1 VARIANT

ONE

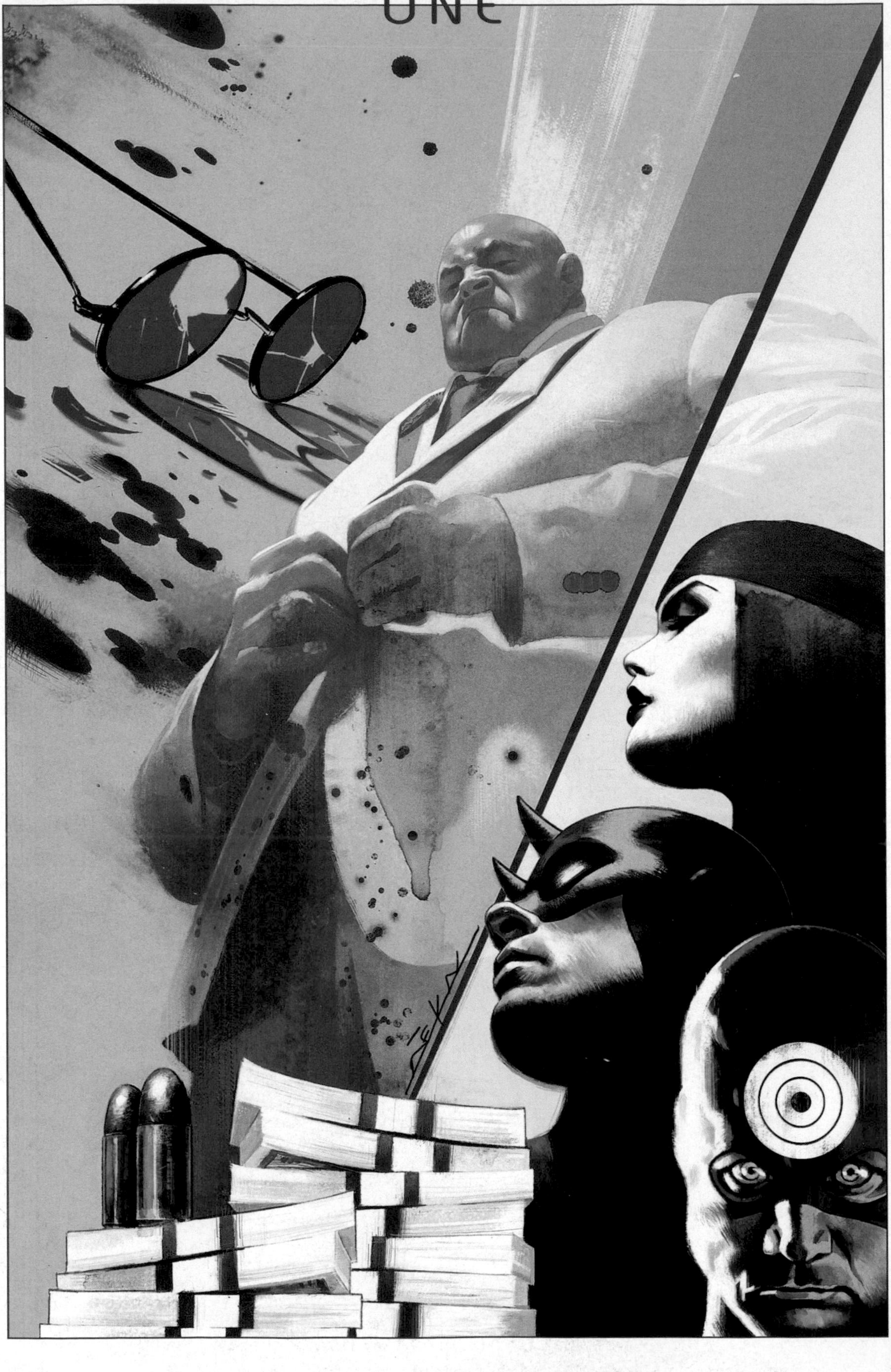

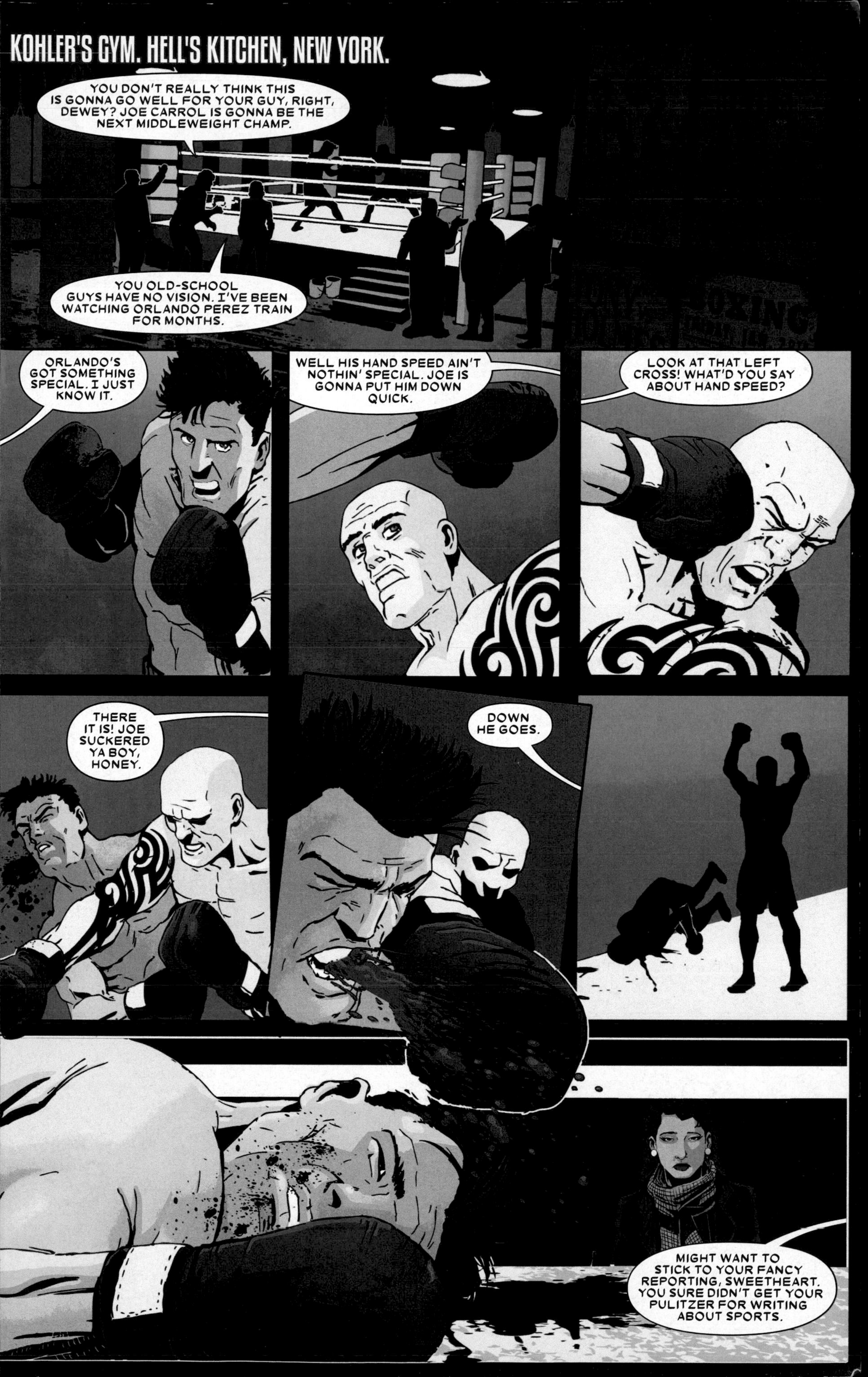
KOHLER'S GYM. HELL'S KITCHEN, NEW YORK.
YOU DON'T REALLY THINK THIS IS GONNA GO WELL FOR YOUR GUY, RIGHT, DEWEY? JOE CARROL IS GONNA BE THE NEXT MIDDLEWEIGHT CHAMP.
YOU OLD-SCHOOL GUYS HAVE NO VISION. I'VE BEEN WATCHING ORLANDO PEREZ TRAIN FOR MONTHS.
ORLANDO'S GOT SOMETHING SPECIAL. I JUST KNOW IT.
WELL HIS HAND SPEED AIN'T NOTHIN' SPECIAL. JOE IS GONNA PUT HIM DOWN QUICK.
LOOK AT THAT LEFT CROSS! WHAT'D YOU SAY ABOUT HAND SPEED?
THERE IT IS! JOE SUCKERED YA BOY, HONEY.
DOWN HE GOES.
MIGHT WANT TO STICK TO YOUR FANCY REPORTING, SWEETHEART. YOU SURE DIDN'T GET YOUR PULITZER FOR WRITING ABOUT SPORTS.

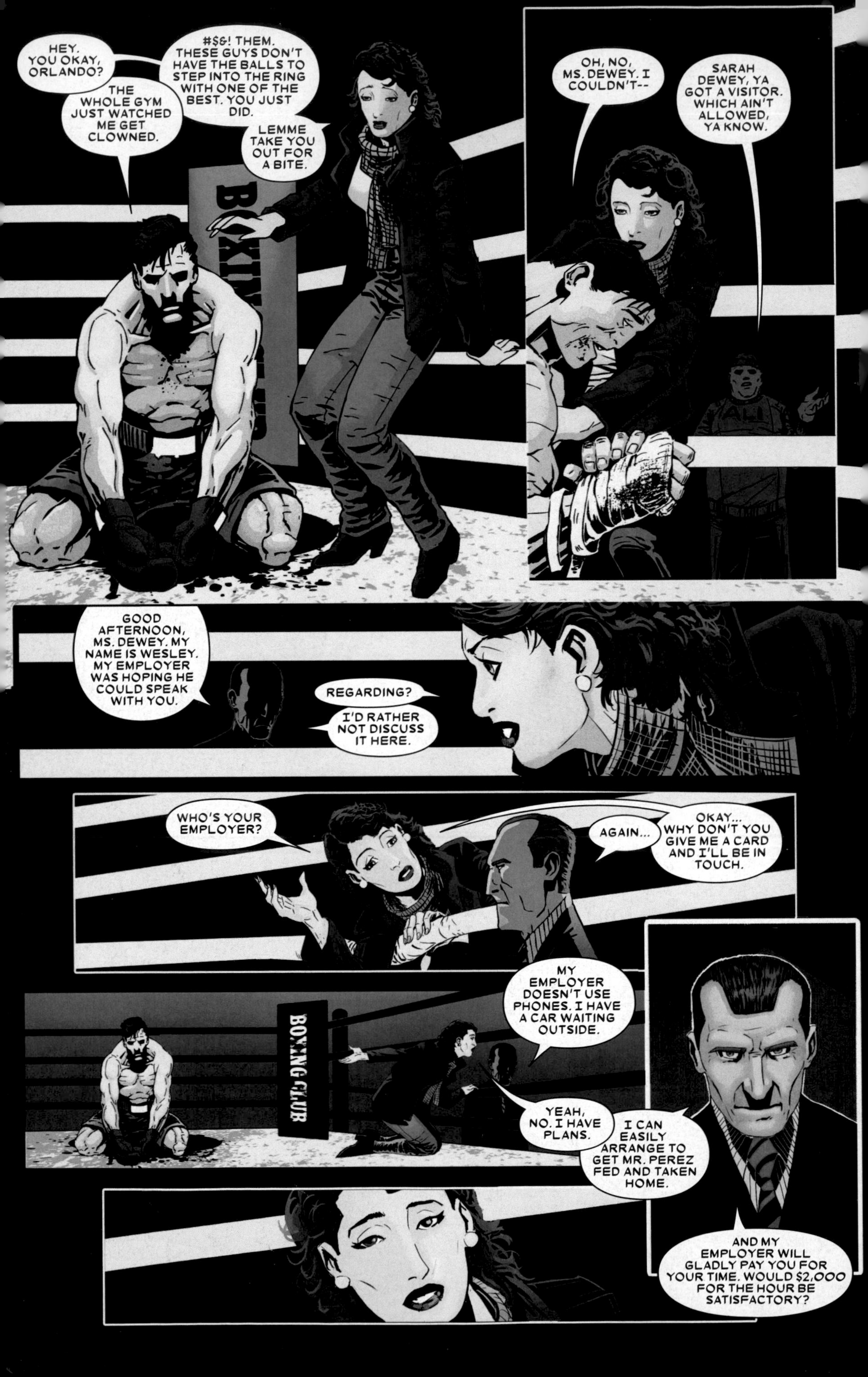
HEY. YOU OKAY, ORLANDO?
THE WHOLE GYM JUST WATCHED ME GET CLOWNED.
#$&! THEM. THESE GUYS DON'T HAVE THE BALLS TO STEP INTO THE RING WITH ONE OF THE BEST. YOU JUST DID.
LEMME TAKE YOU OUT FOR A BITE.
BOXING CLUB
OH, NO, MS. DEWEY. I COULDN'T--
SARAH DEWEY, YA GOT A VISITOR. WHICH AIN'T ALLOWED, YA KNOW.
ALI
GOOD AFTERNOON, MS. DEWEY. MY NAME IS WESLEY. MY EMPLOYER WAS HOPING HE COULD SPEAK WITH YOU.
REGARDING?
I'D RATHER NOT DISCUSS IT HERE.
WHO'S YOUR EMPLOYER?
AGAIN...
OKAY... WHY DON'T YOU GIVE ME A CARD AND I'LL BE IN TOUCH.
MY EMPLOYER DOESN'T USE PHONES. I HAVE A CAR WAITING OUTSIDE.
BOXING CLUB
YEAH, NO. I HAVE PLANS.
I CAN EASILY ARRANGE TO GET MR. PEREZ FED AND TAKEN HOME.
AND MY EMPLOYER WILL GLADLY PAY YOU FOR YOUR TIME. WOULD $2,000 FOR THE HOUR BE SATISFACTORY?

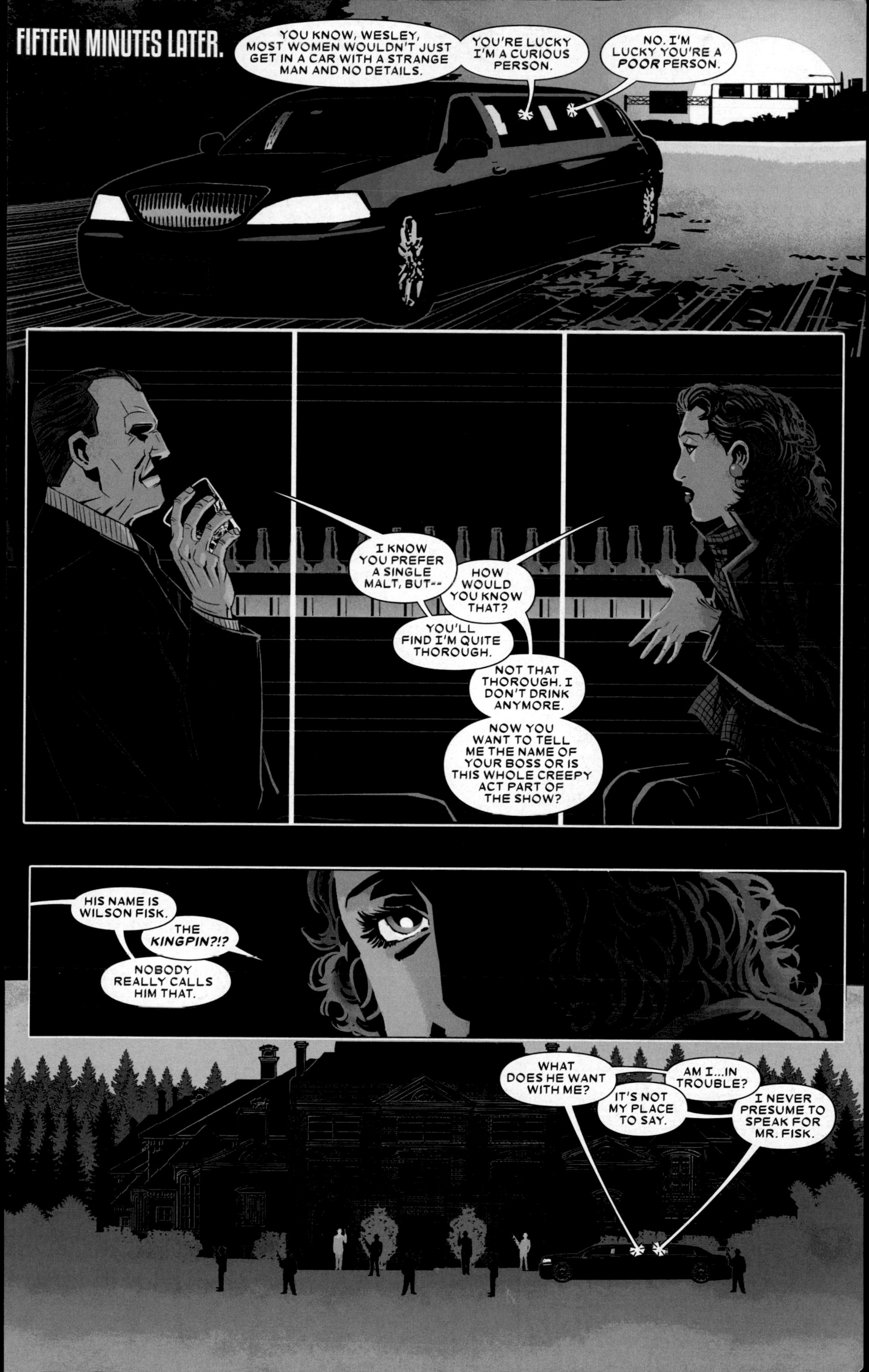
FIFTEEN MINUTES LATER.
YOU KNOW, WESLEY, MOST WOMEN WOULDN'T JUST GET IN A CAR WITH A STRANGE MAN AND NO DETAILS.
YOU'RE LUCKY I'M A CURIOUS PERSON.
NO. I'M LUCKY YOU'RE A POOR PERSON.
I KNOW YOU PREFER A SINGLE MALT, BUT--
HOW WOULD YOU KNOW THAT?
YOU'LL FIND I'M QUITE THOROUGH.
NOT THAT THOROUGH. I DON'T DRINK ANYMORE.
NOW YOU WANT TO TELL ME THE NAME OF YOUR BOSS OR IS THIS WHOLE CREEPY ACT PART OF THE SHOW?
HIS NAME IS WILSON FISK.
THE KINGPIN?!?
NOBODY REALLY CALLS HIM THAT.
WHAT DOES HE WANT WITH ME?
AM I...IN TROUBLE?
IT'S NOT MY PLACE TO SAY.
I NEVER PRESUME TO SPEAK FOR MR. FISK.

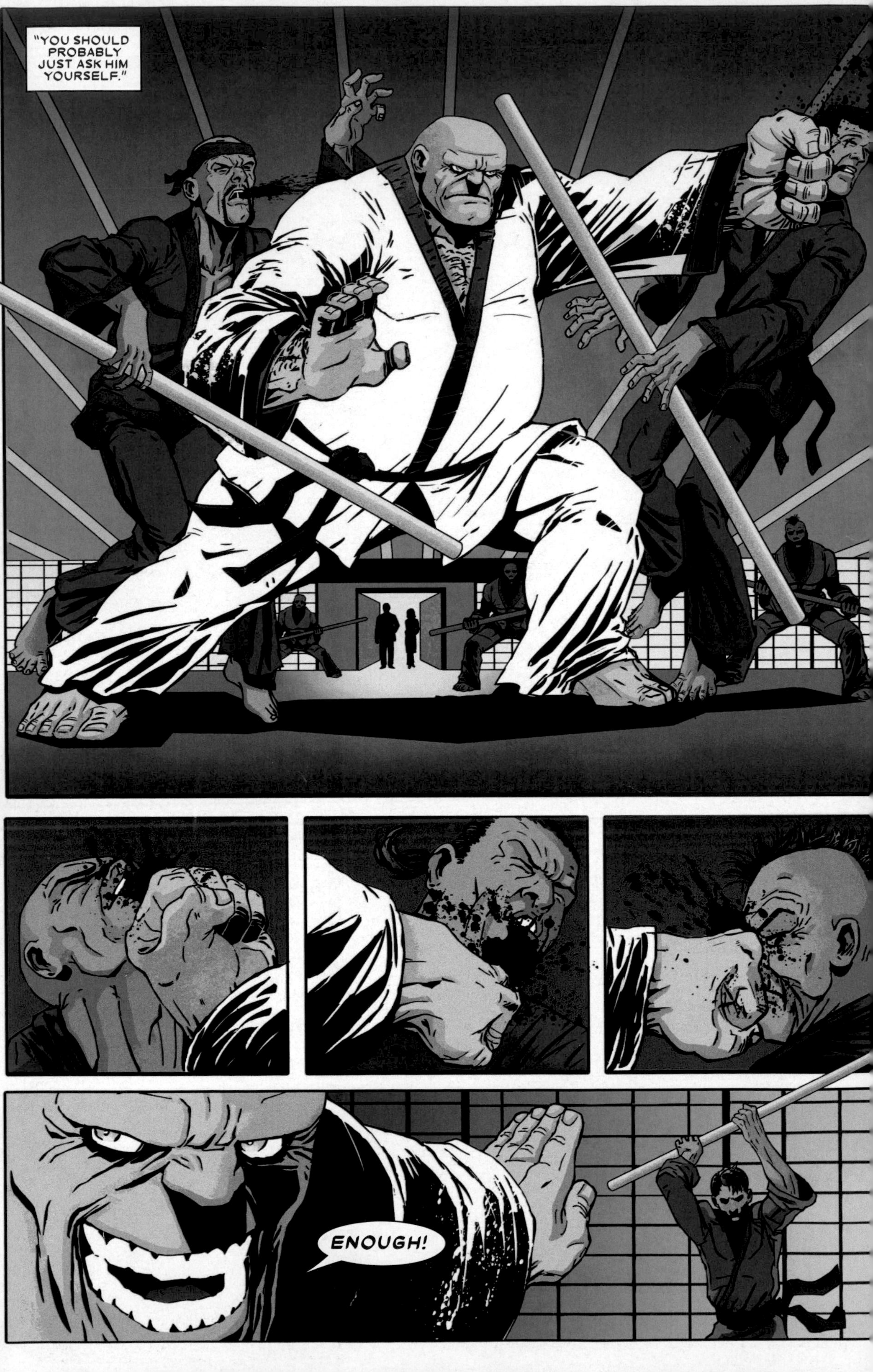
"YOU SHOULD PROBABLY JUST ASK HIM YOURSELF."
ENOUGH!

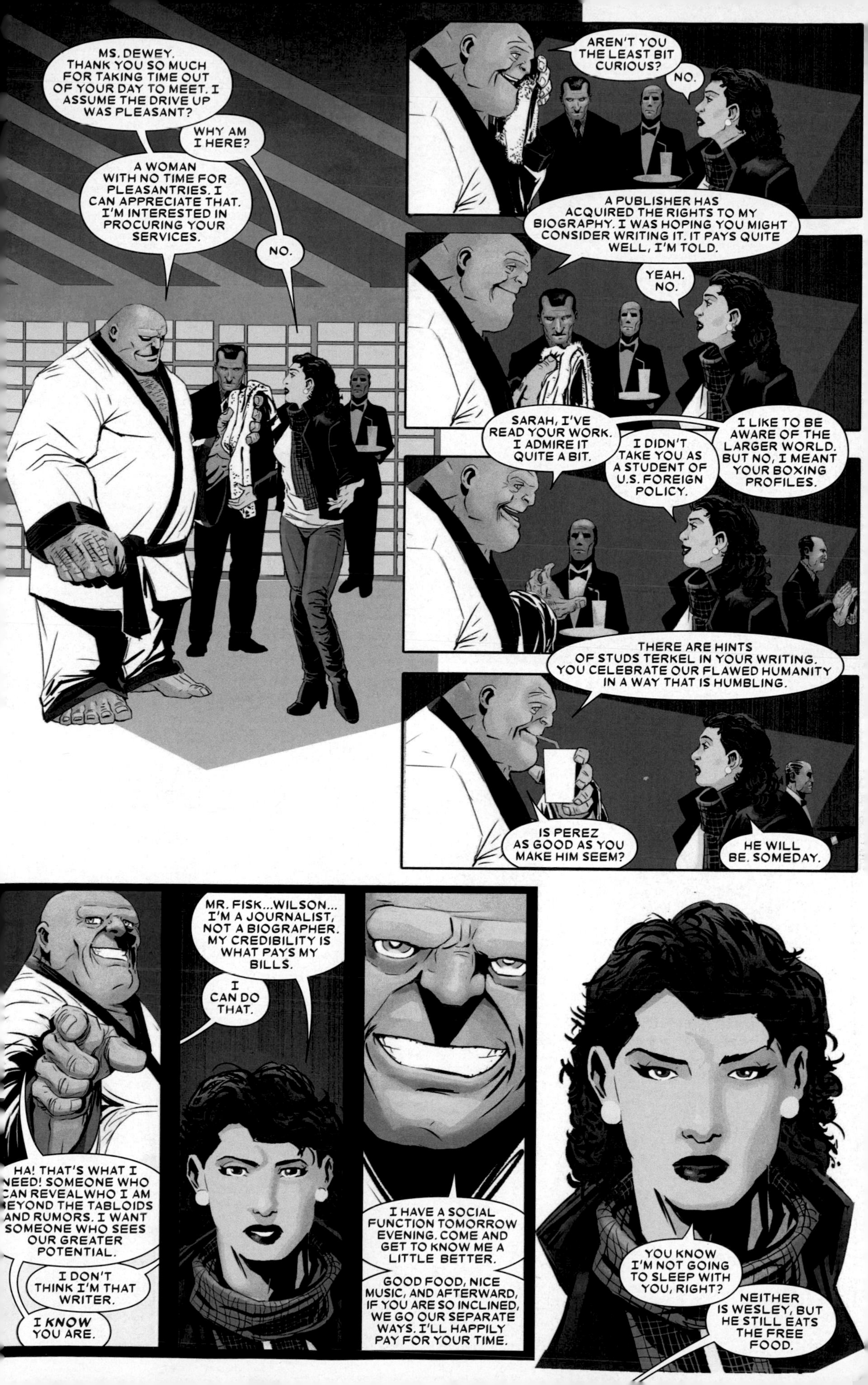
MS. DEWEY. THANK YOU SO MUCH FOR TAKING TIME OUT OF YOUR DAY TO MEET. I ASSUME THE DRIVE UP WAS PLEASANT?
WHY AM I HERE?
A WOMAN WITH NO TIME FOR PLEASANTRIES. I CAN APPRECIATE THAT. I'M INTERESTED IN PROCURING YOUR SERVICES.
NO.
AREN'T YOU THE LEAST BIT CURIOUS?
NO.
A PUBLISHER HAS ACQUIRED THE RIGHTS TO MY BIOGRAPHY. I WAS HOPING YOU MIGHT CONSIDER WRITING IT. IT PAYS QUITE WELL, I'M TOLD.
YEAH. NO.
SARAH, I'VE READ YOUR WORK. I ADMIRE IT QUITE A BIT.
I DIDN'T TAKE YOU AS A STUDENT OF U.S. FOREIGN POLICY.
I LIKE TO BE AWARE OF THE LARGER WORLD. BUT NO, I MEANT YOUR BOXING PROFILES.
THERE ARE HINTS OF STUDS TERKEL IN YOUR WRITING. YOU CELEBRATE OUR FLAWED HUMANITY IN A WAY THAT IS HUMBLING.
IS PEREZ AS GOOD AS YOU MAKE HIM SEEM?
HE WILL BE. SOMEDAY.
HA! THAT'S WHAT I NEED! SOMEONE WHO CAN REVEAL WHO I AM BEYOND THE TABLOIDS AND RUMORS. I WANT SOMEONE WHO SEES OUR GREATER POTENTIAL.
I DON'T THINK I'M THAT WRITER.
I *KNOW* YOU ARE.
MR. FISK...WILSON... I'M A JOURNALIST, NOT A BIOGRAPHER. MY CREDIBILITY IS WHAT PAYS MY BILLS.
I CAN DO THAT.
I HAVE A SOCIAL FUNCTION TOMORROW EVENING. COME AND GET TO KNOW ME A LITTLE BETTER.
GOOD FOOD, NICE MUSIC, AND AFTERWARD, IF YOU ARE SO INCLINED, WE GO OUR SEPARATE WAYS. I'LL HAPPILY PAY FOR YOUR TIME.
YOU KNOW I'M NOT GOING TO SLEEP WITH YOU, RIGHT?
NEITHER IS WESLEY, BUT HE STILL EATS THE FREE FOOD.

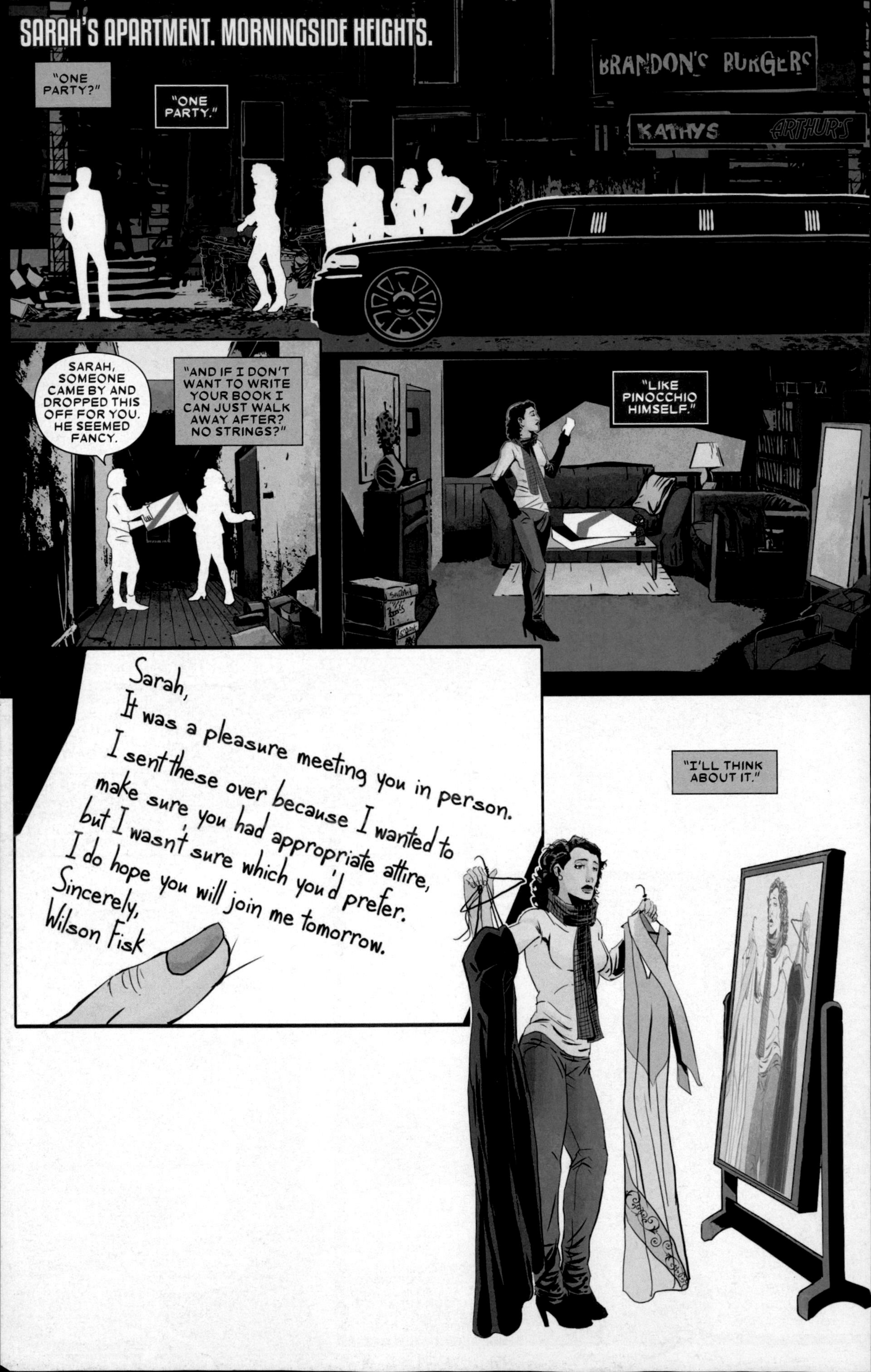
SARAH'S APARTMENT. MORNINGSIDE HEIGHTS.
BRANDON'S BURGERS
KATHYS
ARTHUR'S
"ONE PARTY?"
"ONE PARTY."
SARAH, SOMEONE CAME BY AND DROPPED THIS OFF FOR YOU. HE SEEMED FANCY.
"AND IF I DON'T WANT TO WRITE YOUR BOOK I CAN JUST WALK AWAY AFTER? NO STRINGS?"
"LIKE PINOCCHIO HIMSELF."
Sarah,
It was a pleasure meeting you in person.
I sent these over because I wanted to make sure you had appropriate attire, but I wasn't sure which you'd prefer.
I do hope you will join me tomorrow.
Sincerely,
Wilson Fisk
"I'LL THINK ABOUT IT."

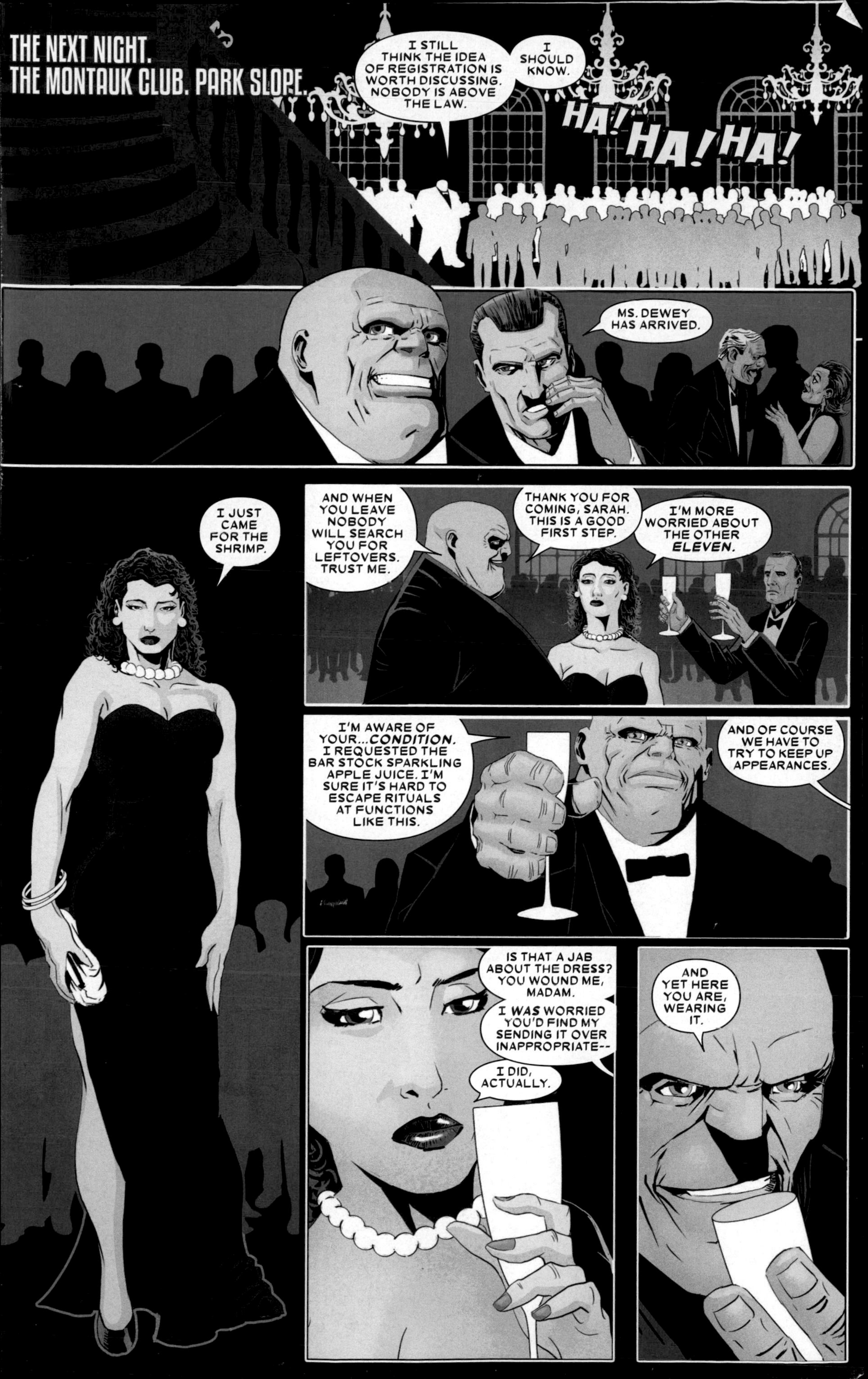
THE NEXT NIGHT. THE MONTAUK CLUB. PARK SLOPE.
I STILL THINK THE IDEA OF REGISTRATION IS WORTH DISCUSSING. NOBODY IS ABOVE THE LAW.
I SHOULD KNOW.
HA! HA! HA!
MS. DEWEY HAS ARRIVED.
I JUST CAME FOR THE SHRIMP.
AND WHEN YOU LEAVE NOBODY WILL SEARCH YOU FOR LEFTOVERS. TRUST ME.
THANK YOU FOR COMING, SARAH. THIS IS A GOOD FIRST STEP.
I'M MORE WORRIED ABOUT THE OTHER ELEVEN.
I'M AWARE OF YOUR...CONDITION. I REQUESTED THE BAR STOCK SPARKLING APPLE JUICE. I'M SURE IT'S HARD TO ESCAPE RITUALS AT FUNCTIONS LIKE THIS.
AND OF COURSE WE HAVE TO TRY TO KEEP UP APPEARANCES.
IS THAT A JAB ABOUT THE DRESS? YOU WOUND ME, MADAM.
I WAS WORRIED YOU'D FIND MY SENDING IT OVER INAPPROPRIATE--
I DID, ACTUALLY.
AND YET HERE YOU ARE, WEARING IT.

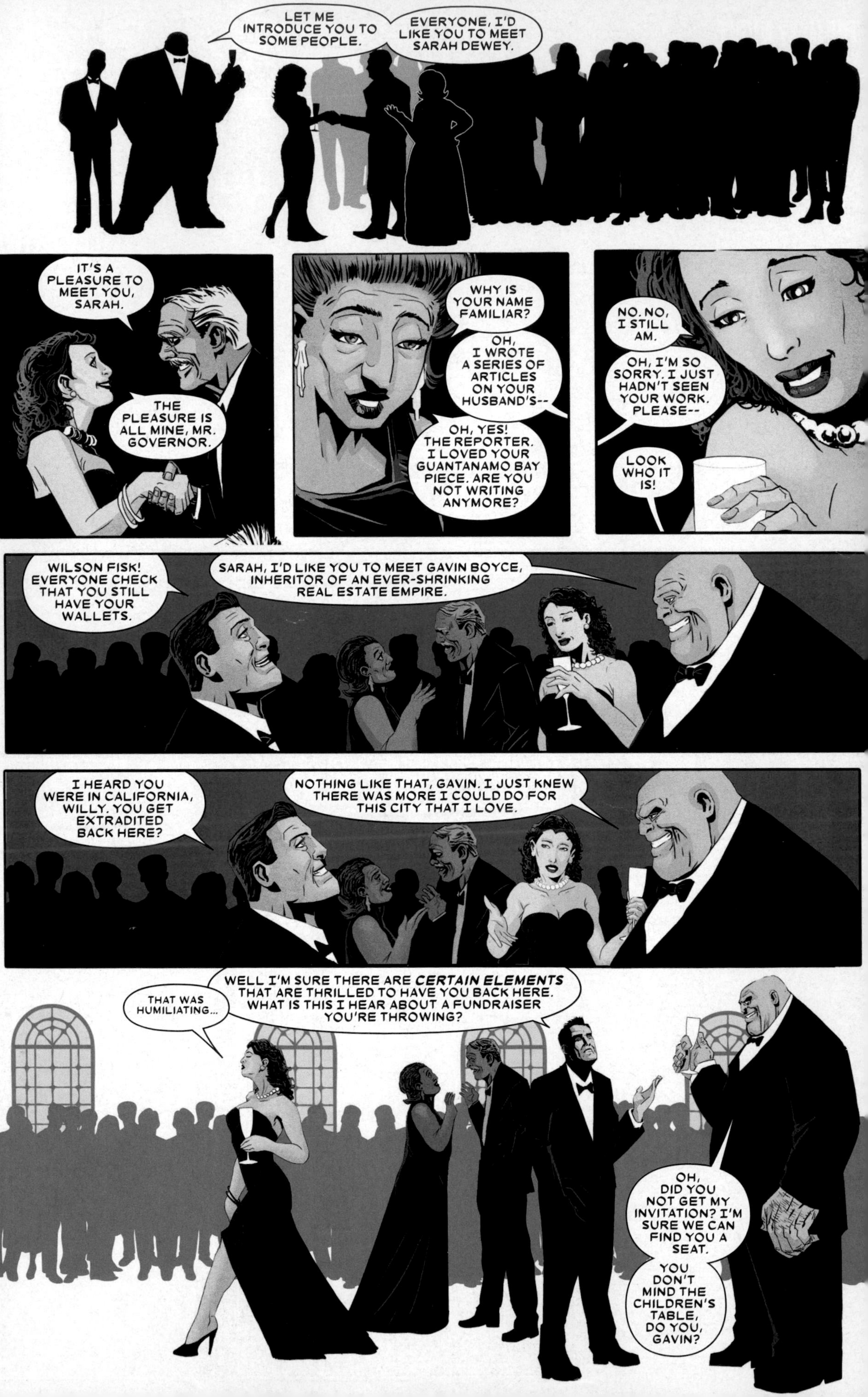
LET ME INTRODUCE YOU TO SOME PEOPLE.
EVERYONE, I'D LIKE YOU TO MEET SARAH DEWEY.
IT'S A PLEASURE TO MEET YOU, SARAH.
THE PLEASURE IS ALL MINE, MR. GOVERNOR.
WHY IS YOUR NAME FAMILIAR?
OH, I WROTE A SERIES OF ARTICLES ON YOUR HUSBAND'S--
OH, YES! THE REPORTER. I LOVED YOUR GUANTANAMO BAY PIECE. ARE YOU NOT WRITING ANYMORE?
NO. NO, I STILL AM.
OH, I'M SO SORRY. I JUST HADN'T SEEN YOUR WORK. PLEASE--
LOOK WHO IT IS!
WILSON FISK! EVERYONE CHECK THAT YOU STILL HAVE YOUR WALLETS.
SARAH, I'D LIKE YOU TO MEET GAVIN BOYCE, INHERITOR OF AN EVER-SHRINKING REAL ESTATE EMPIRE.
I HEARD YOU WERE IN CALIFORNIA, WILLY. YOU GET EXTRADITED BACK HERE?
NOTHING LIKE THAT, GAVIN. I JUST KNEW THERE WAS MORE I COULD DO FOR THIS CITY THAT I LOVE.
THAT WAS HUMILIATING...
WELL I'M SURE THERE ARE *CERTAIN ELEMENTS* THAT ARE THRILLED TO HAVE YOU BACK HERE. WHAT IS THIS I HEAR ABOUT A FUNDRAISER YOU'RE THROWING?
OH, DID YOU NOT GET MY INVITATION? I'M SURE WE CAN FIND YOU A SEAT.
YOU DON'T MIND THE CHILDREN'S TABLE, DO YOU, GAVIN?

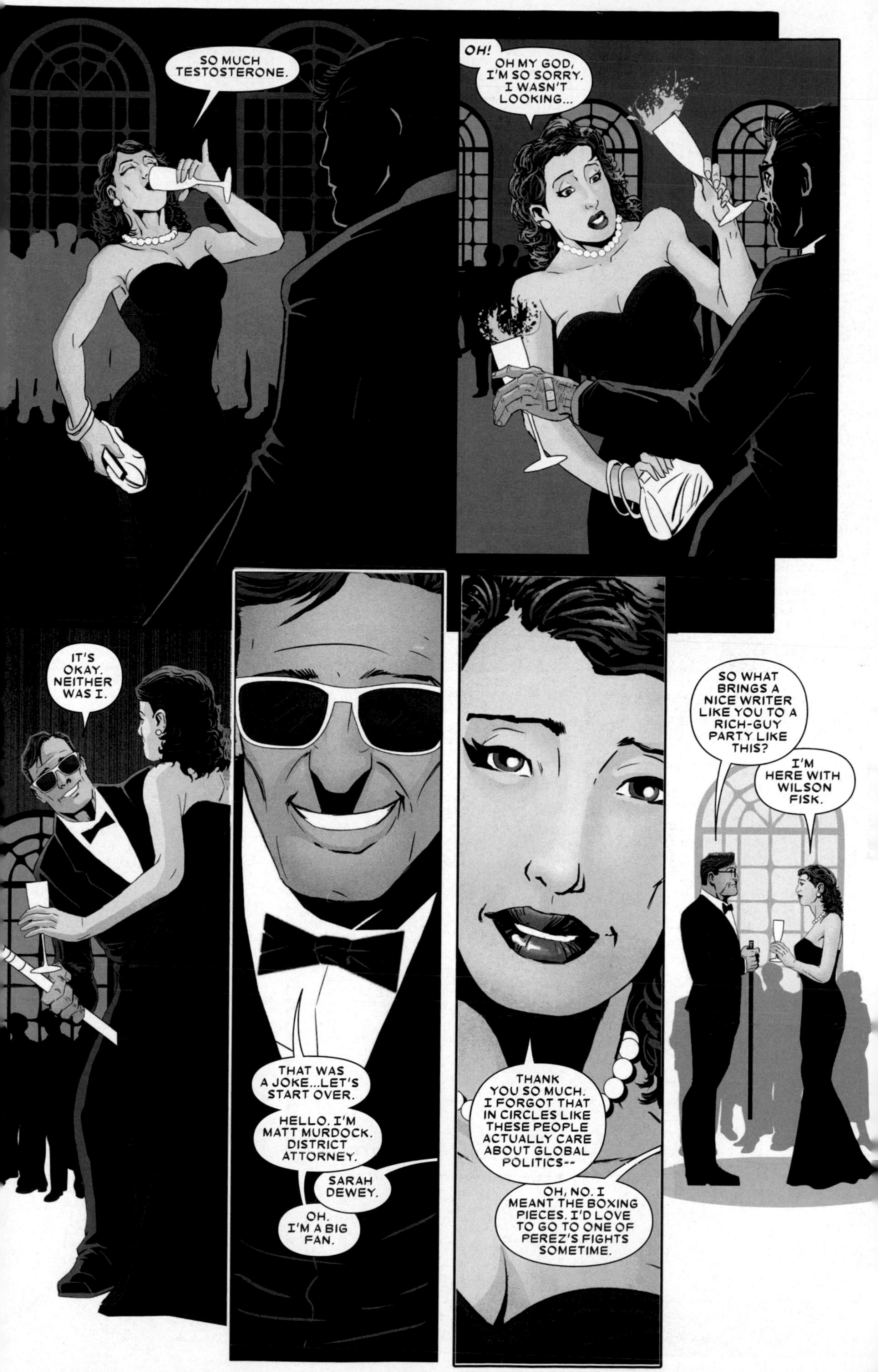
SO MUCH TESTOSTERONE.
OH!
OH MY GOD, I'M SO SORRY. I WASN'T LOOKING...
IT'S OKAY. NEITHER WAS I.
THAT WAS A JOKE...LET'S START OVER.
HELLO. I'M MATT MURDOCK. DISTRICT ATTORNEY.
SARAH DEWEY.
OH. I'M A BIG FAN.
THANK YOU SO MUCH. I FORGOT THAT IN CIRCLES LIKE THESE PEOPLE ACTUALLY CARE ABOUT GLOBAL POLITICS--
OH, NO. I MEANT THE BOXING PIECES. I'D LOVE TO GO TO ONE OF PEREZ'S FIGHTS SOMETIME.
SO WHAT BRINGS A NICE WRITER LIKE YOU TO A RICH-GUY PARTY LIKE THIS?
I'M HERE WITH WILSON FISK.

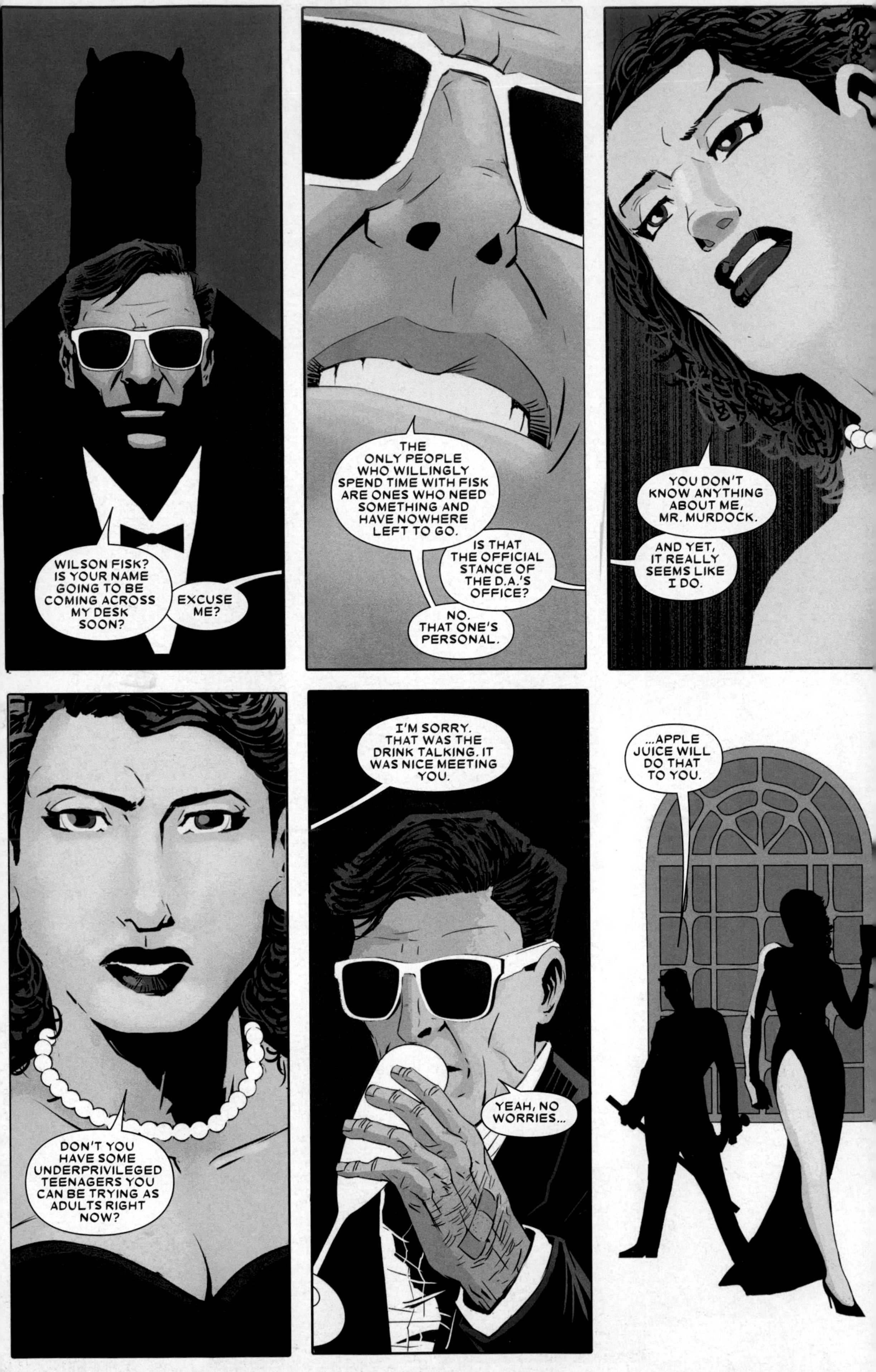

WILSON FISK? IS YOUR NAME GOING TO BE COMING ACROSS MY DESK SOON?
EXCUSE ME?
THE ONLY PEOPLE WHO WILLINGLY SPEND TIME WITH FISK ARE ONES WHO NEED SOMETHING AND HAVE NOWHERE LEFT TO GO.
IS THAT THE OFFICIAL STANCE OF THE D.A.'S OFFICE?
NO. THAT ONE'S PERSONAL.
YOU DON'T KNOW ANYTHING ABOUT ME, MR. MURDOCK.
AND YET, IT REALLY SEEMS LIKE I DO.
DON'T YOU HAVE SOME UNDERPRIVILEGED TEENAGERS YOU CAN BE TRYING AS ADULTS RIGHT NOW?
I'M SORRY. THAT WAS THE DRINK TALKING. IT WAS NICE MEETING YOU.
YEAH, NO WORRIES...
...APPLE JUICE WILL DO THAT TO YOU.

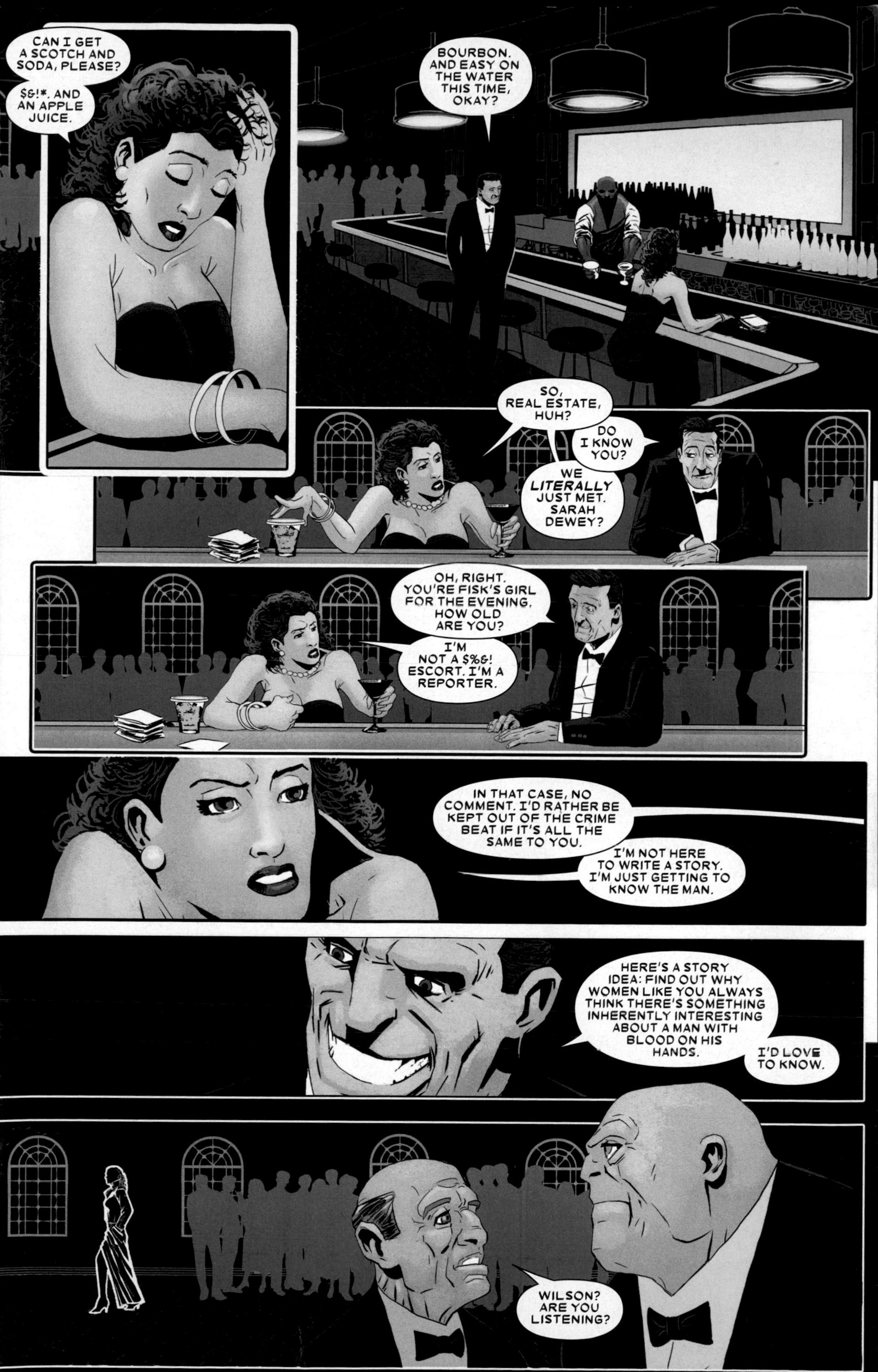
CAN I GET A SCOTCH AND SODA, PLEASE?
$&!*. AND AN APPLE JUICE.
BOURBON. AND EASY ON THE WATER THIS TIME, OKAY?
SO, REAL ESTATE, HUH?
DO I KNOW YOU?
WE LITERALLY JUST MET. SARAH DEWEY?
OH, RIGHT. YOU'RE FISK'S GIRL FOR THE EVENING. HOW OLD ARE YOU?
I'M NOT A $%&! ESCORT. I'M A REPORTER.
IN THAT CASE, NO COMMENT. I'D RATHER BE KEPT OUT OF THE CRIME BEAT IF IT'S ALL THE SAME TO YOU.
I'M NOT HERE TO WRITE A STORY. I'M JUST GETTING TO KNOW THE MAN.
HERE'S A STORY IDEA: FIND OUT WHY WOMEN LIKE YOU ALWAYS THINK THERE'S SOMETHING INHERENTLY INTERESTING ABOUT A MAN WITH BLOOD ON HIS HANDS.
I'D LOVE TO KNOW.
WILSON? ARE YOU LISTENING?

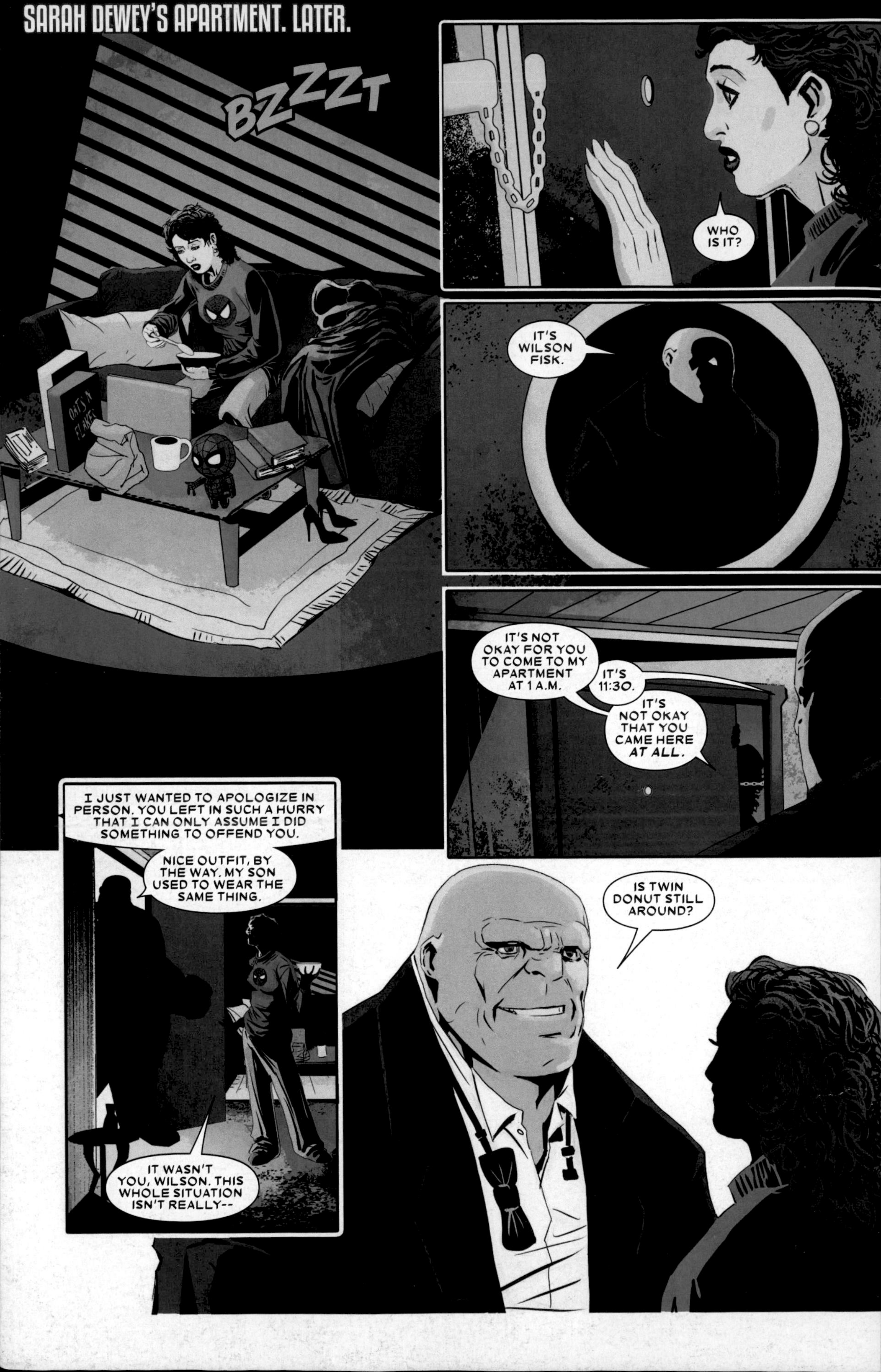
SARAH DEWEY'S APARTMENT. LATER.
BZZZT
WHO IS IT?
IT'S WILSON FISK.
IT'S NOT OKAY FOR YOU TO COME TO MY APARTMENT AT 1 A.M.
IT'S 11:30.
IT'S NOT OKAY THAT YOU CAME HERE AT ALL.
I JUST WANTED TO APOLOGIZE IN PERSON. YOU LEFT IN SUCH A HURRY THAT I CAN ONLY ASSUME I DID SOMETHING TO OFFEND YOU.
NICE OUTFIT, BY THE WAY. MY SON USED TO WEAR THE SAME THING.
IT WASN'T YOU, WILSON. THIS WHOLE SITUATION ISN'T REALLY--
IS TWIN DONUT STILL AROUND?

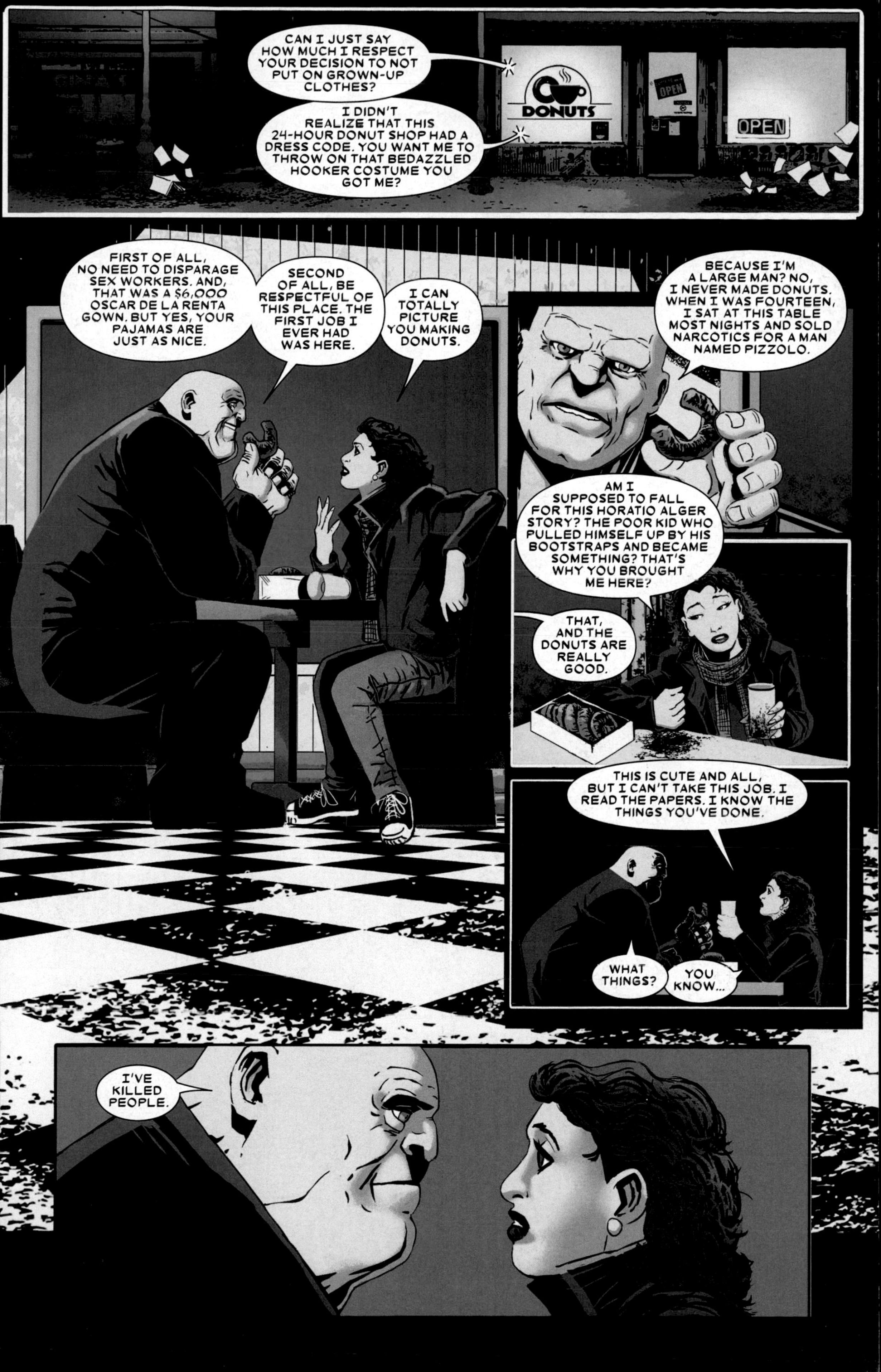
CAN I JUST SAY HOW MUCH I RESPECT YOUR DECISION TO NOT PUT ON GROWN-UP CLOTHES?
DONUTS
OPEN
OPEN
I DIDN'T REALIZE THAT THIS 24-HOUR DONUT SHOP HAD A DRESS CODE. YOU WANT ME TO THROW ON THAT BEDAZZLED HOOKER COSTUME YOU GOT ME?
FIRST OF ALL, NO NEED TO DISPARAGE SEX WORKERS. AND, THAT WAS A $6,000 OSCAR DE LA RENTA GOWN. BUT YES, YOUR PAJAMAS ARE JUST AS NICE.
SECOND OF ALL, BE RESPECTFUL OF THIS PLACE. THE FIRST JOB I EVER HAD WAS HERE.
I CAN TOTALLY PICTURE YOU MAKING DONUTS.
BECAUSE I'M A LARGE MAN? NO, I NEVER MADE DONUTS. WHEN I WAS FOURTEEN, I SAT AT THIS TABLE MOST NIGHTS AND SOLD NARCOTICS FOR A MAN NAMED PIZZOLO.
AM I SUPPOSED TO FALL FOR THIS HORATIO ALGER STORY? THE POOR KID WHO PULLED HIMSELF UP BY HIS BOOTSTRAPS AND BECAME SOMETHING? THAT'S WHY YOU BROUGHT ME HERE?
THAT, AND THE DONUTS ARE REALLY GOOD.
THIS IS CUTE AND ALL, BUT I CAN'T TAKE THIS JOB. I READ THE PAPERS. I KNOW THE THINGS YOU'VE DONE.
WHAT THINGS?
YOU KNOW...
I'VE KILLED PEOPLE.

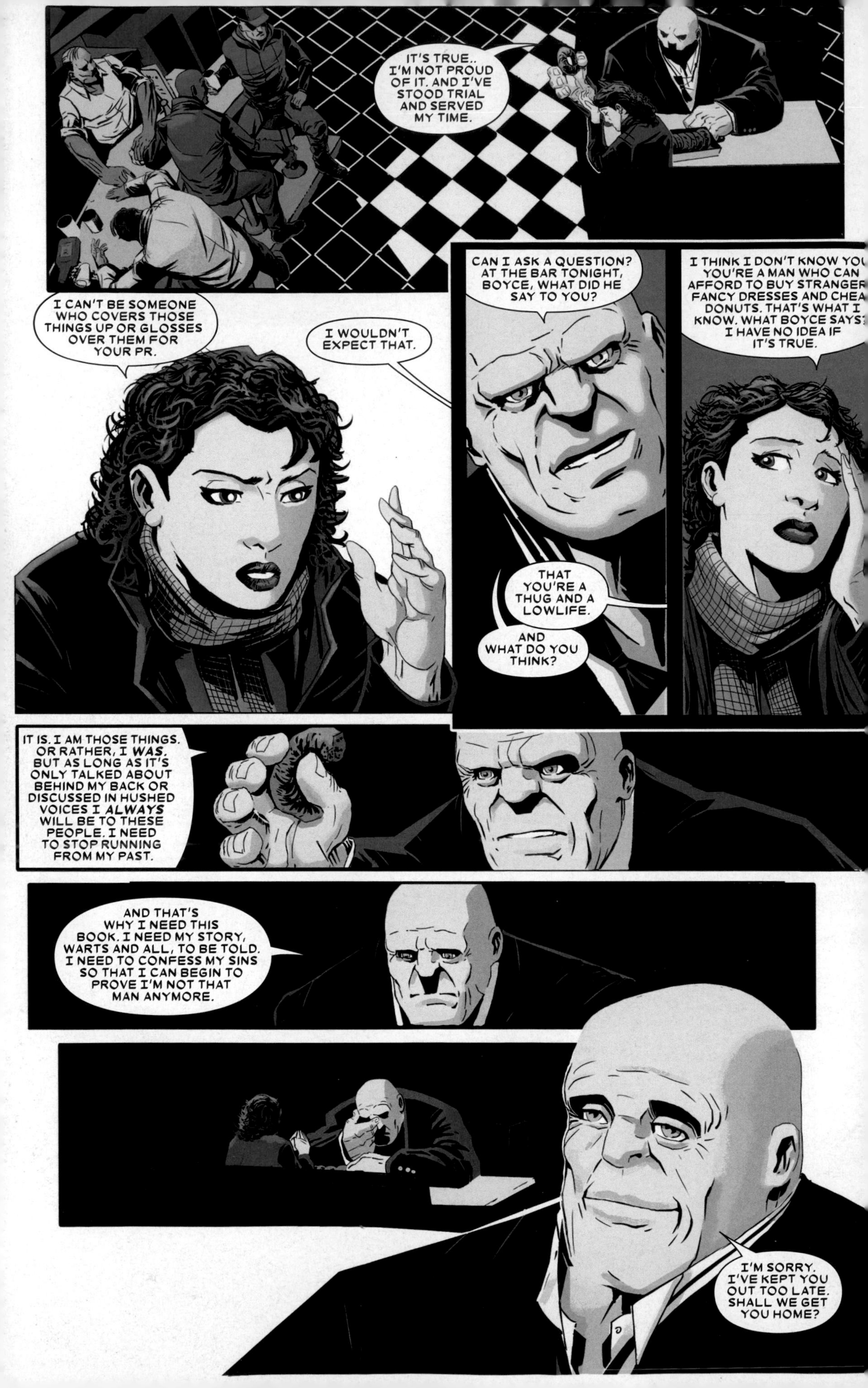
IT'S TRUE.. I'M NOT PROUD OF IT. AND I'VE STOOD TRIAL AND SERVED MY TIME.
I CAN'T BE SOMEONE WHO COVERS THOSE THINGS UP OR GLOSSES OVER THEM FOR YOUR PR.
I WOULDN'T EXPECT THAT.
CAN I ASK A QUESTION? AT THE BAR TONIGHT, BOYCE, WHAT DID HE SAY TO YOU?
THAT YOU'RE A THUG AND A LOWLIFE.
AND WHAT DO YOU THINK?
I THINK I DON'T KNOW YOU. YOU'RE A MAN WHO CAN AFFORD TO BUY STRANGERS FANCY DRESSES AND CHEAP DONUTS. THAT'S WHAT I KNOW. WHAT BOYCE SAYS? I HAVE NO IDEA IF IT'S TRUE.
IT IS. I AM THOSE THINGS. OR RATHER, I *WAS*. BUT AS LONG AS IT'S ONLY TALKED ABOUT BEHIND MY BACK OR DISCUSSED IN HUSHED VOICES I *ALWAYS* WILL BE TO THESE PEOPLE. I NEED TO STOP RUNNING FROM MY PAST.
AND THAT'S WHY I NEED THIS BOOK. I NEED MY STORY, WARTS AND ALL, TO BE TOLD. I NEED TO CONFESS MY SINS SO THAT I CAN BEGIN TO PROVE I'M NOT THAT MAN ANYMORE.
I'M SORRY. I'VE KEPT YOU OUT TOO LATE. SHALL WE GET YOU HOME?

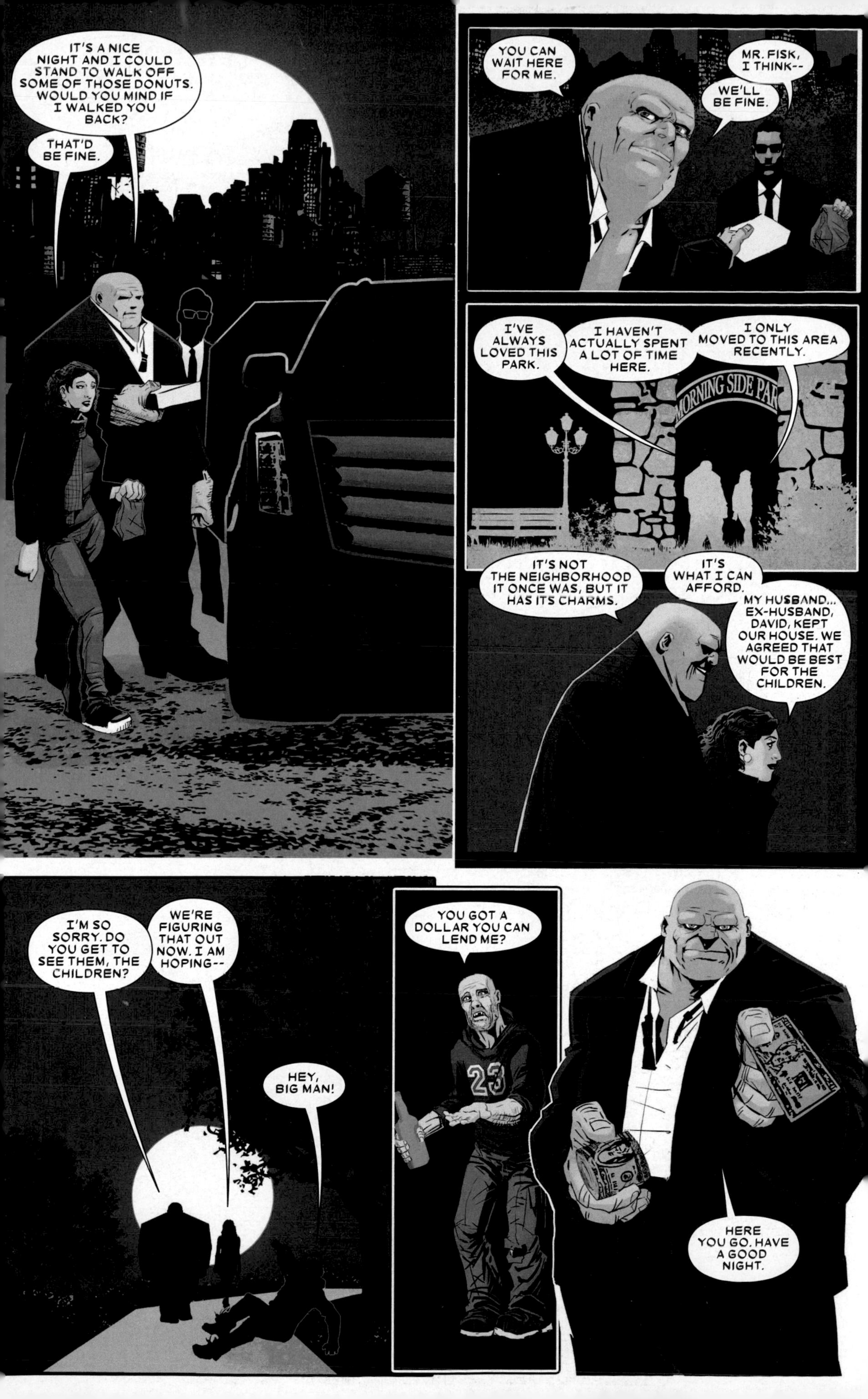
IT'S A NICE NIGHT AND I COULD STAND TO WALK OFF SOME OF THOSE DONUTS. WOULD YOU MIND IF I WALKED YOU BACK?
THAT'D BE FINE.
YOU CAN WAIT HERE FOR ME.
MR. FISK, I THINK--
WE'LL BE FINE.
I'VE ALWAYS LOVED THIS PARK.
I HAVEN'T ACTUALLY SPENT A LOT OF TIME HERE.
I ONLY MOVED TO THIS AREA RECENTLY.
MORNING SIDE PAR
IT'S NOT THE NEIGHBORHOOD IT ONCE WAS, BUT IT HAS ITS CHARMS.
IT'S WHAT I CAN AFFORD.
MY HUSBAND... EX-HUSBAND, DAVID, KEPT OUR HOUSE. WE AGREED THAT WOULD BE BEST FOR THE CHILDREN.
I'M SO SORRY. DO YOU GET TO SEE THEM, THE CHILDREN?
WE'RE FIGURING THAT OUT NOW. I AM HOPING--
HEY, BIG MAN!
YOU GOT A DOLLAR YOU CAN LEND ME?
23
HERE YOU GO. HAVE A GOOD NIGHT.

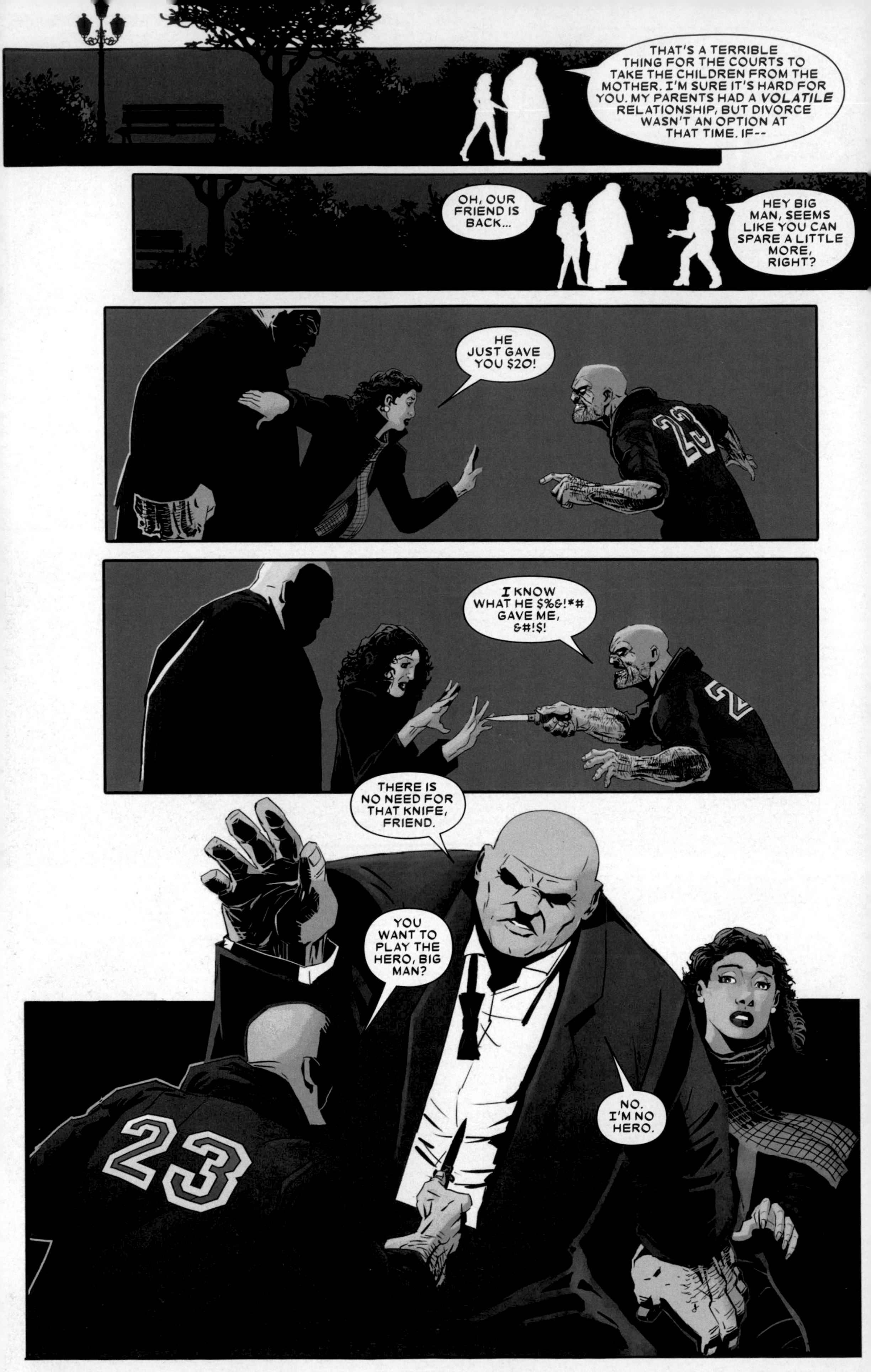
THAT'S A TERRIBLE THING FOR THE COURTS TO TAKE THE CHILDREN FROM THE MOTHER. I'M SURE IT'S HARD FOR YOU. MY PARENTS HAD A VOLATILE RELATIONSHIP, BUT DIVORCE WASN'T AN OPTION AT THAT TIME. IF--
OH, OUR FRIEND IS BACK...
HEY BIG MAN, SEEMS LIKE YOU CAN SPARE A LITTLE MORE, RIGHT?
HE JUST GAVE YOU $20!
I KNOW WHAT HE $%&!*# GAVE ME, &#!$!
THERE IS NO NEED FOR THAT KNIFE, FRIEND.
YOU WANT TO PLAY THE HERO, BIG MAN?
NO. I'M NO HERO.

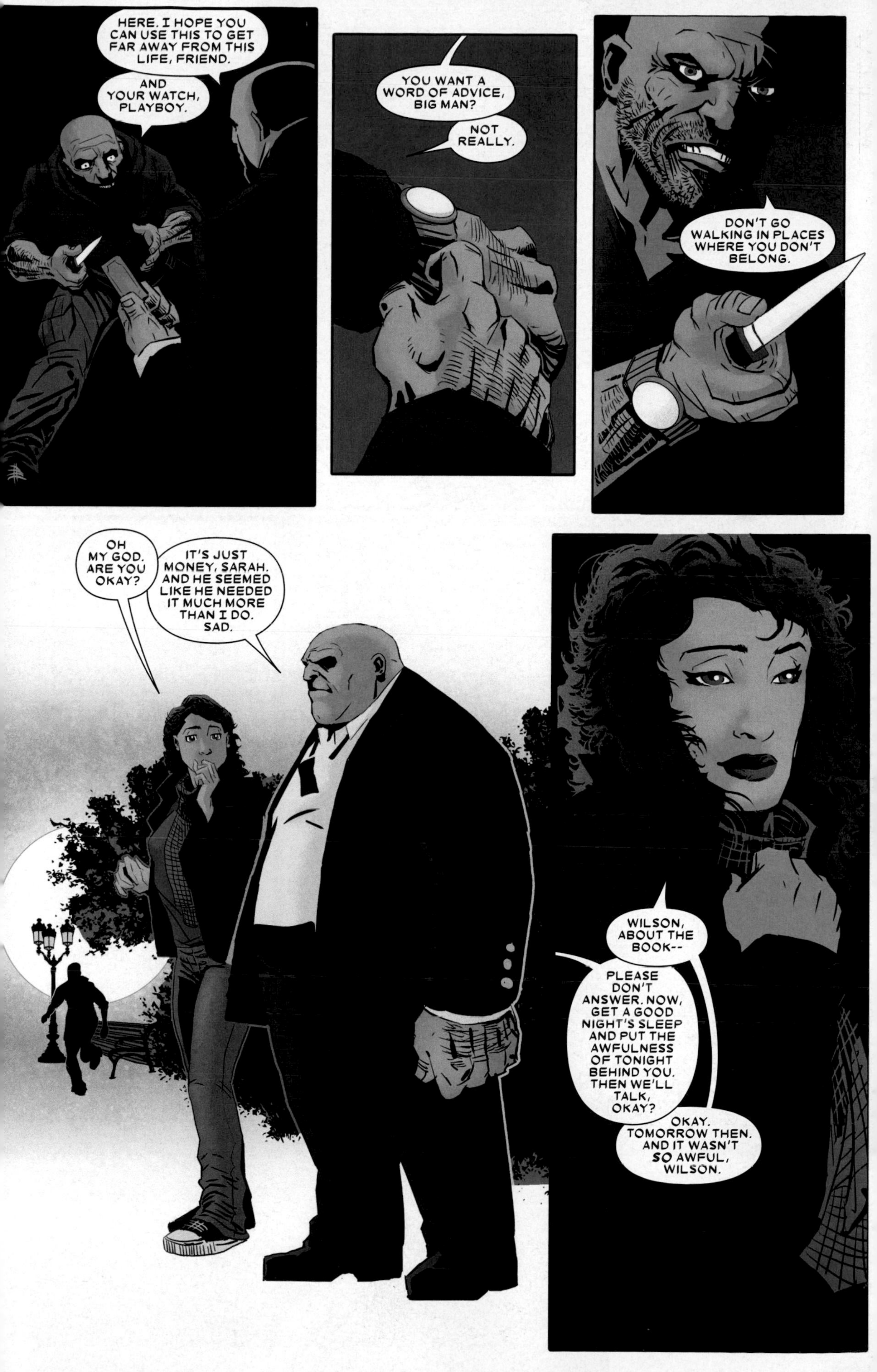
HERE. I HOPE YOU CAN USE THIS TO GET FAR AWAY FROM THIS LIFE, FRIEND.
AND YOUR WATCH, PLAYBOY.
YOU WANT A WORD OF ADVICE, BIG MAN?
NOT REALLY.
DON'T GO WALKING IN PLACES WHERE YOU DON'T BELONG.
OH MY GOD. ARE YOU OKAY?
IT'S JUST MONEY, SARAH. AND HE SEEMED LIKE HE NEEDED IT MUCH MORE THAN I DO. SAD.
WILSON, ABOUT THE BOOK--
PLEASE DON'T ANSWER. NOW, GET A GOOD NIGHT'S SLEEP AND PUT THE AWFULNESS OF TONIGHT BEHIND YOU. THEN WE'LL TALK, OKAY?
OKAY. TOMORROW THEN. AND IT WASN'T SO AWFUL, WILSON.

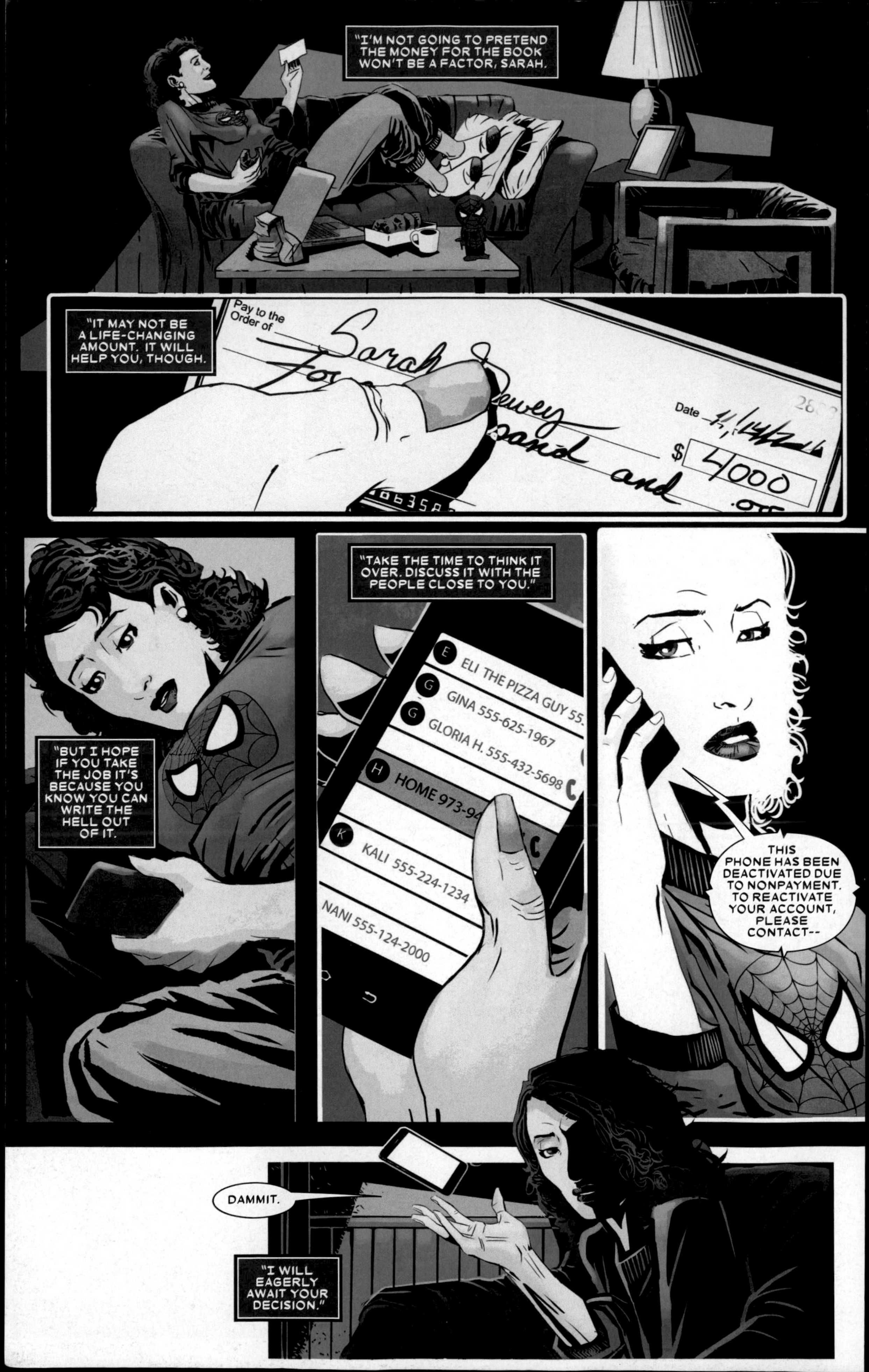
"I'M NOT GOING TO PRETEND THE MONEY FOR THE BOOK WON'T BE A FACTOR, SARAH.
"IT MAY NOT BE A LIFE-CHANGING AMOUNT. IT WILL HELP YOU, THOUGH.
Pay to the Order of
Sarah Dewey
Date
$ 4000
"BUT I HOPE IF YOU TAKE THE JOB IT'S BECAUSE YOU KNOW YOU CAN WRITE THE HELL OUT OF IT.
"TAKE THE TIME TO THINK IT OVER. DISCUSS IT WITH THE PEOPLE CLOSE TO YOU."
ELI THE PIZZA GUY
GINA 555-625-1967
GLORIA H. 555-432-5698
KALI 555-224-1234
NANI 555-124-2000
THIS PHONE HAS BEEN DEACTIVATED DUE TO NONPAYMENT. TO REACTIVATE YOUR ACCOUNT, PLEASE CONTACT--
DAMMIT.
"I WILL EAGERLY AWAIT YOUR DECISION."

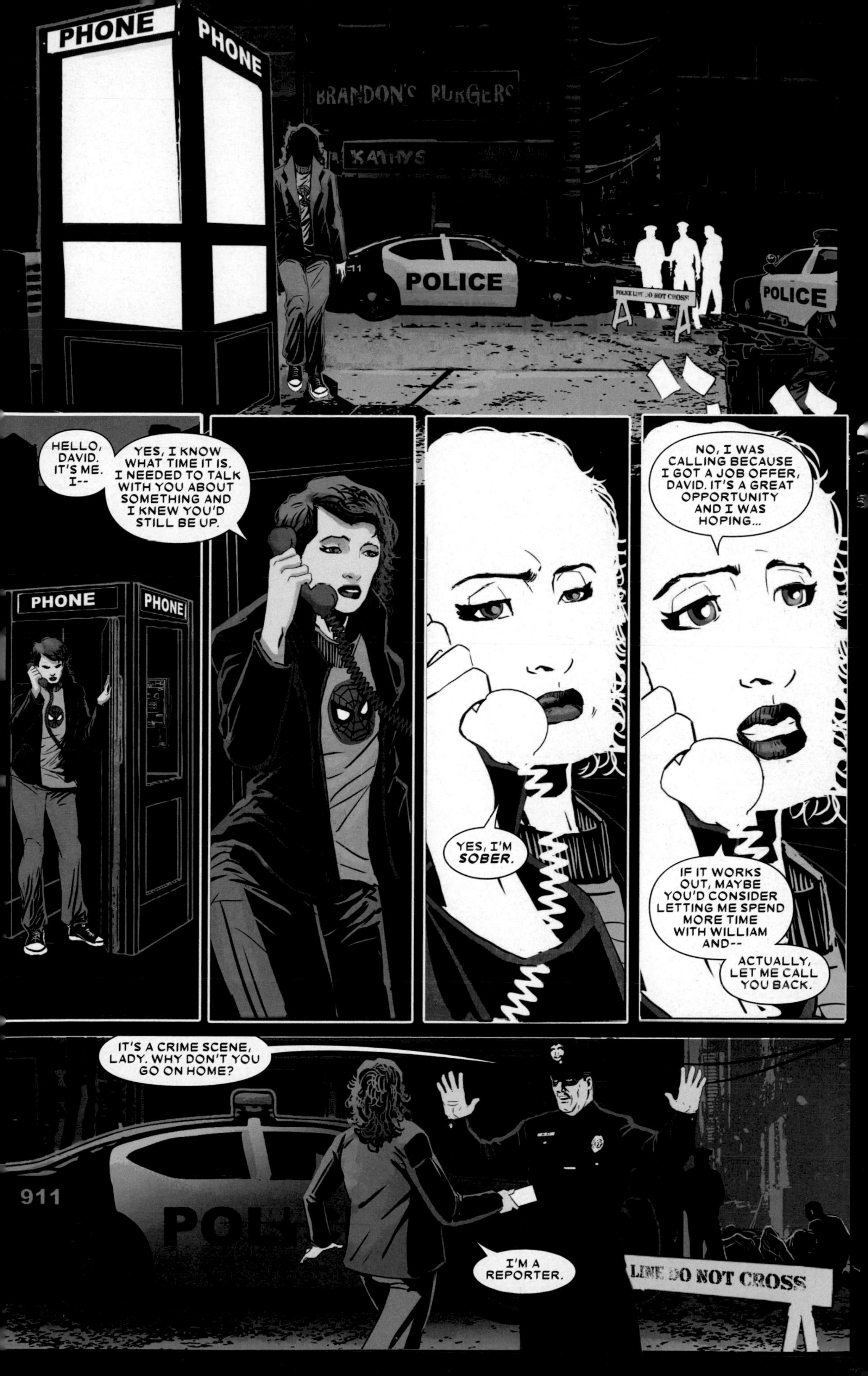
PHONE
PHONE
BRANDON'S BURGERS
KATHYS
POLICE
POLICE LINE DO NOT CROSS
POLICE
HELLO, DAVID. IT'S ME. I--
YES, I KNOW WHAT TIME IT IS. I NEEDED TO TALK WITH YOU ABOUT SOMETHING AND I KNEW YOU'D STILL BE UP.
PHONE
PHONE
YES, I'M *SOBER*.
NO, I WAS CALLING BECAUSE I GOT A JOB OFFER, DAVID. IT'S A GREAT OPPORTUNITY AND I WAS HOPING...
IF IT WORKS OUT, MAYBE YOU'D CONSIDER LETTING ME SPEND MORE TIME WITH WILLIAM AND--
ACTUALLY, LET ME CALL YOU BACK.
IT'S A CRIME SCENE, LADY. WHY DON'T YOU GO ON HOME?
911
I'M A REPORTER.
LINE DO NOT CROSS

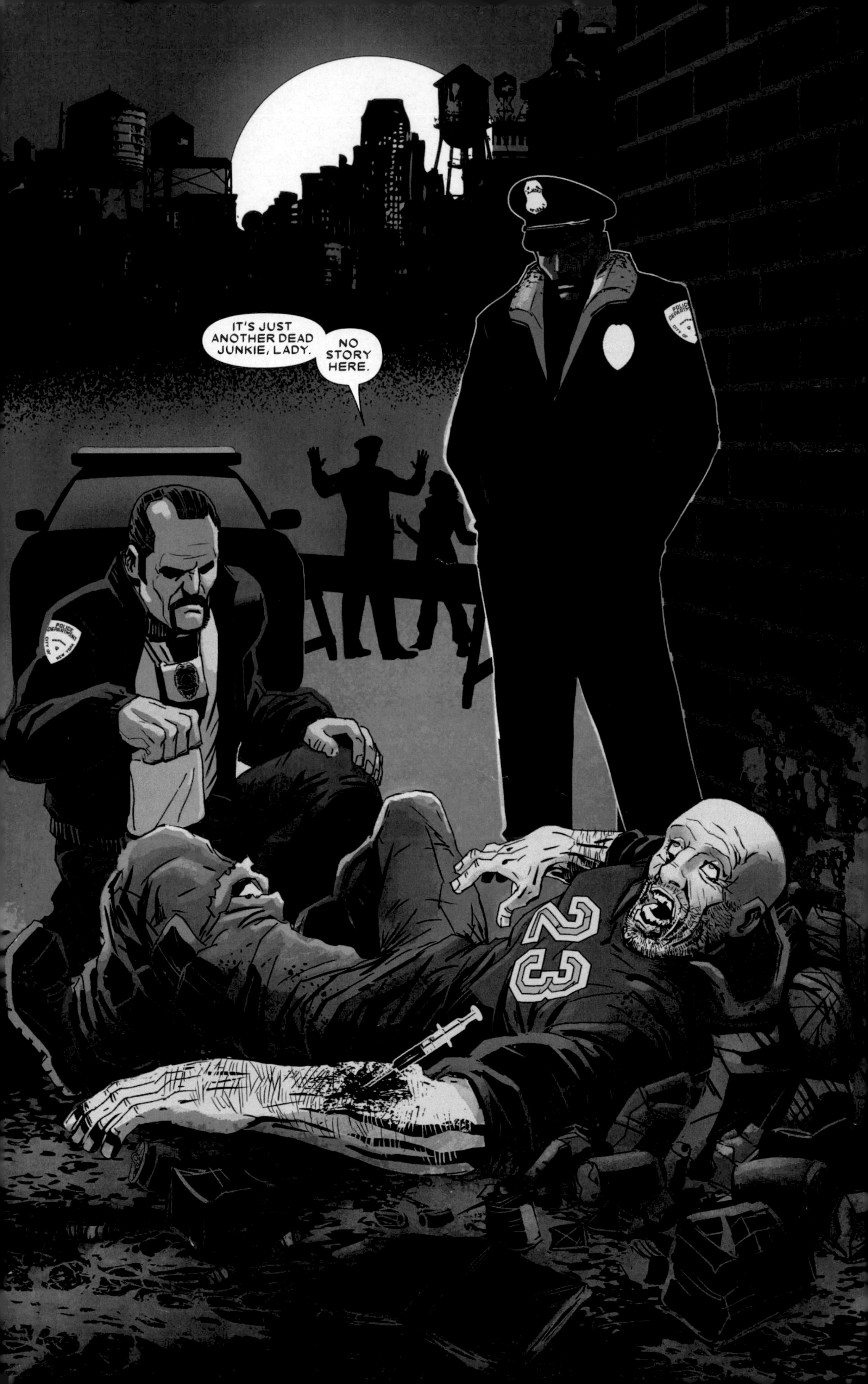
IT'S JUST ANOTHER DEAD JUNKIE, LADY.
NO STORY HERE.

TWO

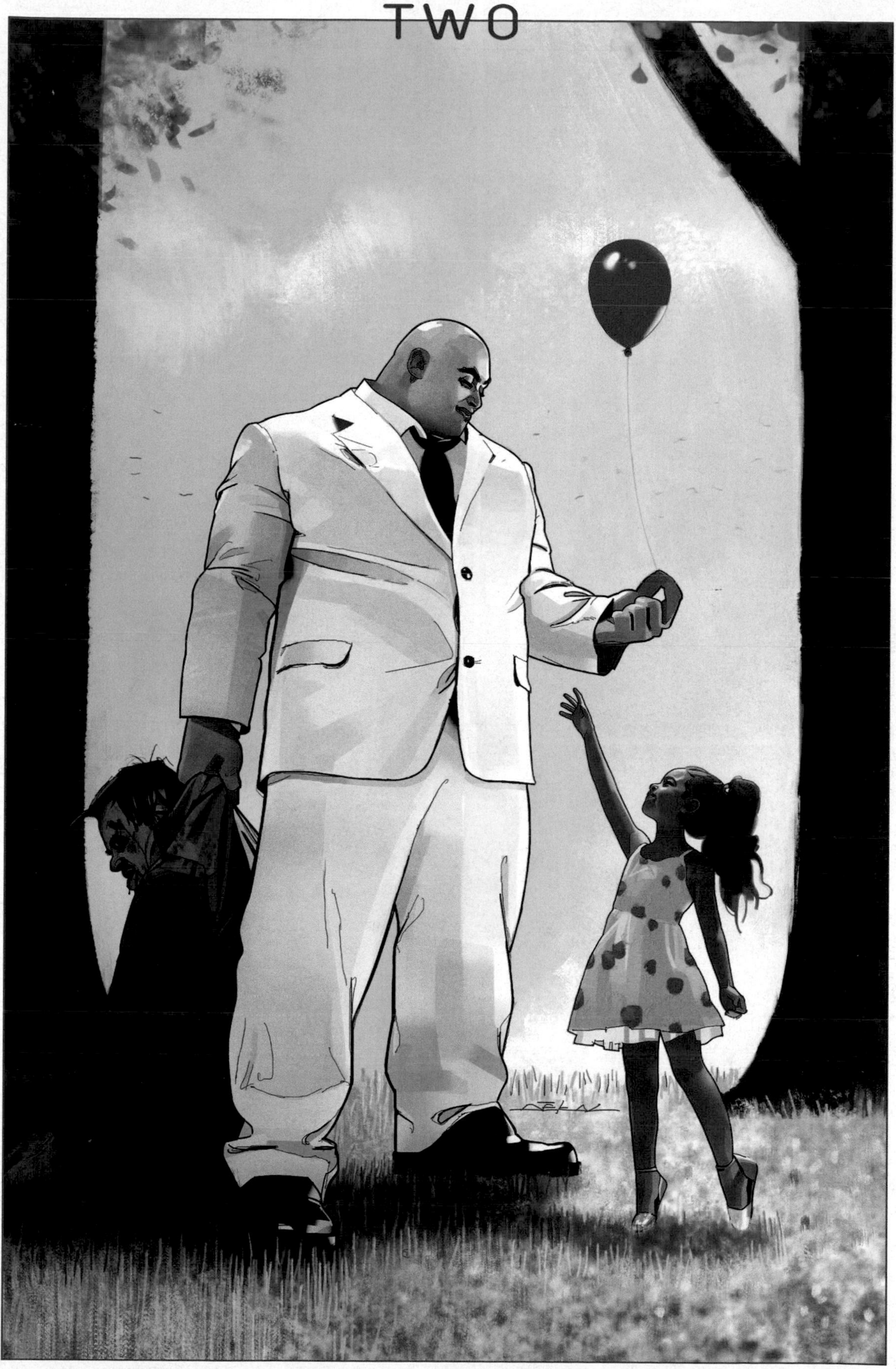

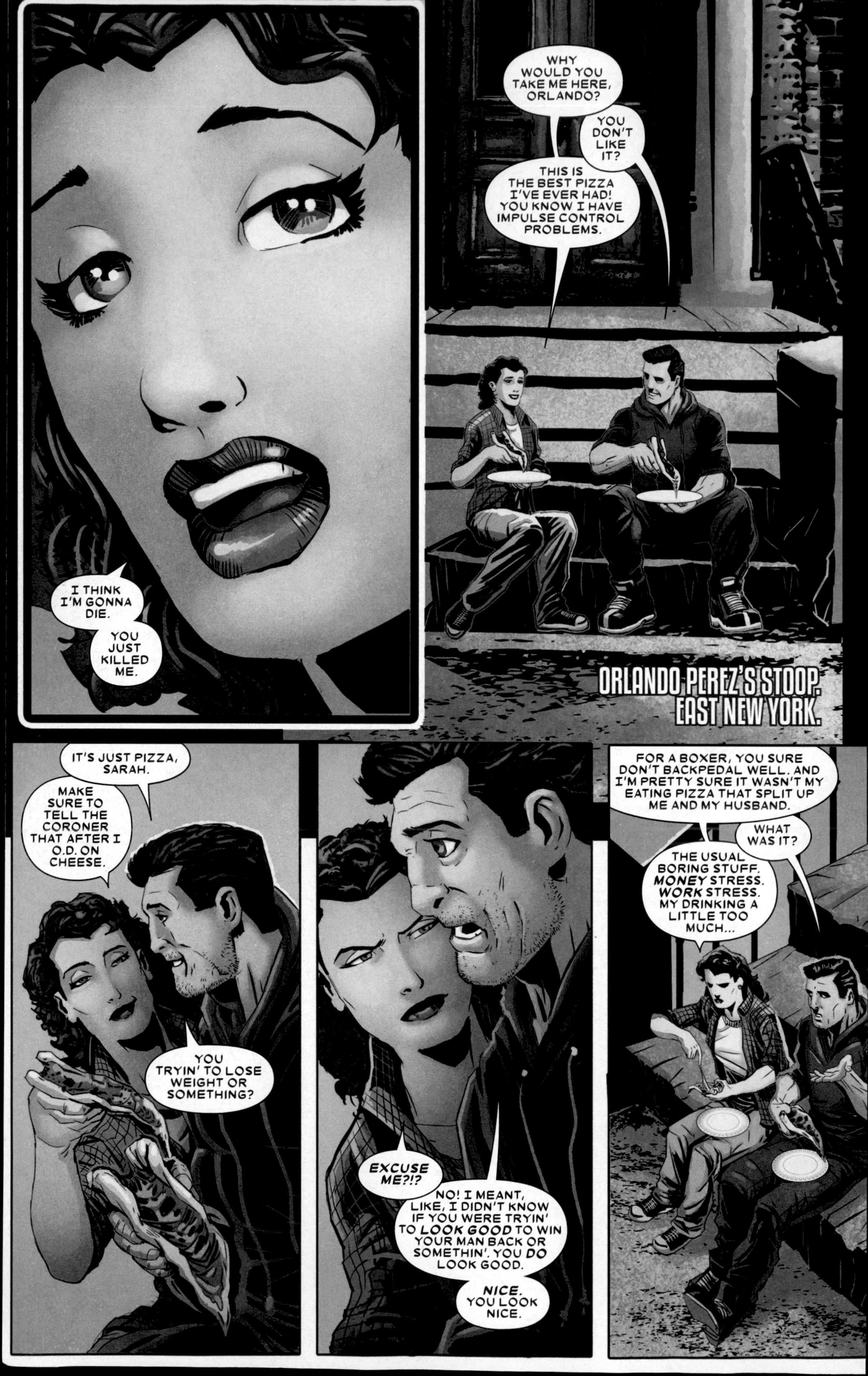
I THINK I'M GONNA DIE.
YOU JUST KILLED ME.
WHY WOULD YOU TAKE ME HERE, ORLANDO?
YOU DON'T LIKE IT?
THIS IS THE BEST PIZZA I'VE EVER HAD! YOU KNOW I HAVE IMPULSE CONTROL PROBLEMS.
ORLANDO PEREZ'S STOOP. EAST NEW YORK.
IT'S JUST PIZZA, SARAH.
MAKE SURE TO TELL THE CORONER THAT AFTER I O.D. ON CHEESE.
YOU TRYIN' TO LOSE WEIGHT OR SOMETHING?
EXCUSE ME?!?
NO! I MEANT, LIKE, I DIDN'T KNOW IF YOU WERE TRYIN' TO LOOK GOOD TO WIN YOUR MAN BACK OR SOMETHIN'. YOU DO LOOK GOOD.
NICE. YOU LOOK NICE.
FOR A BOXER, YOU SURE DON'T BACKPEDAL WELL. AND I'M PRETTY SURE IT WASN'T MY EATING PIZZA THAT SPLIT UP ME AND MY HUSBAND.
WHAT WAS IT?
THE USUAL BORING STUFF. MONEY STRESS. WORK STRESS. MY DRINKING A LITTLE TOO MUCH...

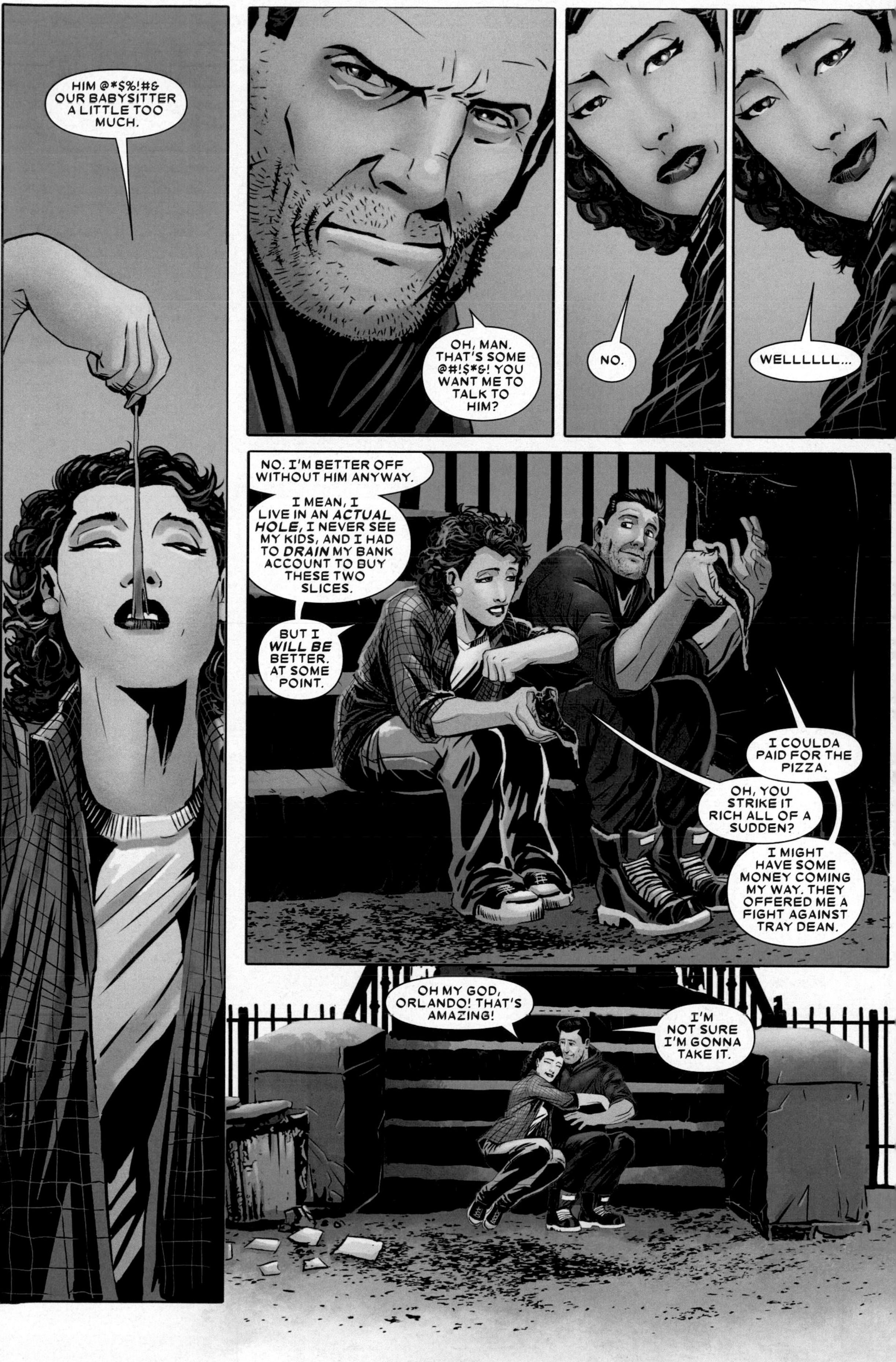

HIM @*$%!#& OUR BABYSITTER A LITTLE TOO MUCH.
OH, MAN. THAT'S SOME @#!$*&! YOU WANT ME TO TALK TO HIM?
NO.
WELLLLLL...
NO. I'M BETTER OFF WITHOUT HIM ANYWAY.
I MEAN, I LIVE IN AN ACTUAL HOLE, I NEVER SEE MY KIDS, AND I HAD TO DRAIN MY BANK ACCOUNT TO BUY THESE TWO SLICES.
BUT I WILL BE BETTER. AT SOME POINT.
I COULDA PAID FOR THE PIZZA.
OH, YOU STRIKE IT RICH ALL OF A SUDDEN?
I MIGHT HAVE SOME MONEY COMING MY WAY. THEY OFFERED ME A FIGHT AGAINST TRAY DEAN.
OH MY GOD, ORLANDO! THAT'S AMAZING!
I'M NOT SURE I'M GONNA TAKE IT.

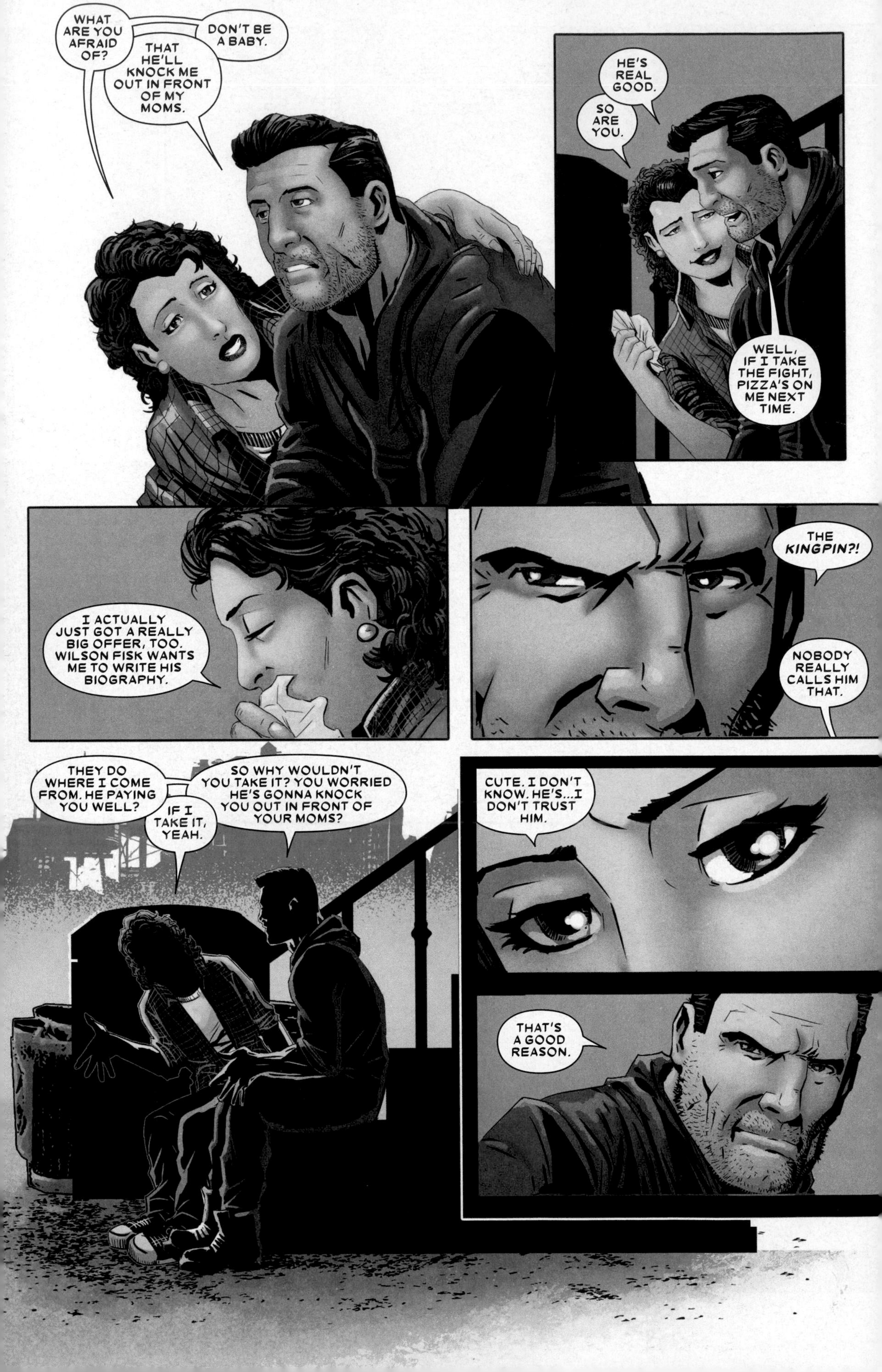
WHAT ARE YOU AFRAID OF?
DON'T BE A BABY.
THAT HE'LL KNOCK ME OUT IN FRONT OF MY MOMS.
HE'S REAL GOOD.
SO ARE YOU.
WELL, IF I TAKE THE FIGHT, PIZZA'S ON ME NEXT TIME.
I ACTUALLY JUST GOT A REALLY BIG OFFER, TOO. WILSON FISK WANTS ME TO WRITE HIS BIOGRAPHY.
THE KINGPIN?!
NOBODY REALLY CALLS HIM THAT.
THEY DO WHERE I COME FROM. HE PAYING YOU WELL?
IF I TAKE IT, YEAH.
SO WHY WOULDN'T YOU TAKE IT? YOU WORRIED HE'S GONNA KNOCK YOU OUT IN FRONT OF YOUR MOMS?
CUTE. I DON'T KNOW. HE'S...I DON'T TRUST HIM.
THAT'S A GOOD REASON.

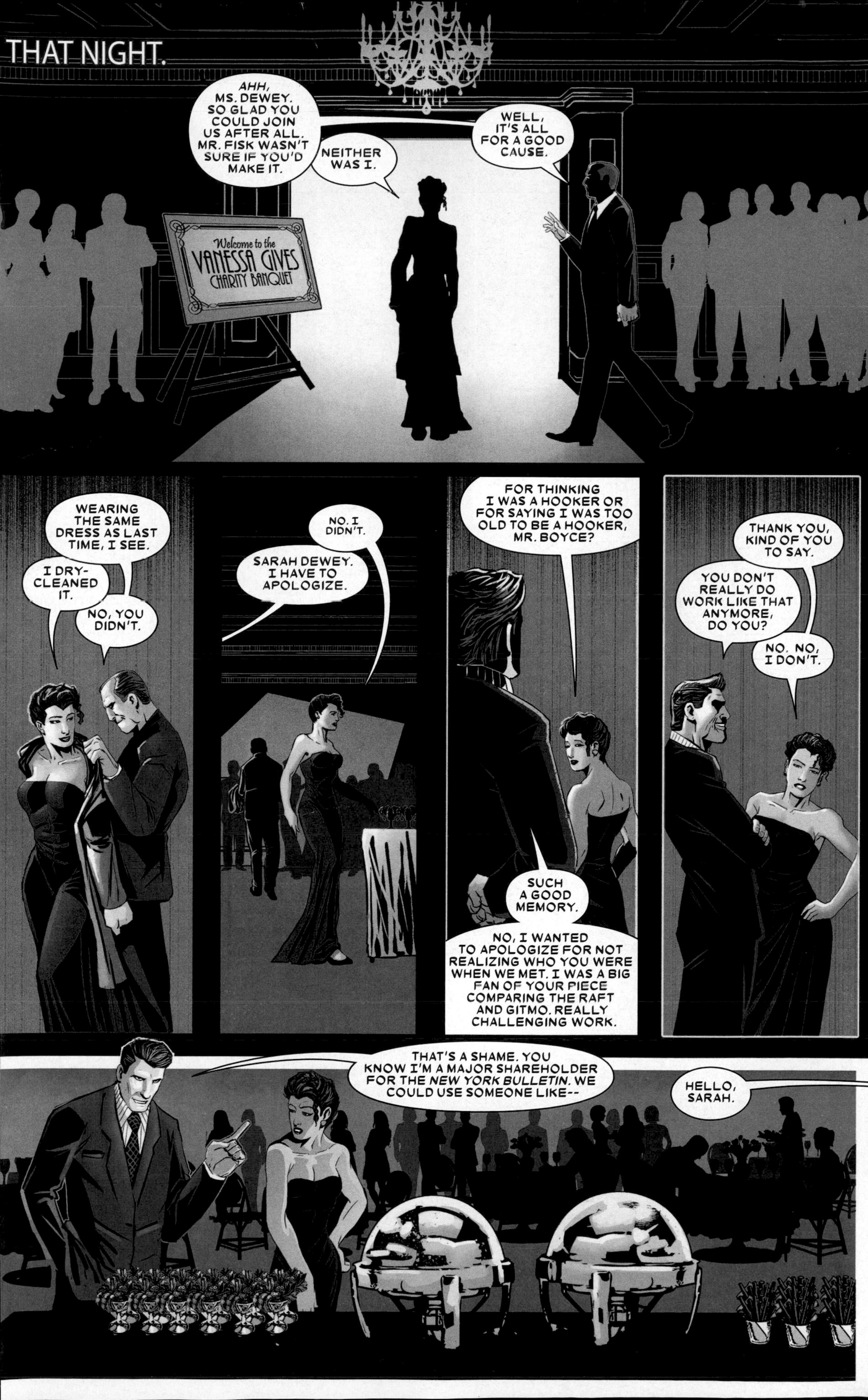
THAT NIGHT.
AHH, MS. DEWEY. SO GLAD YOU COULD JOIN US AFTER ALL. MR. FISK WASN'T SURE IF YOU'D MAKE IT.
NEITHER WAS I.
WELL, IT'S ALL FOR A GOOD CAUSE.
Welcome to the VANESSA GIVES CHARITY BANQUET
WEARING THE SAME DRESS AS LAST TIME, I SEE.
I DRY-CLEANED IT.
NO, YOU DIDN'T.
SARAH DEWEY. I HAVE TO APOLOGIZE.
NO. I DIDN'T.
FOR THINKING I WAS A HOOKER OR FOR SAYING I WAS TOO OLD TO BE A HOOKER, MR. BOYCE?
SUCH A GOOD MEMORY.
NO, I WANTED TO APOLOGIZE FOR NOT REALIZING WHO YOU WERE WHEN WE MET. I WAS A BIG FAN OF YOUR PIECE COMPARING THE RAFT AND GITMO. REALLY CHALLENGING WORK.
THANK YOU, KIND OF YOU TO SAY.
YOU DON'T REALLY DO WORK LIKE THAT ANYMORE, DO YOU?
NO. NO, I DON'T.
THAT'S A SHAME. YOU KNOW I'M A MAJOR SHAREHOLDER FOR THE *NEW YORK BULLETIN*. WE COULD USE SOMEONE LIKE--
HELLO, SARAH.

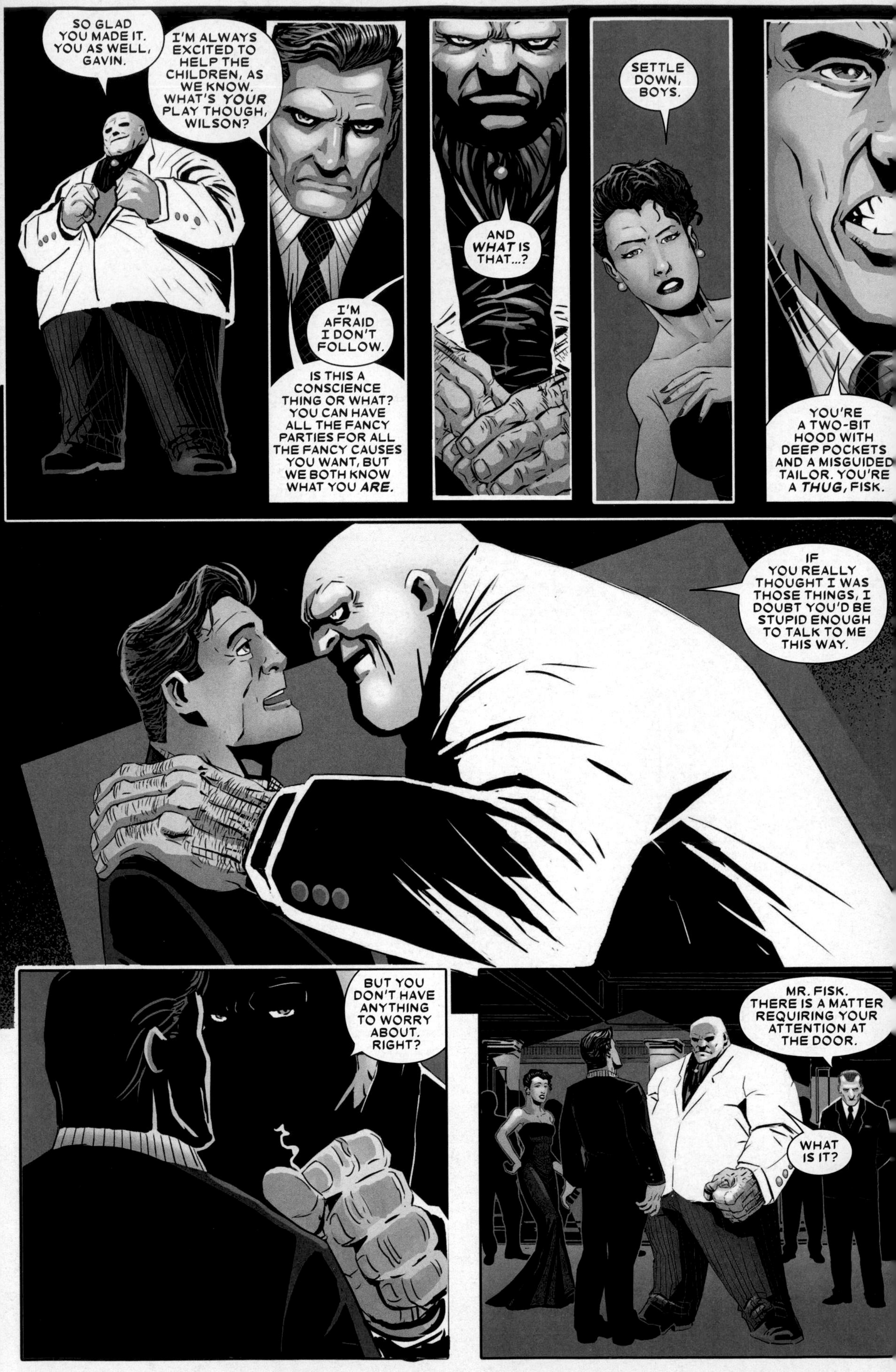
SO GLAD YOU MADE IT. YOU AS WELL, GAVIN.
I'M ALWAYS EXCITED TO HELP THE CHILDREN, AS WE KNOW. WHAT'S *YOUR* PLAY THOUGH, WILSON?
I'M AFRAID I DON'T FOLLOW.
IS THIS A CONSCIENCE THING OR WHAT? YOU CAN HAVE ALL THE FANCY PARTIES FOR ALL THE FANCY CAUSES YOU WANT, BUT WE BOTH KNOW WHAT YOU *ARE.*
AND *WHAT* IS THAT...?
SETTLE DOWN, BOYS.
YOU'RE A TWO-BIT HOOD WITH DEEP POCKETS AND A MISGUIDED TAILOR. YOU'RE A *THUG,* FISK.
IF YOU REALLY THOUGHT I WAS THOSE THINGS, I DOUBT YOU'D BE STUPID ENOUGH TO TALK TO ME THIS WAY.
BUT YOU DON'T HAVE ANYTHING TO WORRY ABOUT. RIGHT?
MR. FISK. THERE IS A MATTER REQUIRING YOUR ATTENTION AT THE DOOR.
WHAT IS IT?

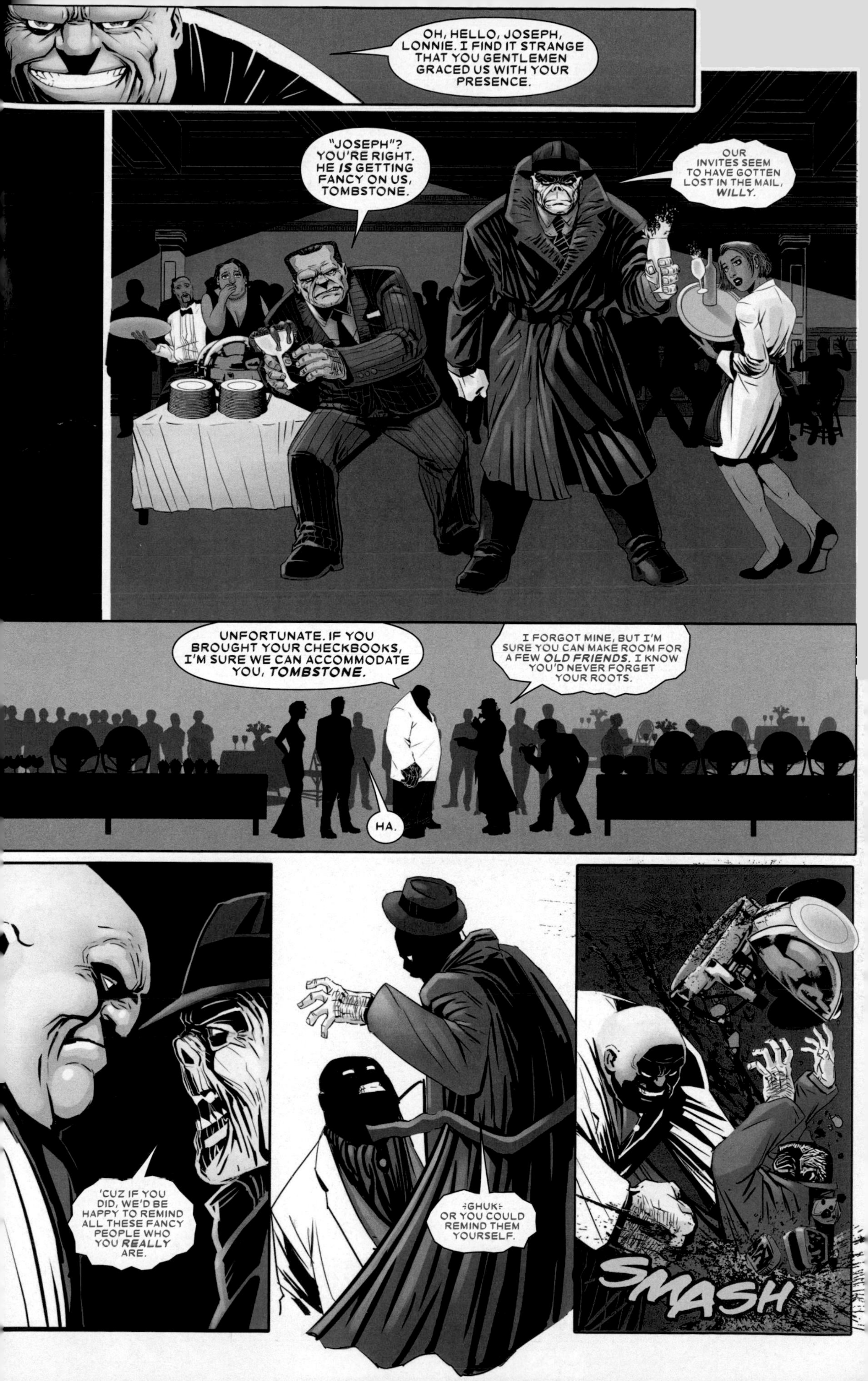
OH, HELLO, JOSEPH, LONNIE. I FIND IT STRANGE THAT YOU GENTLEMEN GRACED US WITH YOUR PRESENCE.
"JOSEPH"? YOU'RE RIGHT. HE *IS* GETTING FANCY ON US, TOMBSTONE.
OUR INVITES SEEM TO HAVE GOTTEN LOST IN THE MAIL, *WILLY*.
UNFORTUNATE. IF YOU BROUGHT YOUR CHECKBOOKS, I'M SURE WE CAN ACCOMMODATE YOU, *TOMBSTONE.*
I FORGOT MINE, BUT I'M SURE YOU CAN MAKE ROOM FOR A FEW *OLD FRIENDS*. I KNOW YOU'D NEVER FORGET YOUR ROOTS.
HA.
'CUZ IF YOU DID, WE'D BE HAPPY TO REMIND ALL THESE FANCY PEOPLE WHO YOU *REALLY* ARE.
⁂GHUK⁂ OR YOU COULD REMIND THEM YOURSELF.
SMASH

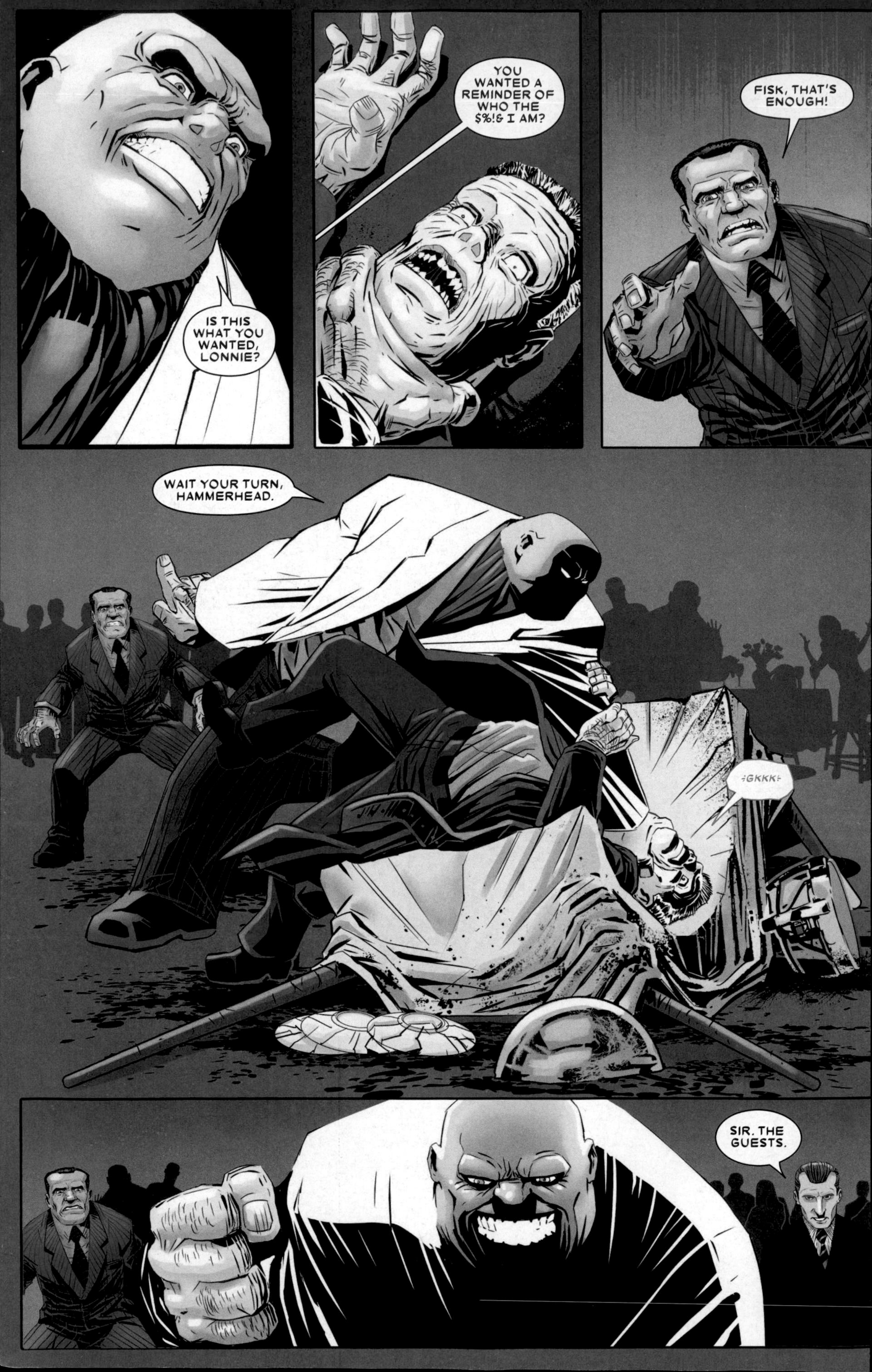
IS THIS WHAT YOU WANTED, LONNIE?
YOU WANTED A REMINDER OF WHO THE $%!& I AM?
FISK, THAT'S ENOUGH!
WAIT YOUR TURN, HAMMERHEAD.
GKKK
SIR. THE GUESTS.

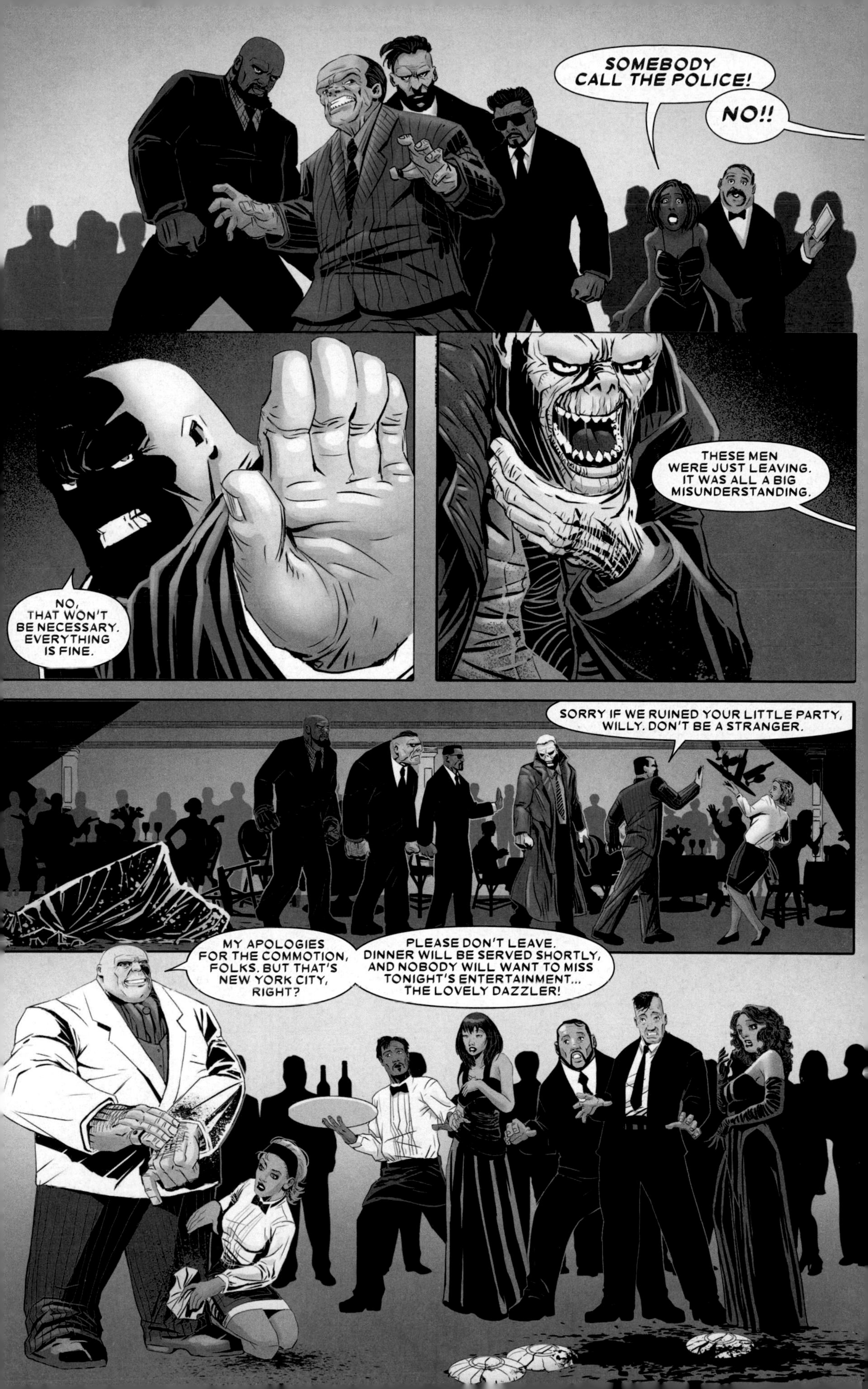

SOMEBODY CALL THE POLICE!
NO!!
NO, THAT WON'T BE NECESSARY. EVERYTHING IS FINE.
THESE MEN WERE JUST LEAVING. IT WAS ALL A BIG MISUNDERSTANDING.
SORRY IF WE RUINED YOUR LITTLE PARTY, WILLY. DON'T BE A STRANGER.
MY APOLOGIES FOR THE COMMOTION, FOLKS. BUT THAT'S NEW YORK CITY, RIGHT?
PLEASE DON'T LEAVE. DINNER WILL BE SERVED SHORTLY, AND NOBODY WILL WANT TO MISS TONIGHT'S ENTERTAINMENT... THE LOVELY DAZZLER!

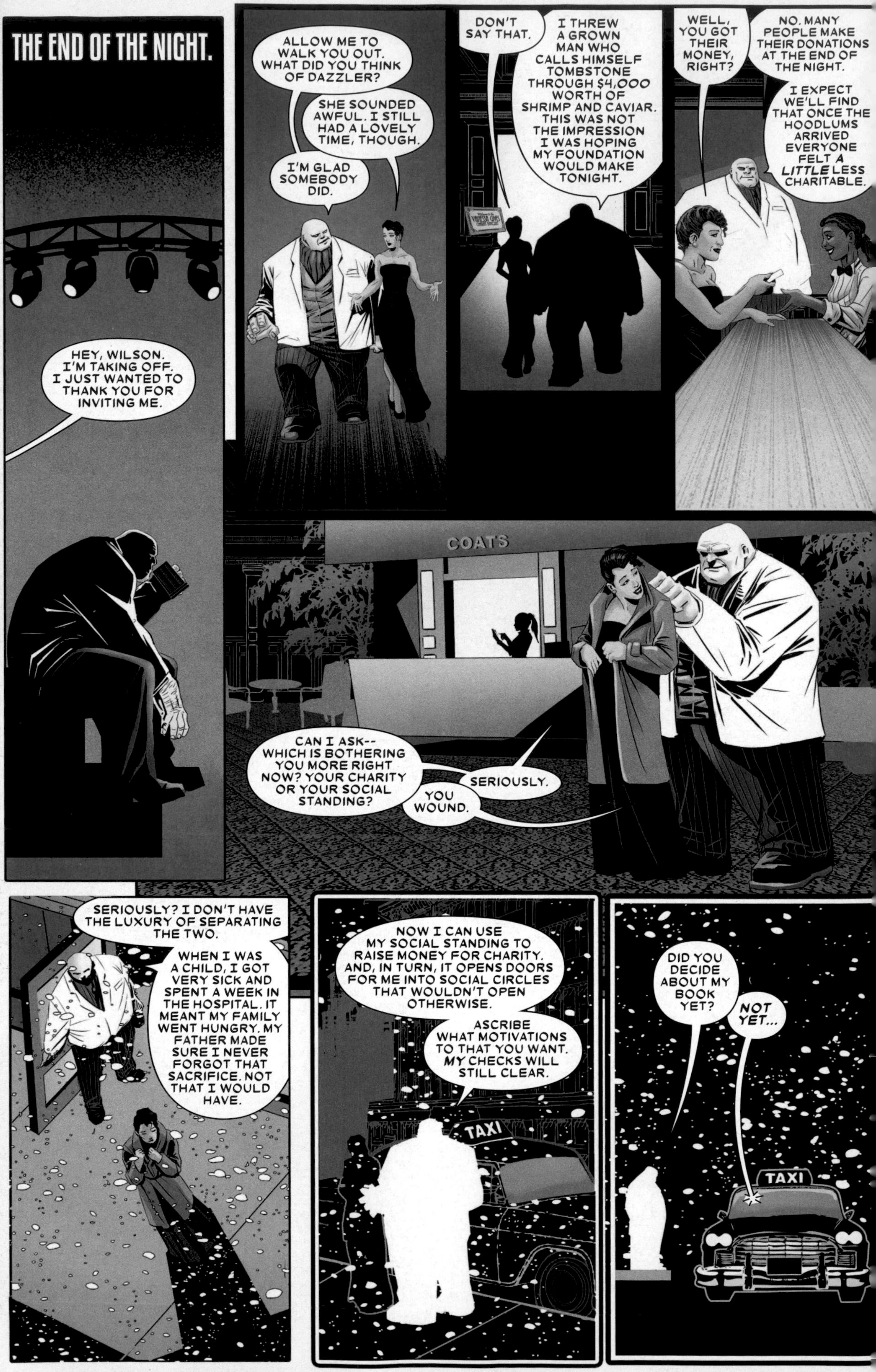
THE END OF THE NIGHT.
HEY, WILSON. I'M TAKING OFF. I JUST WANTED TO THANK YOU FOR INVITING ME.
ALLOW ME TO WALK YOU OUT. WHAT DID YOU THINK OF DAZZLER?
SHE SOUNDED AWFUL. I STILL HAD A LOVELY TIME, THOUGH.
I'M GLAD SOMEBODY DID.
I THREW A GROWN MAN WHO CALLS HIMSELF TOMBSTONE THROUGH $4,000 WORTH OF SHRIMP AND CAVIAR. THIS WAS NOT THE IMPRESSION I WAS HOPING MY FOUNDATION WOULD MAKE TONIGHT.
DON'T SAY THAT.
WELL, YOU GOT THEIR MONEY, RIGHT?
NO. MANY PEOPLE MAKE THEIR DONATIONS AT THE END OF THE NIGHT.
I EXPECT WE'LL FIND THAT ONCE THE HOODLUMS ARRIVED EVERYONE FELT A *LITTLE* LESS CHARITABLE.
COATS
CAN I ASK-- WHICH IS BOTHERING YOU MORE RIGHT NOW? YOUR CHARITY OR YOUR SOCIAL STANDING?
YOU WOUND.
SERIOUSLY.
SERIOUSLY? I DON'T HAVE THE LUXURY OF SEPARATING THE TWO.
WHEN I WAS A CHILD, I GOT VERY SICK AND SPENT A WEEK IN THE HOSPITAL. IT MEANT MY FAMILY WENT HUNGRY. MY FATHER MADE SURE I NEVER FORGOT THAT SACRIFICE. NOT THAT I WOULD HAVE.
NOW I CAN USE MY SOCIAL STANDING TO RAISE MONEY FOR CHARITY. AND, IN TURN, IT OPENS DOORS FOR ME INTO SOCIAL CIRCLES THAT WOULDN'T OPEN OTHERWISE.
ASCRIBE WHAT MOTIVATIONS TO THAT YOU WANT. *MY* CHECKS WILL STILL CLEAR.
TAXI
DID YOU DECIDE ABOUT MY BOOK YET?
NOT YET...
TAXI

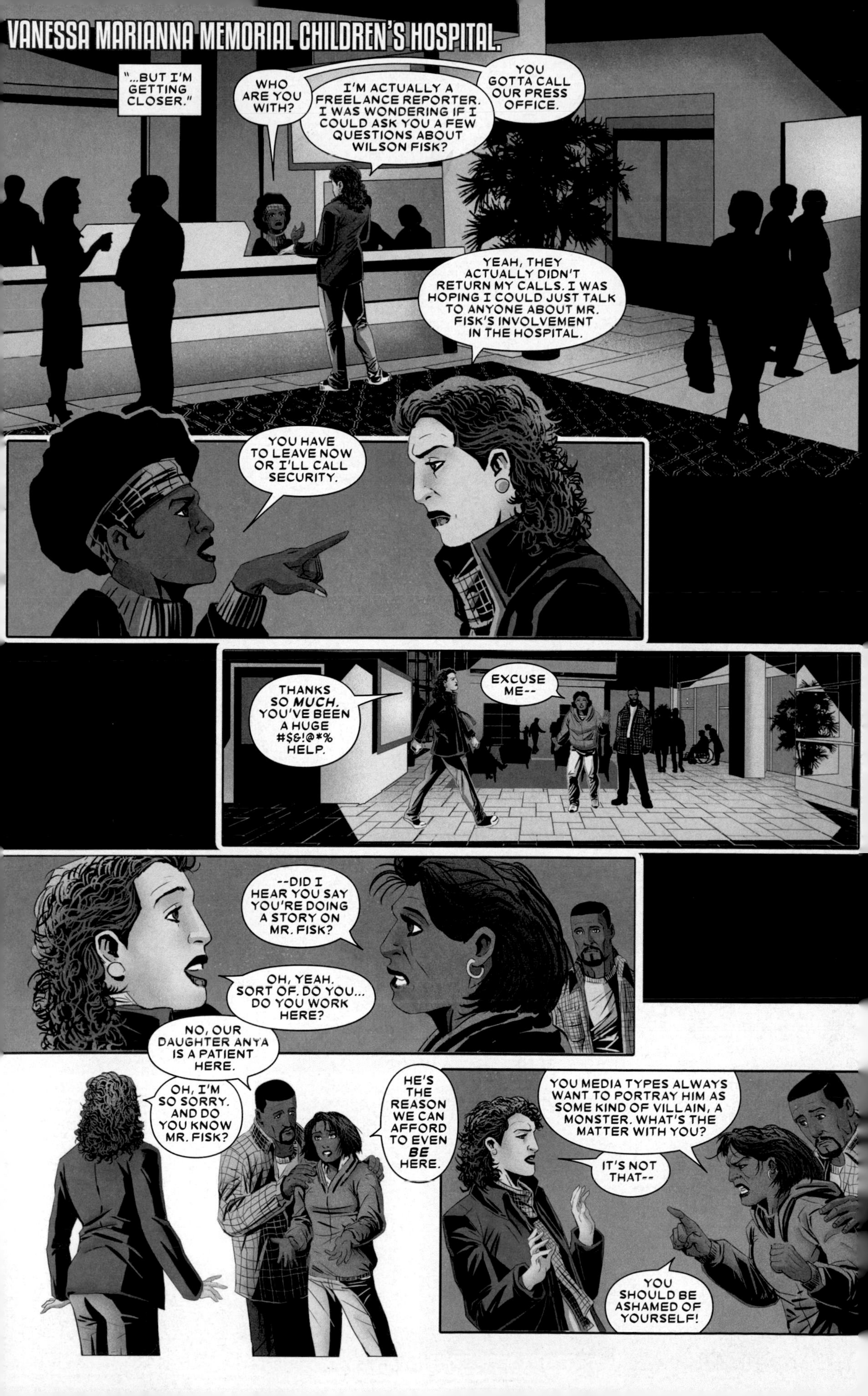
VANESSA MARIANNA MEMORIAL CHILDREN'S HOSPITAL.
"...BUT I'M GETTING CLOSER."
WHO ARE YOU WITH?
I'M ACTUALLY A FREELANCE REPORTER. I WAS WONDERING IF I COULD ASK YOU A FEW QUESTIONS ABOUT WILSON FISK?
YOU GOTTA CALL OUR PRESS OFFICE.
YEAH, THEY ACTUALLY DIDN'T RETURN MY CALLS. I WAS HOPING I COULD JUST TALK TO ANYONE ABOUT MR. FISK'S INVOLVEMENT IN THE HOSPITAL.
YOU HAVE TO LEAVE NOW OR I'LL CALL SECURITY.
THANKS SO MUCH. YOU'VE BEEN A HUGE #$&!@*% HELP.
EXCUSE ME--
--DID I HEAR YOU SAY YOU'RE DOING A STORY ON MR. FISK?
OH, YEAH. SORT OF. DO YOU... DO YOU WORK HERE?
NO, OUR DAUGHTER ANYA IS A PATIENT HERE.
OH, I'M SO SORRY. AND DO YOU KNOW MR. FISK?
HE'S THE REASON WE CAN AFFORD TO EVEN BE HERE.
YOU MEDIA TYPES ALWAYS WANT TO PORTRAY HIM AS SOME KIND OF VILLAIN, A MONSTER. WHAT'S THE MATTER WITH YOU?
IT'S NOT THAT--
YOU SHOULD BE ASHAMED OF YOURSELF!

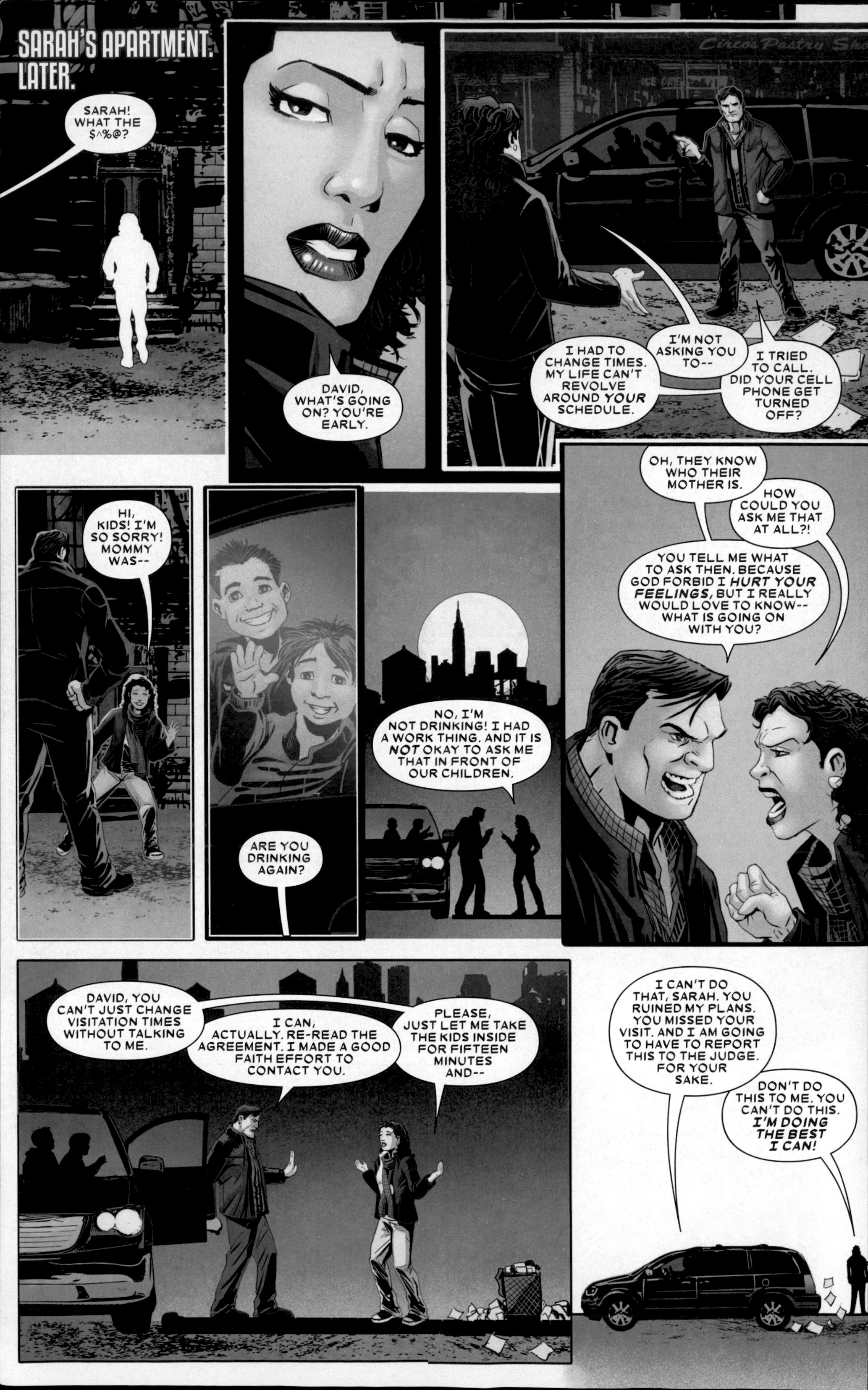
SARAH'S APARTMENT. LATER.
SARAH! WHAT THE $^%@?
DAVID, WHAT'S GOING ON? YOU'RE EARLY.
I HAD TO CHANGE TIMES. MY LIFE CAN'T REVOLVE AROUND YOUR SCHEDULE.
I'M NOT ASKING YOU TO--
I TRIED TO CALL. DID YOUR CELL PHONE GET TURNED OFF?
HI, KIDS! I'M SO SORRY! MOMMY WAS--
ARE YOU DRINKING AGAIN?
NO, I'M NOT DRINKING! I HAD A WORK THING. AND IT IS NOT OKAY TO ASK ME THAT IN FRONT OF OUR CHILDREN.
OH, THEY KNOW WHO THEIR MOTHER IS.
HOW COULD YOU ASK ME THAT AT ALL?!
YOU TELL ME WHAT TO ASK THEN. BECAUSE GOD FORBID I HURT YOUR FEELINGS, BUT I REALLY WOULD LOVE TO KNOW-- WHAT IS GOING ON WITH YOU?
DAVID, YOU CAN'T JUST CHANGE VISITATION TIMES WITHOUT TALKING TO ME.
I CAN, ACTUALLY. RE-READ THE AGREEMENT. I MADE A GOOD FAITH EFFORT TO CONTACT YOU.
PLEASE, JUST LET ME TAKE THE KIDS INSIDE FOR FIFTEEN MINUTES AND--
I CAN'T DO THAT, SARAH. YOU RUINED MY PLANS. YOU MISSED YOUR VISIT. AND I AM GOING TO HAVE TO REPORT THIS TO THE JUDGE. FOR YOUR SAKE.
DON'T DO THIS TO ME. YOU CAN'T DO THIS. I'M DOING THE BEST I CAN!

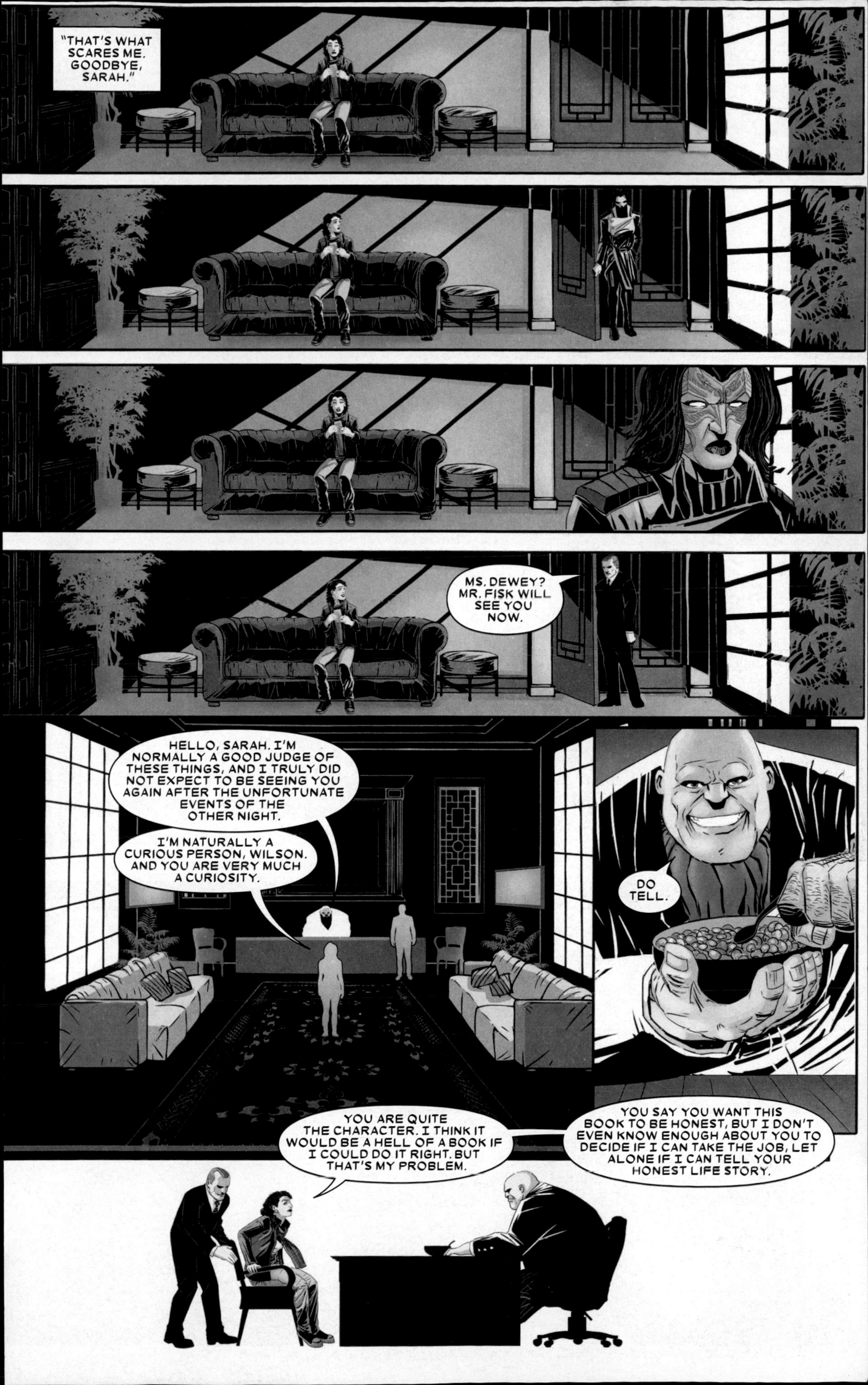

"THAT'S WHAT SCARES ME. GOODBYE, SARAH."
MS. DEWEY? MR. FISK WILL SEE YOU NOW.
HELLO, SARAH. I'M NORMALLY A GOOD JUDGE OF THESE THINGS, AND I TRULY DID NOT EXPECT TO BE SEEING YOU AGAIN AFTER THE UNFORTUNATE EVENTS OF THE OTHER NIGHT.
I'M NATURALLY A CURIOUS PERSON, WILSON. AND YOU ARE VERY MUCH A CURIOSITY.
DO TELL.
YOU ARE QUITE THE CHARACTER. I THINK IT WOULD BE A HELL OF A BOOK IF I COULD DO IT RIGHT. BUT THAT'S MY PROBLEM.
YOU SAY YOU WANT THIS BOOK TO BE HONEST, BUT I DON'T EVEN KNOW ENOUGH ABOUT YOU TO DECIDE IF I CAN TAKE THE JOB, LET ALONE IF I CAN TELL YOUR HONEST LIFE STORY.

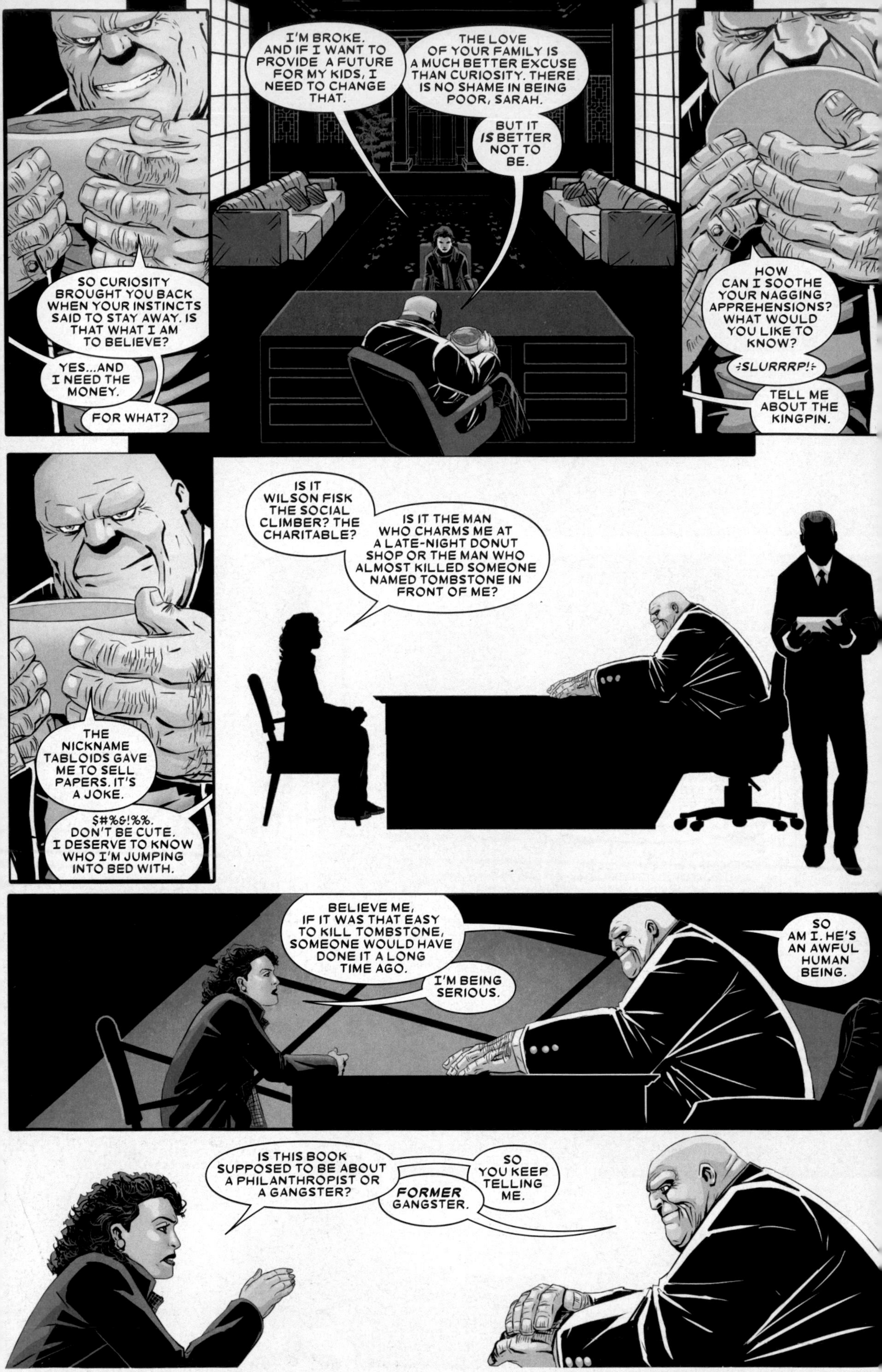
I'M BROKE. AND IF I WANT TO PROVIDE A FUTURE FOR MY KIDS, I NEED TO CHANGE THAT.
THE LOVE OF YOUR FAMILY IS A MUCH BETTER EXCUSE THAN CURIOSITY. THERE IS NO SHAME IN BEING POOR, SARAH.
BUT IT *IS* BETTER NOT TO BE.
SO CURIOSITY BROUGHT YOU BACK WHEN YOUR INSTINCTS SAID TO STAY AWAY. IS THAT WHAT I AM TO BELIEVE?
YES...AND I NEED THE MONEY.
FOR WHAT?
HOW CAN I SOOTHE YOUR NAGGING APPREHENSIONS? WHAT WOULD YOU LIKE TO KNOW?
SLURRRP!
TELL ME ABOUT THE KINGPIN.
THE NICKNAME TABLOIDS GAVE ME TO SELL PAPERS. IT'S A JOKE.
$#%&!%%. DON'T BE CUTE. I DESERVE TO KNOW WHO I'M JUMPING INTO BED WITH.
IS IT WILSON FISK THE SOCIAL CLIMBER? THE CHARITABLE?
IS IT THE MAN WHO CHARMS ME AT A LATE-NIGHT DONUT SHOP OR THE MAN WHO ALMOST KILLED SOMEONE NAMED TOMBSTONE IN FRONT OF ME?
BELIEVE ME, IF IT WAS THAT EASY TO KILL TOMBSTONE, SOMEONE WOULD HAVE DONE IT A LONG TIME AGO.
I'M BEING SERIOUS.
SO AM I. HE'S AN AWFUL HUMAN BEING.
IS THIS BOOK SUPPOSED TO BE ABOUT A PHILANTHROPIST OR A GANGSTER?
FORMER GANGSTER.
SO YOU KEEP TELLING ME.

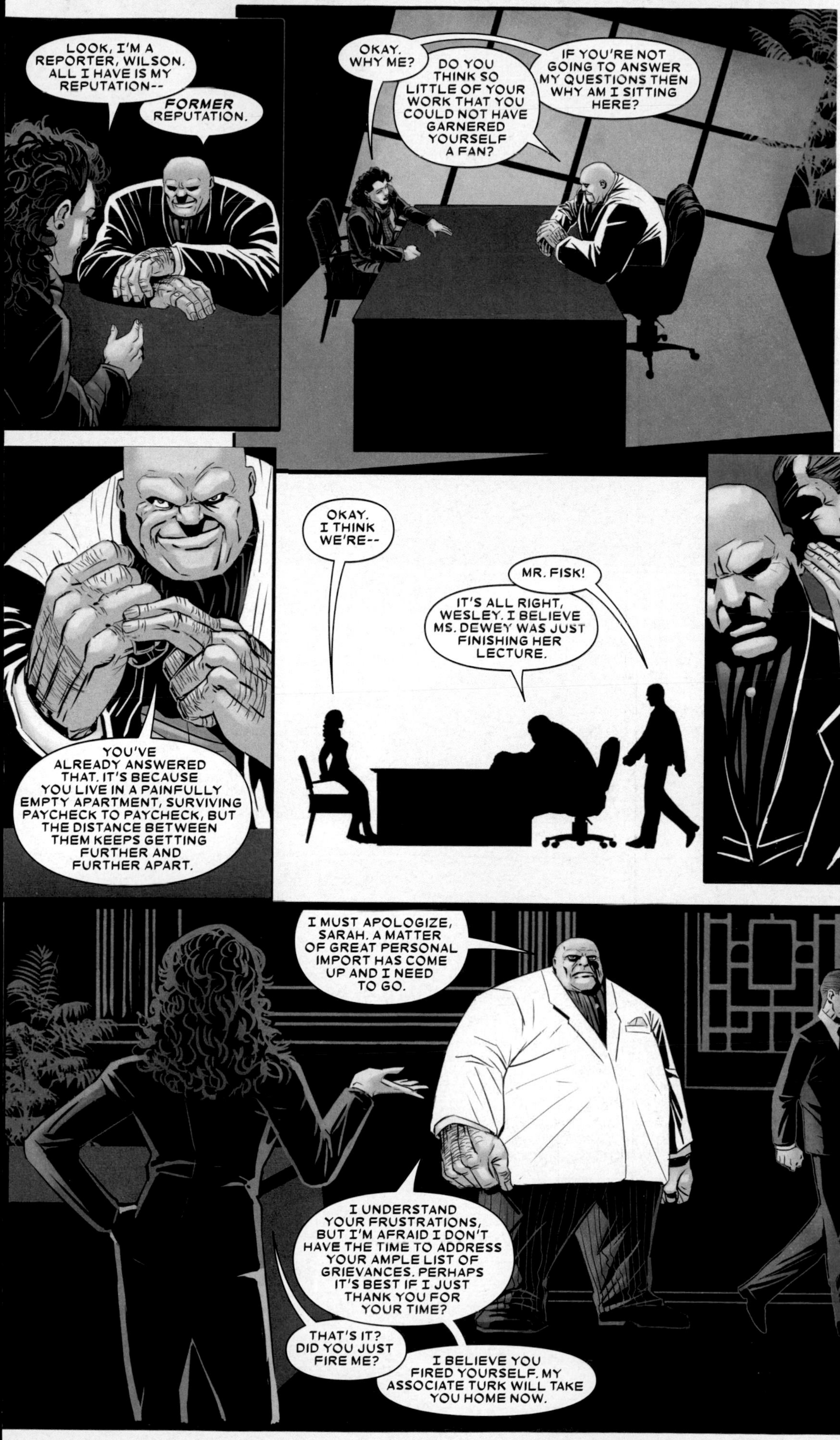
LOOK, I'M A REPORTER, WILSON. ALL I HAVE IS MY REPUTATION--
FORMER REPUTATION.
OKAY. WHY ME?
DO YOU THINK SO LITTLE OF YOUR WORK THAT YOU COULD NOT HAVE GARNERED YOURSELF A FAN?
IF YOU'RE NOT GOING TO ANSWER MY QUESTIONS THEN WHY AM I SITTING HERE?
YOU'VE ALREADY ANSWERED THAT. IT'S BECAUSE YOU LIVE IN A PAINFULLY EMPTY APARTMENT, SURVIVING PAYCHECK TO PAYCHECK, BUT THE DISTANCE BETWEEN THEM KEEPS GETTING FURTHER AND FURTHER APART.
OKAY. I THINK WE'RE--
MR. FISK!
IT'S ALL RIGHT, WESLEY. I BELIEVE MS. DEWEY WAS JUST FINISHING HER LECTURE.
I MUST APOLOGIZE, SARAH. A MATTER OF GREAT PERSONAL IMPORT HAS COME UP AND I NEED TO GO.
I UNDERSTAND YOUR FRUSTRATIONS, BUT I'M AFRAID I DON'T HAVE THE TIME TO ADDRESS YOUR AMPLE LIST OF GRIEVANCES. PERHAPS IT'S BEST IF I JUST THANK YOU FOR YOUR TIME?
THAT'S IT? DID YOU JUST FIRE ME?
I BELIEVE YOU FIRED YOURSELF. MY ASSOCIATE TURK WILL TAKE YOU HOME NOW.

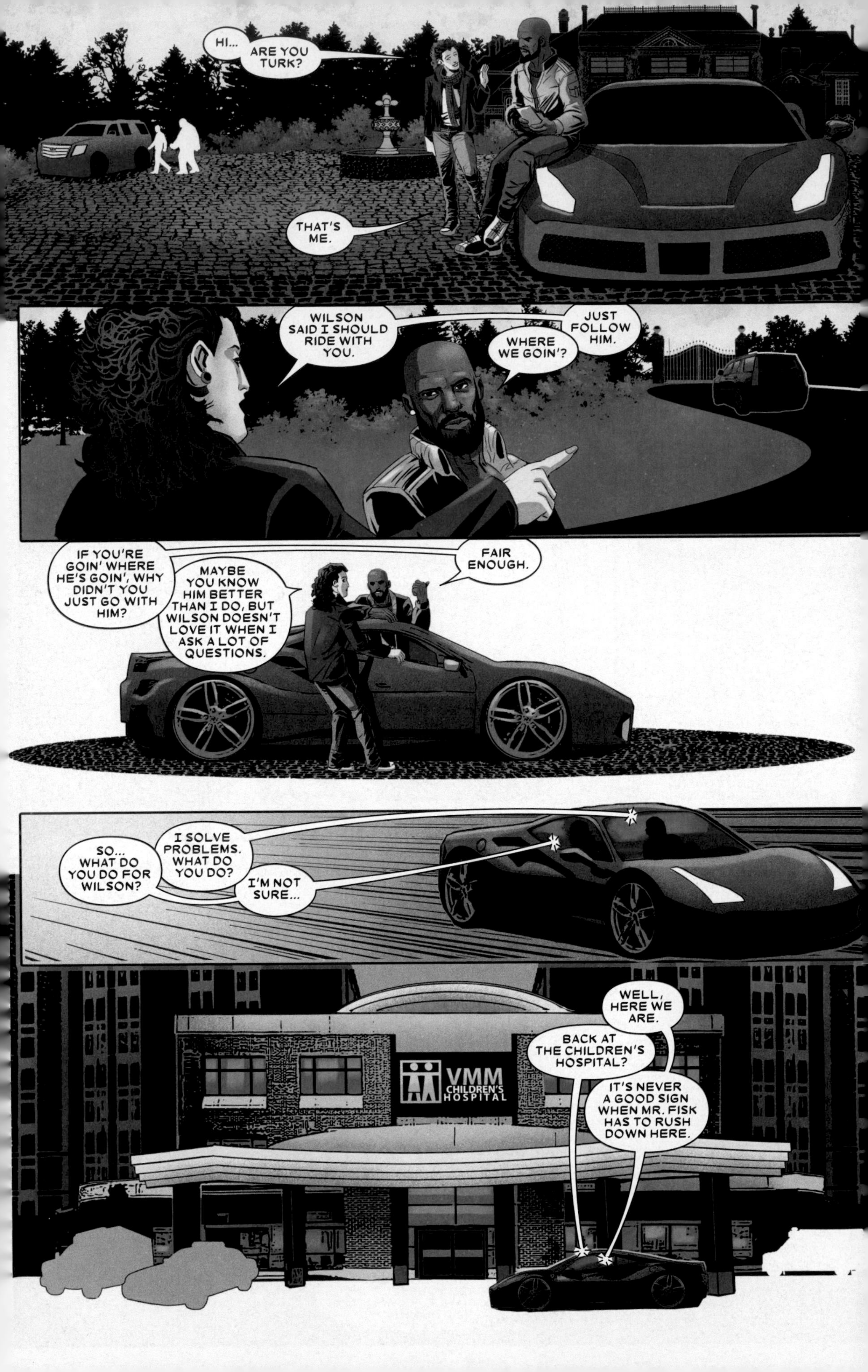
HI... ARE YOU TURK?
THAT'S ME.
WILSON SAID I SHOULD RIDE WITH YOU.
WHERE WE GOIN'?
JUST FOLLOW HIM.
IF YOU'RE GOIN' WHERE HE'S GOIN', WHY DIDN'T YOU JUST GO WITH HIM?
MAYBE YOU KNOW HIM BETTER THAN I DO, BUT WILSON DOESN'T LOVE IT WHEN I ASK A LOT OF QUESTIONS.
FAIR ENOUGH.
SO... WHAT DO YOU DO FOR WILSON?
I SOLVE PROBLEMS. WHAT DO YOU DO?
I'M NOT SURE...
VMM CHILDREN'S HOSPITAL
WELL, HERE WE ARE.
BACK AT THE CHILDREN'S HOSPITAL?
IT'S NEVER A GOOD SIGN WHEN MR. FISK HAS TO RUSH DOWN HERE.

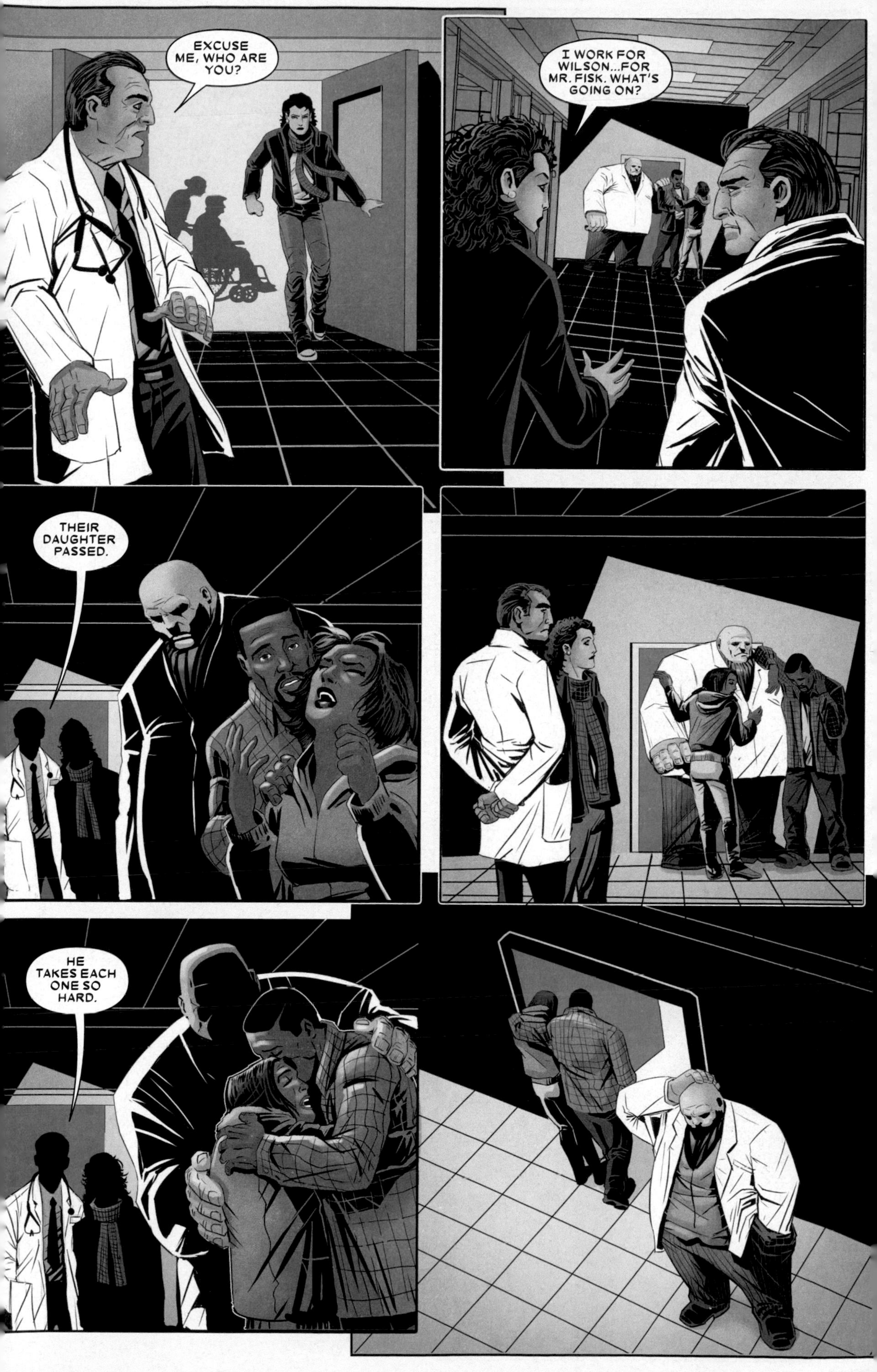
EXCUSE ME, WHO ARE YOU?
I WORK FOR WILSON...FOR MR. FISK. WHAT'S GOING ON?
THEIR DAUGHTER PASSED.
HE TAKES EACH ONE SO HARD.

YOU MIGHT WANT TO WAIT HERE.

MR. FISK, I'M--

DOCTOR D'AMICO, WHAT DID YOU TELL ME ABOUT THAT LITTLE GIRL?

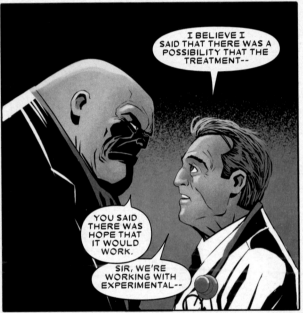

I BELIEVE I SAID THAT THERE WAS A POSSIBILITY THAT THE TREATMENT--

YOU SAID THERE WAS HOPE THAT IT WOULD WORK.

SIR, WE'RE WORKING WITH EXPERIMENTAL--

DID THAT LOOK LIKE HOPE TO YOU? I TOLD THEM WHAT YOU SAID. I GAVE THEM MY WORD THERE WAS STILL HOPE. AND WHAT DID YOUR HOPE GET THAT FAMILY?

I'M SORRY, SIR.

IT'S ALL RIGHT, DOCTOR. MY EMOTIONS GET THE BEST OF ME SOMETIMES. PLEASE FORGIVE ME.

OF COURSE.

PLEASE MAKE SURE THAT ALL OF THEIR BILLS ARE SENT TO ME.

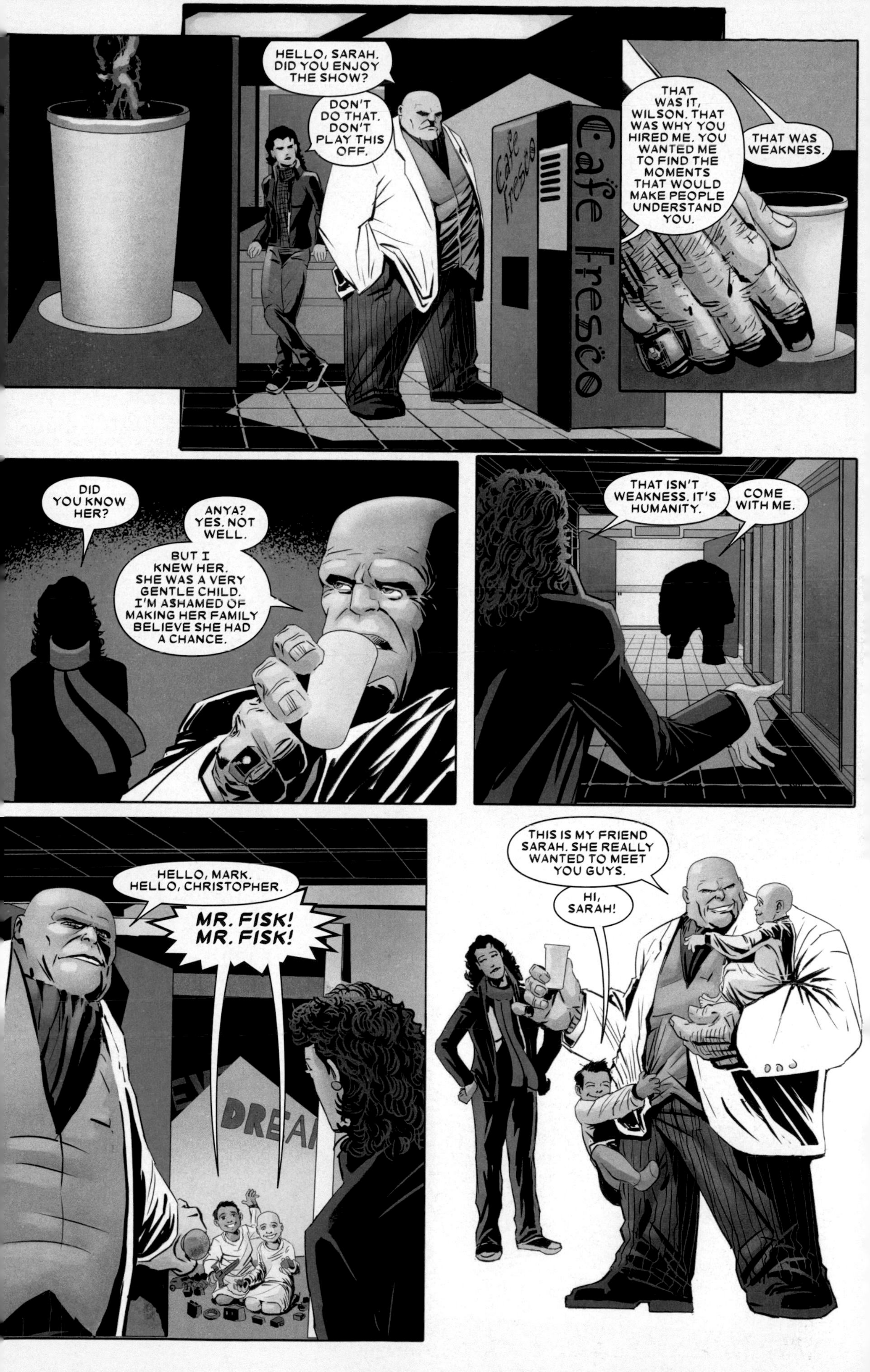
HELLO, SARAH. DID YOU ENJOY THE SHOW?
DON'T DO THAT. DON'T PLAY THIS OFF.
Cafe Fresco
Café Fresco
THAT WAS IT, WILSON. THAT WAS WHY YOU HIRED ME. YOU WANTED ME TO FIND THE MOMENTS THAT WOULD MAKE PEOPLE UNDERSTAND YOU.
THAT WAS WEAKNESS.
DID YOU KNOW HER?
ANYA? YES. NOT WELL.
BUT I KNEW HER. SHE WAS A VERY GENTLE CHILD. I'M ASHAMED OF MAKING HER FAMILY BELIEVE SHE HAD A CHANCE.
THAT ISN'T WEAKNESS. IT'S HUMANITY.
COME WITH ME.
HELLO, MARK. HELLO, CHRISTOPHER.
MR. FISK! MR. FISK!
DREA
THIS IS MY FRIEND SARAH. SHE REALLY WANTED TO MEET YOU GUYS.
HI, SARAH!

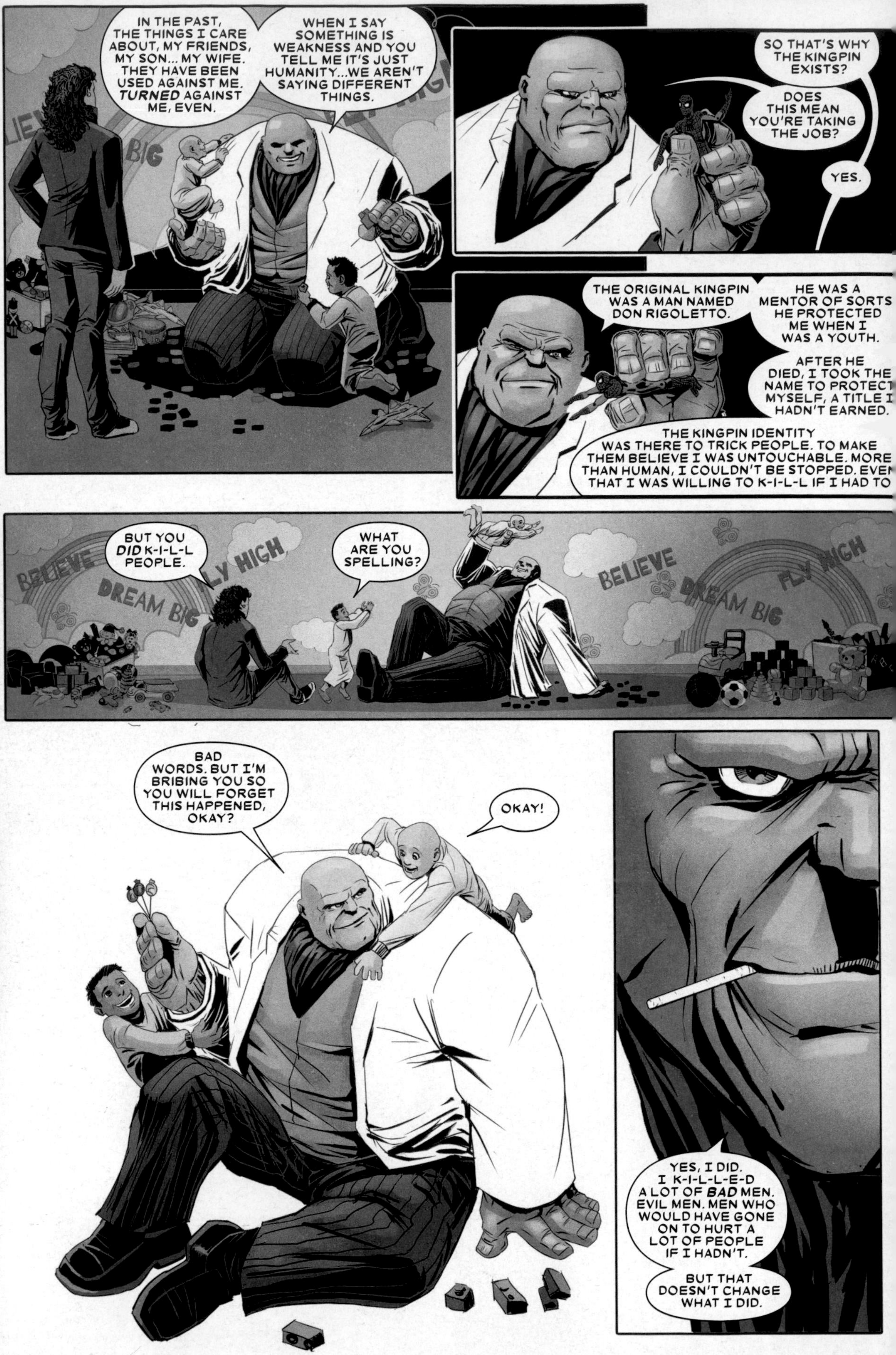
IN THE PAST, THE THINGS I CARE ABOUT, MY FRIENDS, MY SON... MY WIFE. THEY HAVE BEEN USED AGAINST ME. *TURNED* AGAINST ME, EVEN.
WHEN I SAY SOMETHING IS WEAKNESS AND YOU TELL ME IT'S JUST HUMANITY...WE AREN'T SAYING DIFFERENT THINGS.
SO THAT'S WHY THE KINGPIN EXISTS?
DOES THIS MEAN YOU'RE TAKING THE JOB?
YES.
THE ORIGINAL KINGPIN WAS A MAN NAMED DON RIGOLETTO.
HE WAS A MENTOR OF SORTS. HE PROTECTED ME WHEN I WAS A YOUTH.
AFTER HE DIED, I TOOK THE NAME TO PROTECT MYSELF, A TITLE I HADN'T EARNED.
THE KINGPIN IDENTITY WAS THERE TO TRICK PEOPLE. TO MAKE THEM BELIEVE I WAS UNTOUCHABLE. MORE THAN HUMAN, I COULDN'T BE STOPPED. EVEN THAT I WAS WILLING TO K-I-L-L IF I HAD TO.
BELIEVE
DREAM BIG
FLY HIGH
BUT YOU *DID* K-I-L-L PEOPLE.
WHAT ARE YOU SPELLING?
BAD WORDS. BUT I'M BRIBING YOU SO YOU WILL FORGET THIS HAPPENED, OKAY?
OKAY!
YES, I DID. I K-I-L-L-E-D A LOT OF *BAD* MEN. EVIL MEN. MEN WHO WOULD HAVE GONE ON TO HURT A LOT OF PEOPLE IF I HADN'T.
BUT THAT DOESN'T CHANGE WHAT I DID.

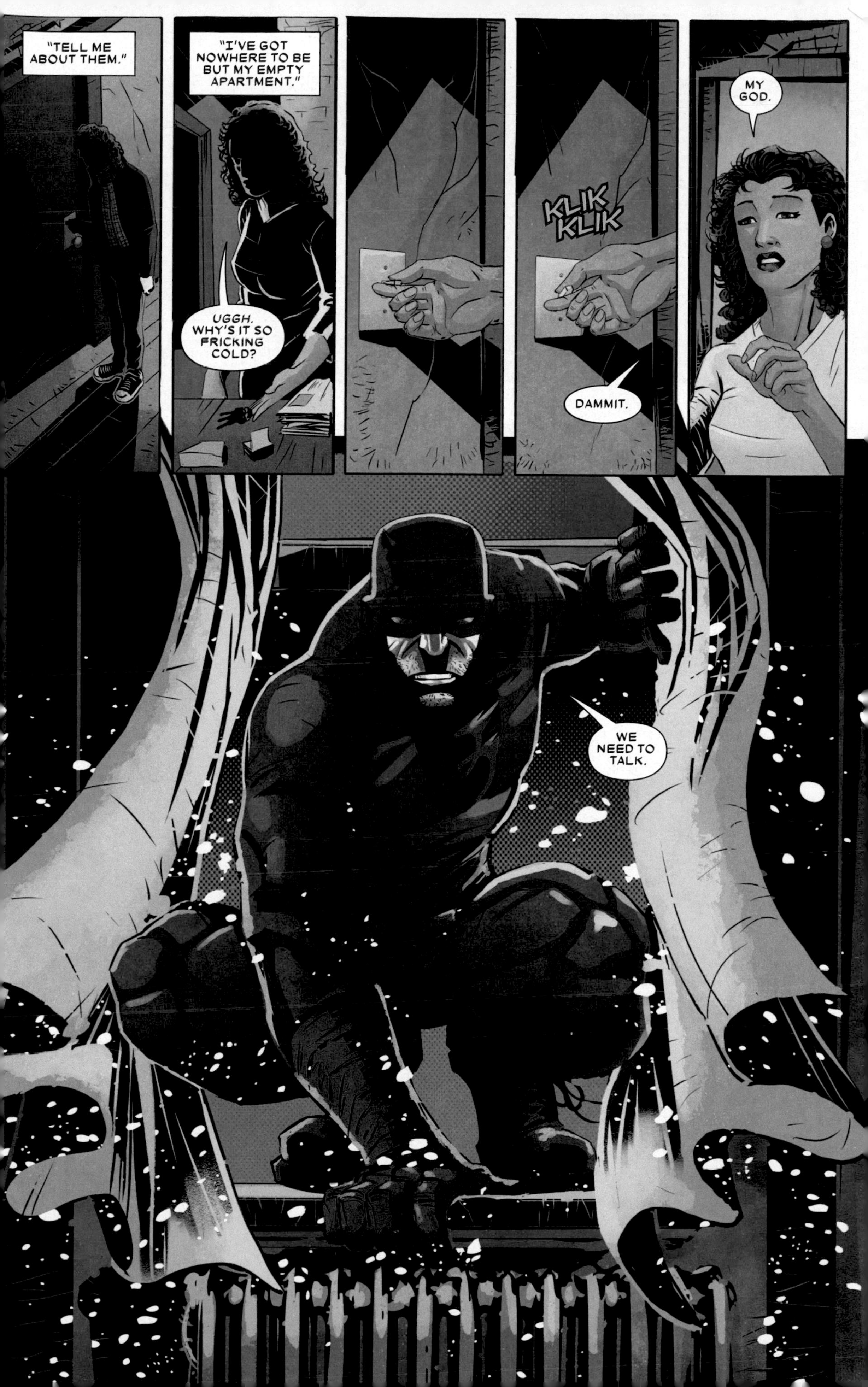
"TELL ME ABOUT THEM."
"I'VE GOT NOWHERE TO BE BUT MY EMPTY APARTMENT."
UGGH. WHY'S IT SO FRICKING COLD?
KLIK KLIK
DAMMIT.
MY GOD.
WE NEED TO TALK.

THREE

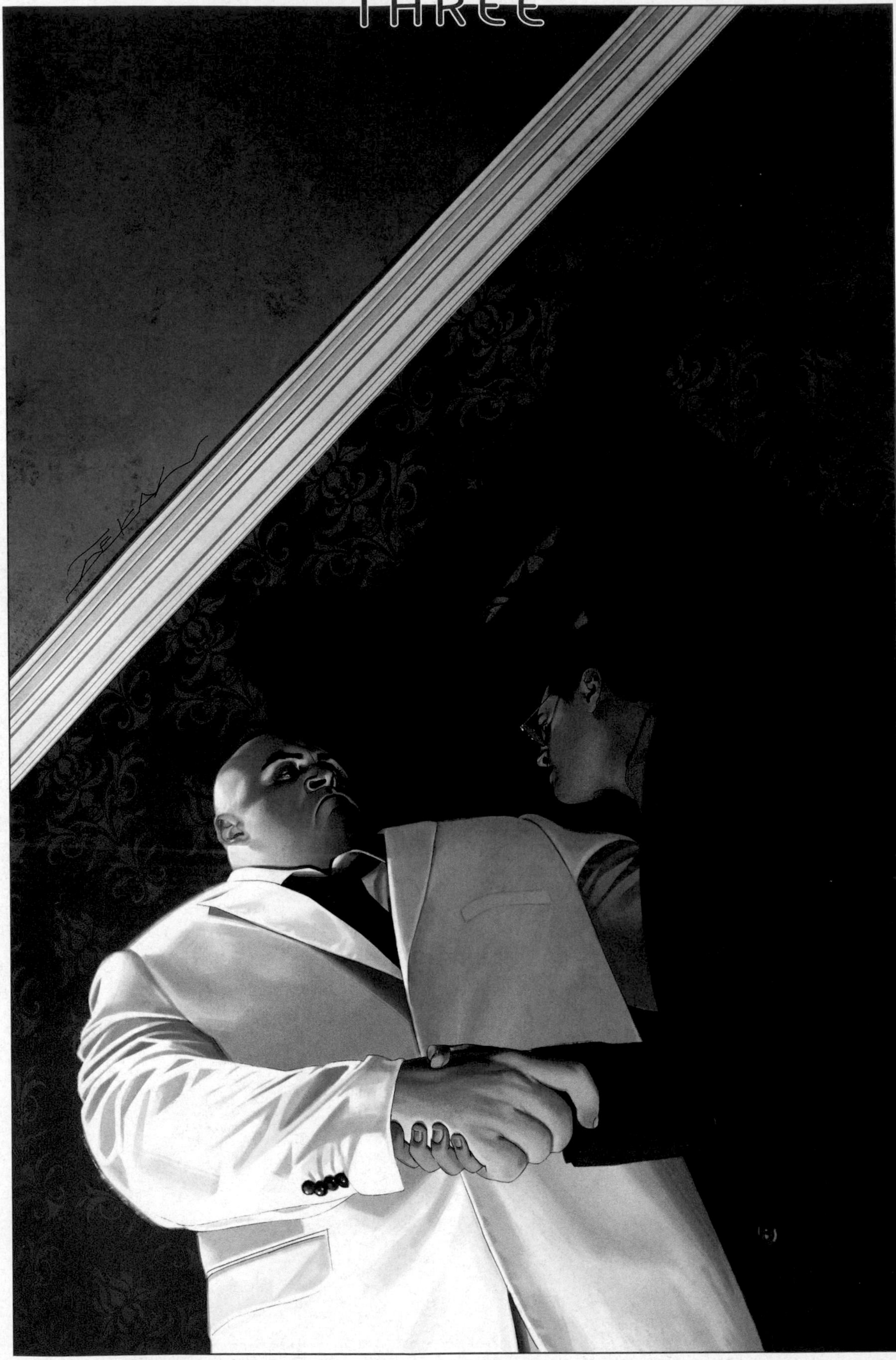

SARAH DEWEY'S APARTMENT. MORNINGSIDE HEIGHTS. LATE.
GET THE $%*! OUT!
I'M NOT HERE TO HURT YOU, MS. DEWEY.
I'M HERE BECAUSE OF WILSON FISK.
THEN YOU'RE IN THE WRONG APARTMENT.

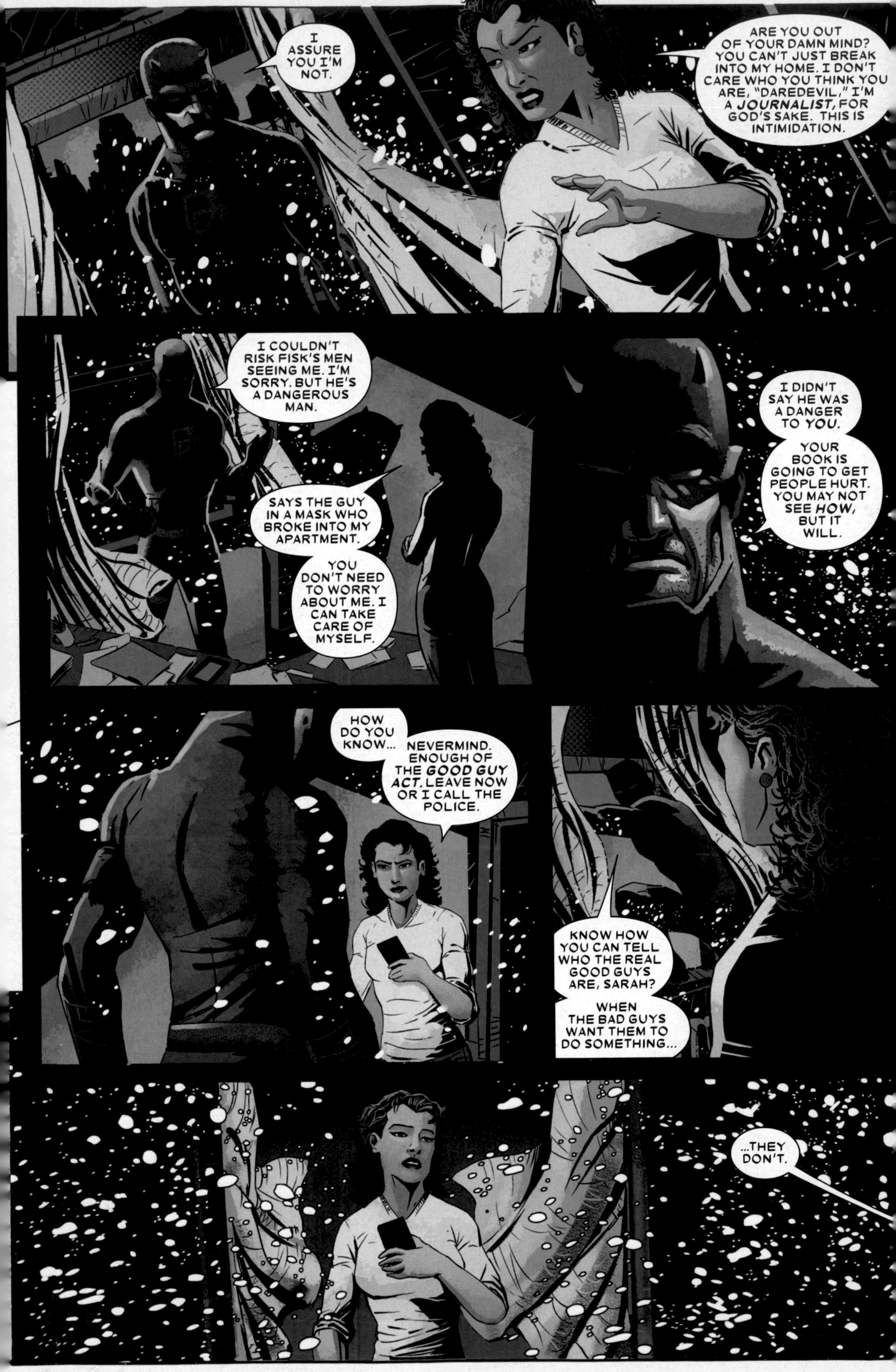
ARE YOU OUT OF YOUR DAMN MIND? YOU CAN'T JUST BREAK INTO MY HOME. I DON'T CARE WHO YOU THINK YOU ARE, "DAREDEVIL," I'M A *JOURNALIST*, FOR GOD'S SAKE. THIS IS INTIMIDATION.
I ASSURE YOU I'M NOT.
I COULDN'T RISK FISK'S MEN SEEING ME. I'M SORRY. BUT HE'S A DANGEROUS MAN.
SAYS THE GUY IN A MASK WHO BROKE INTO MY APARTMENT.
YOU DON'T NEED TO WORRY ABOUT ME. I CAN TAKE CARE OF MYSELF.
I DIDN'T SAY HE WAS A DANGER TO *YOU*.
YOUR BOOK IS GOING TO GET PEOPLE HURT. YOU MAY NOT SEE *HOW*, BUT IT WILL.
HOW DO YOU KNOW...
NEVERMIND. ENOUGH OF THE *GOOD GUY ACT*. LEAVE NOW OR I CALL THE POLICE.
KNOW HOW YOU CAN TELL WHO THE REAL GOOD GUYS ARE, SARAH?
WHEN THE BAD GUYS WANT THEM TO DO SOMETHING...
...THEY DON'T.

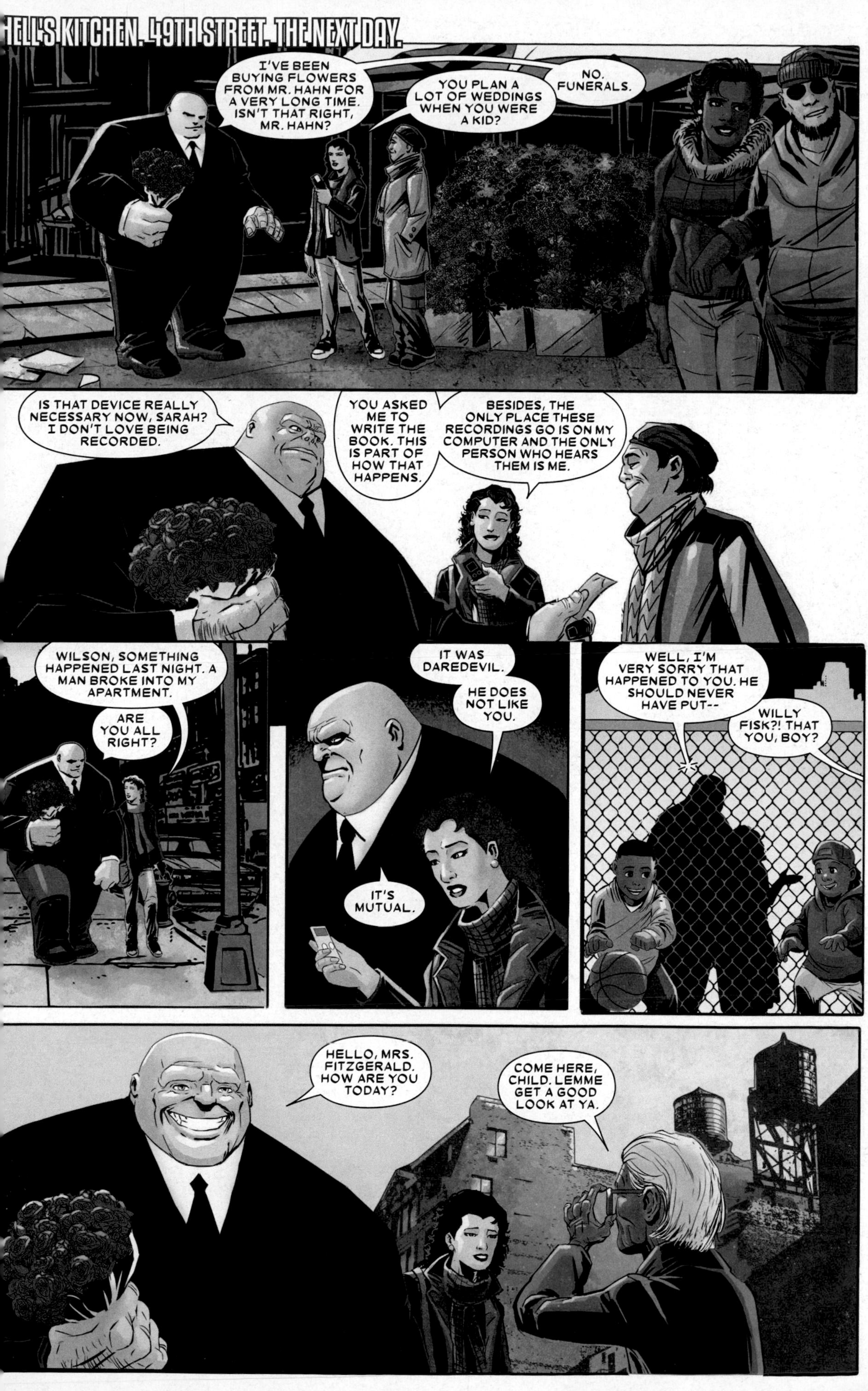
HELL'S KITCHEN. 49TH STREET. THE NEXT DAY.
I'VE BEEN BUYING FLOWERS FROM MR. HAHN FOR A VERY LONG TIME. ISN'T THAT RIGHT, MR. HAHN?
YOU PLAN A LOT OF WEDDINGS WHEN YOU WERE A KID?
NO. FUNERALS.
IS THAT DEVICE REALLY NECESSARY NOW, SARAH? I DON'T LOVE BEING RECORDED.
YOU ASKED ME TO WRITE THE BOOK. THIS IS PART OF HOW THAT HAPPENS.
BESIDES, THE ONLY PLACE THESE RECORDINGS GO IS ON MY COMPUTER AND THE ONLY PERSON WHO HEARS THEM IS ME.
WILSON, SOMETHING HAPPENED LAST NIGHT. A MAN BROKE INTO MY APARTMENT.
ARE YOU ALL RIGHT?
IT WAS DAREDEVIL.
HE DOES NOT LIKE YOU.
IT'S MUTUAL.
WELL, I'M VERY SORRY THAT HAPPENED TO YOU. HE SHOULD NEVER HAVE PUT--
WILLY FISK?! THAT YOU, BOY?
HELLO, MRS. FITZGERALD. HOW ARE YOU TODAY?
COME HERE, CHILD. LEMME GET A GOOD LOOK AT YA.

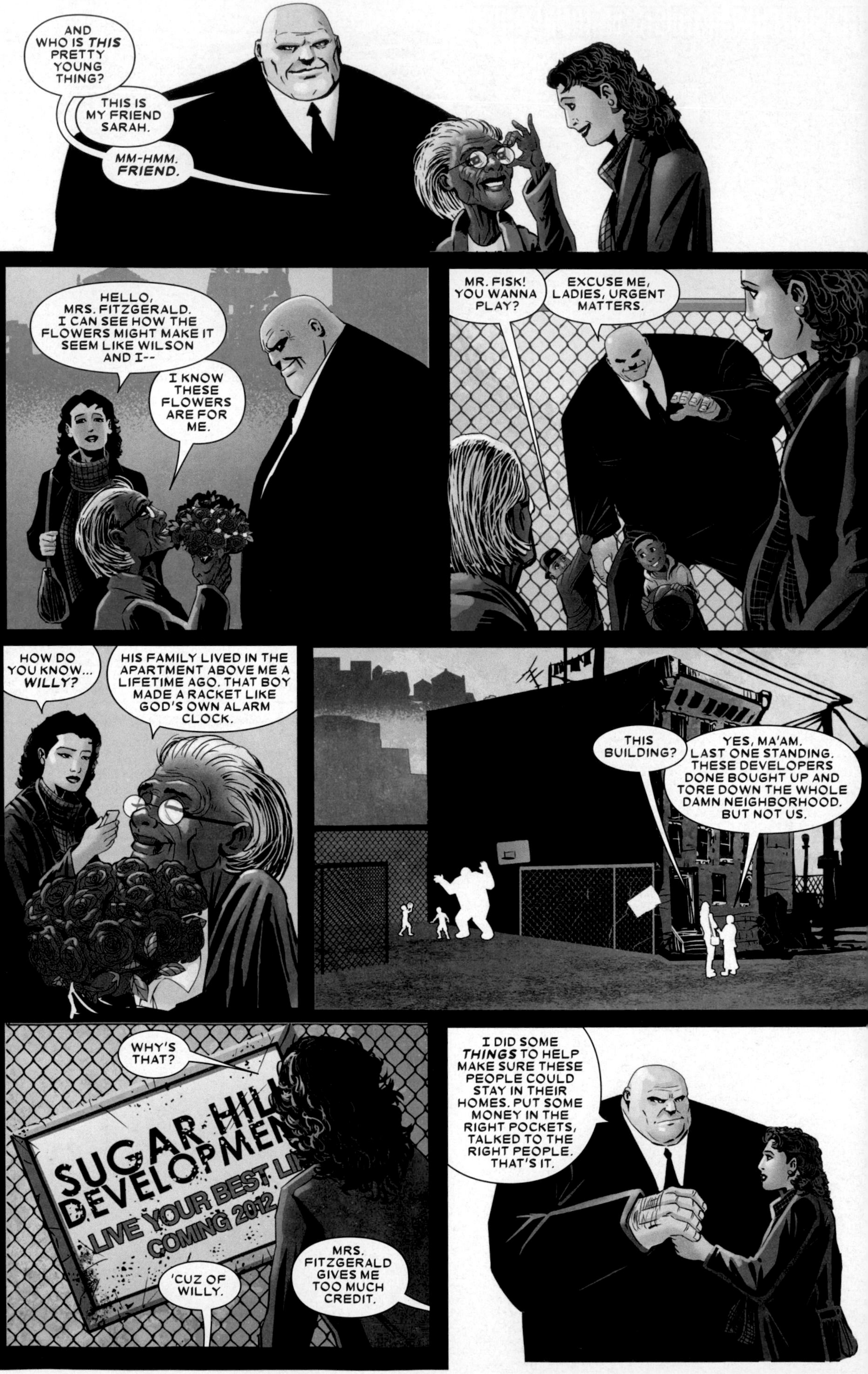
AND WHO IS *THIS* PRETTY YOUNG THING?
THIS IS MY FRIEND SARAH.
MM-HMM. *FRIEND.*
HELLO, MRS. FITZGERALD. I CAN SEE HOW THE FLOWERS MIGHT MAKE IT SEEM LIKE WILSON AND I--
I KNOW THESE FLOWERS ARE FOR ME.
MR. FISK! YOU WANNA PLAY?
EXCUSE ME, LADIES, URGENT MATTERS.
HOW DO YOU KNOW... *WILLY?*
HIS FAMILY LIVED IN THE APARTMENT ABOVE ME A LIFETIME AGO. THAT BOY MADE A RACKET LIKE GOD'S OWN ALARM CLOCK.
THIS BUILDING?
YES, MA'AM. LAST ONE STANDING. THESE DEVELOPERS DONE BOUGHT UP AND TORE DOWN THE WHOLE DAMN NEIGHBORHOOD. BUT NOT US.
WHY'S THAT?
SUGAR HIL
DEVELOPMEN
LIVE YOUR BEST LI
COMING 2012
'CUZ OF WILLY.
MRS. FITZGERALD GIVES ME TOO MUCH CREDIT.
I DID SOME *THINGS* TO HELP MAKE SURE THESE PEOPLE COULD STAY IN THEIR HOMES. PUT SOME MONEY IN THE RIGHT POCKETS, TALKED TO THE RIGHT PEOPLE. THAT'S IT.

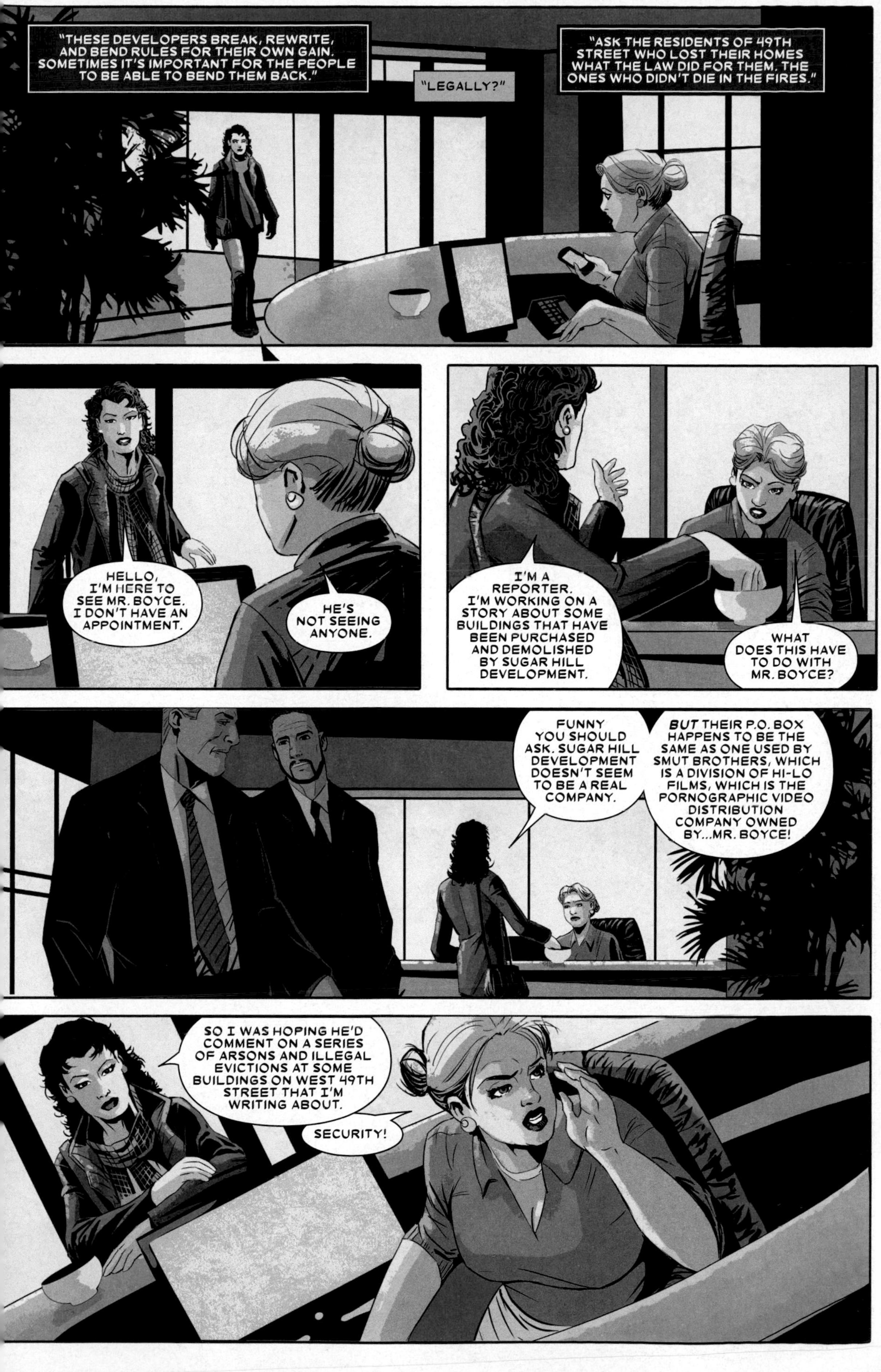
"THESE DEVELOPERS BREAK, REWRITE, AND BEND RULES FOR THEIR OWN GAIN. SOMETIMES IT'S IMPORTANT FOR THE PEOPLE TO BE ABLE TO BEND THEM BACK."
"LEGALLY?"
"ASK THE RESIDENTS OF 49TH STREET WHO LOST THEIR HOMES WHAT THE LAW DID FOR THEM. THE ONES WHO DIDN'T DIE IN THE FIRES."
HELLO, I'M HERE TO SEE MR. BOYCE. I DON'T HAVE AN APPOINTMENT.
HE'S NOT SEEING ANYONE.
I'M A REPORTER. I'M WORKING ON A STORY ABOUT SOME BUILDINGS THAT HAVE BEEN PURCHASED AND DEMOLISHED BY SUGAR HILL DEVELOPMENT.
WHAT DOES THIS HAVE TO DO WITH MR. BOYCE?
FUNNY YOU SHOULD ASK. SUGAR HILL DEVELOPMENT DOESN'T SEEM TO BE A REAL COMPANY.
BUT THEIR P.O. BOX HAPPENS TO BE THE SAME AS ONE USED BY SMUT BROTHERS, WHICH IS A DIVISION OF HI-LO FILMS, WHICH IS THE PORNOGRAPHIC VIDEO DISTRIBUTION COMPANY OWNED BY...MR. BOYCE!
SO I WAS HOPING HE'D COMMENT ON A SERIES OF ARSONS AND ILLEGAL EVICTIONS AT SOME BUILDINGS ON WEST 49TH STREET THAT I'M WRITING ABOUT.
SECURITY!

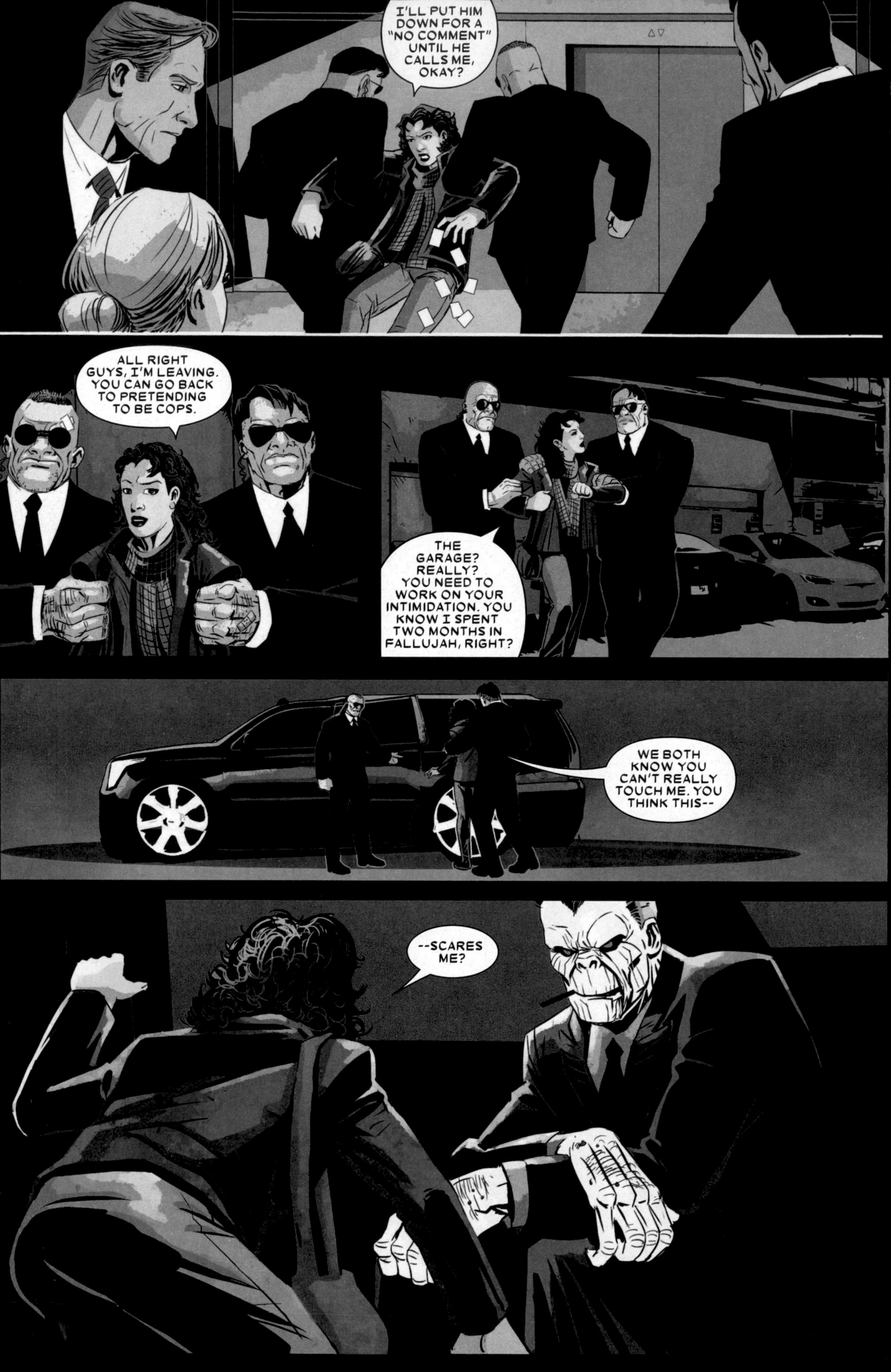
I'LL PUT HIM DOWN FOR A "NO COMMENT" UNTIL HE CALLS ME, OKAY?
ALL RIGHT GUYS, I'M LEAVING. YOU CAN GO BACK TO PRETENDING TO BE COPS.
THE GARAGE? REALLY? YOU NEED TO WORK ON YOUR INTIMIDATION. YOU KNOW I SPENT TWO MONTHS IN FALLUJAH, RIGHT?
WE BOTH KNOW YOU CAN'T REALLY TOUCH ME. YOU THINK THIS--
--SCARES ME?

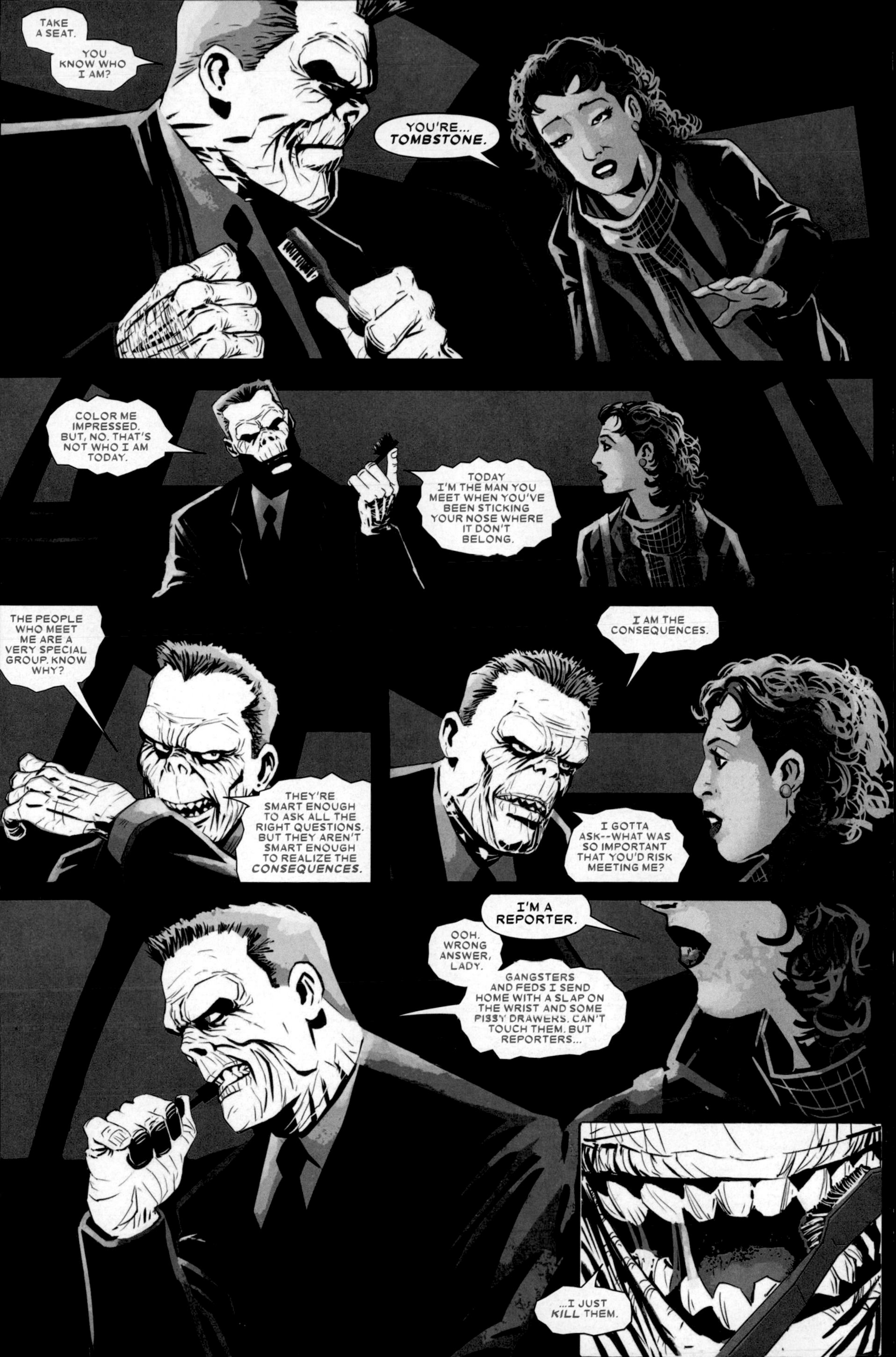

TAKE A SEAT.
YOU KNOW WHO I AM?
YOU'RE... TOMBSTONE.
COLOR ME IMPRESSED. BUT, NO. THAT'S NOT WHO I AM TODAY.
TODAY I'M THE MAN YOU MEET WHEN YOU'VE BEEN STICKING YOUR NOSE WHERE IT DON'T BELONG.
THE PEOPLE WHO MEET ME ARE A VERY SPECIAL GROUP. KNOW WHY?
THEY'RE SMART ENOUGH TO ASK ALL THE RIGHT QUESTIONS. BUT THEY AREN'T SMART ENOUGH TO REALIZE THE CONSEQUENCES.
I AM THE CONSEQUENCES.
I GOTTA ASK--WHAT WAS SO IMPORTANT THAT YOU'D RISK MEETING ME?
I'M A REPORTER.
OOH. WRONG ANSWER, LADY.
GANGSTERS AND FEDS I SEND HOME WITH A SLAP ON THE WRIST AND SOME PISSY DRAWERS. CAN'T TOUCH THEM. BUT REPORTERS...
...I JUST KILL THEM.

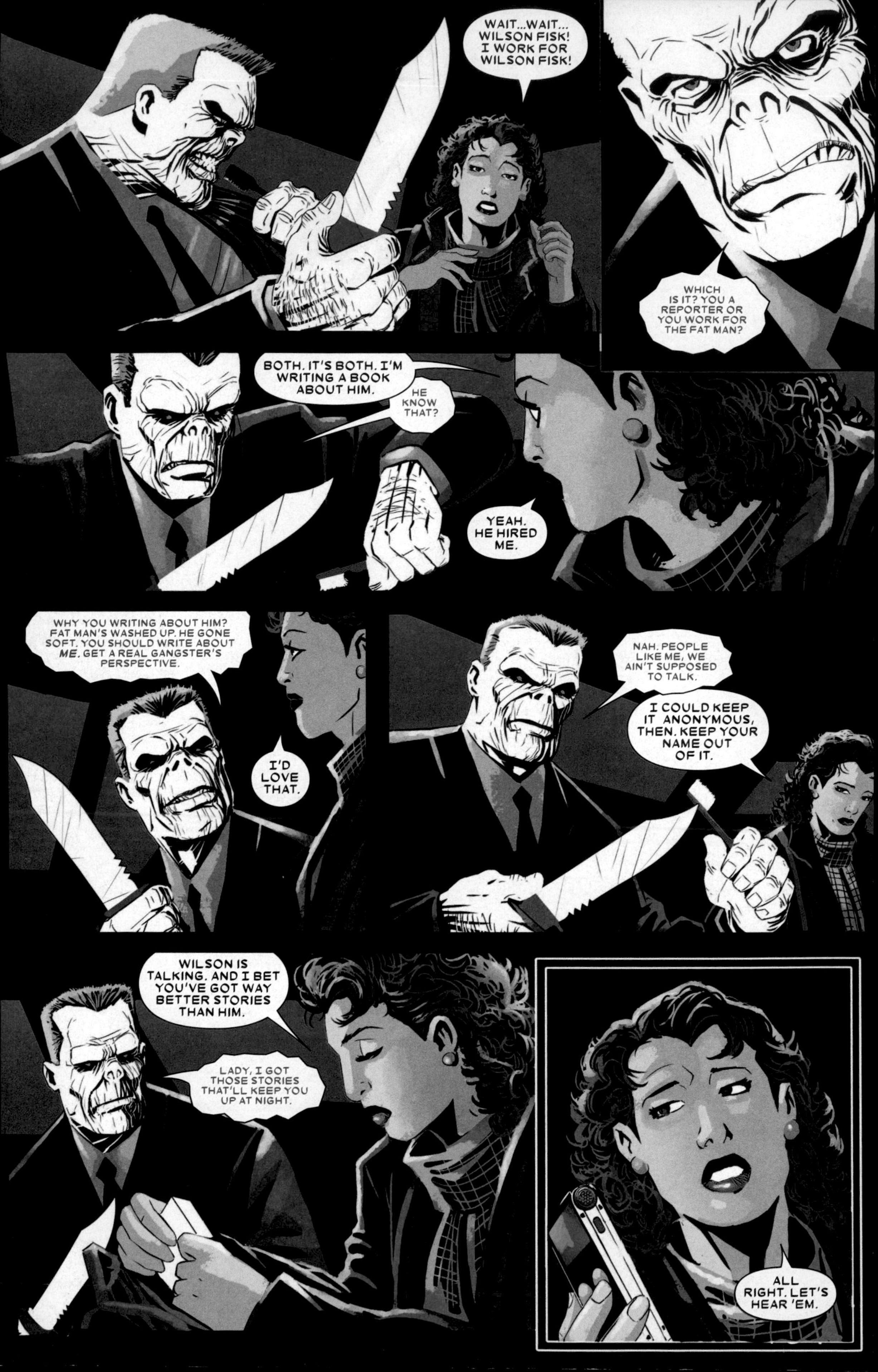
WAIT...WAIT... WILSON FISK! I WORK FOR WILSON FISK!
WHICH IS IT? YOU A REPORTER OR YOU WORK FOR THE FAT MAN?
BOTH. IT'S BOTH. I'M WRITING A BOOK ABOUT HIM.
HE KNOW THAT?
YEAH. HE HIRED ME.
WHY YOU WRITING ABOUT HIM? FAT MAN'S WASHED UP. HE GONE SOFT. YOU SHOULD WRITE ABOUT ME. GET A REAL GANGSTER'S PERSPECTIVE.
I'D LOVE THAT.
NAH. PEOPLE LIKE ME, WE AIN'T SUPPOSED TO TALK.
I COULD KEEP IT ANONYMOUS, THEN. KEEP YOUR NAME OUT OF IT.
WILSON IS TALKING. AND I BET YOU'VE GOT WAY BETTER STORIES THAN HIM.
LADY, I GOT THOSE STORIES THAT'LL KEEP YOU UP AT NIGHT.
ALL RIGHT. LET'S HEAR 'EM.

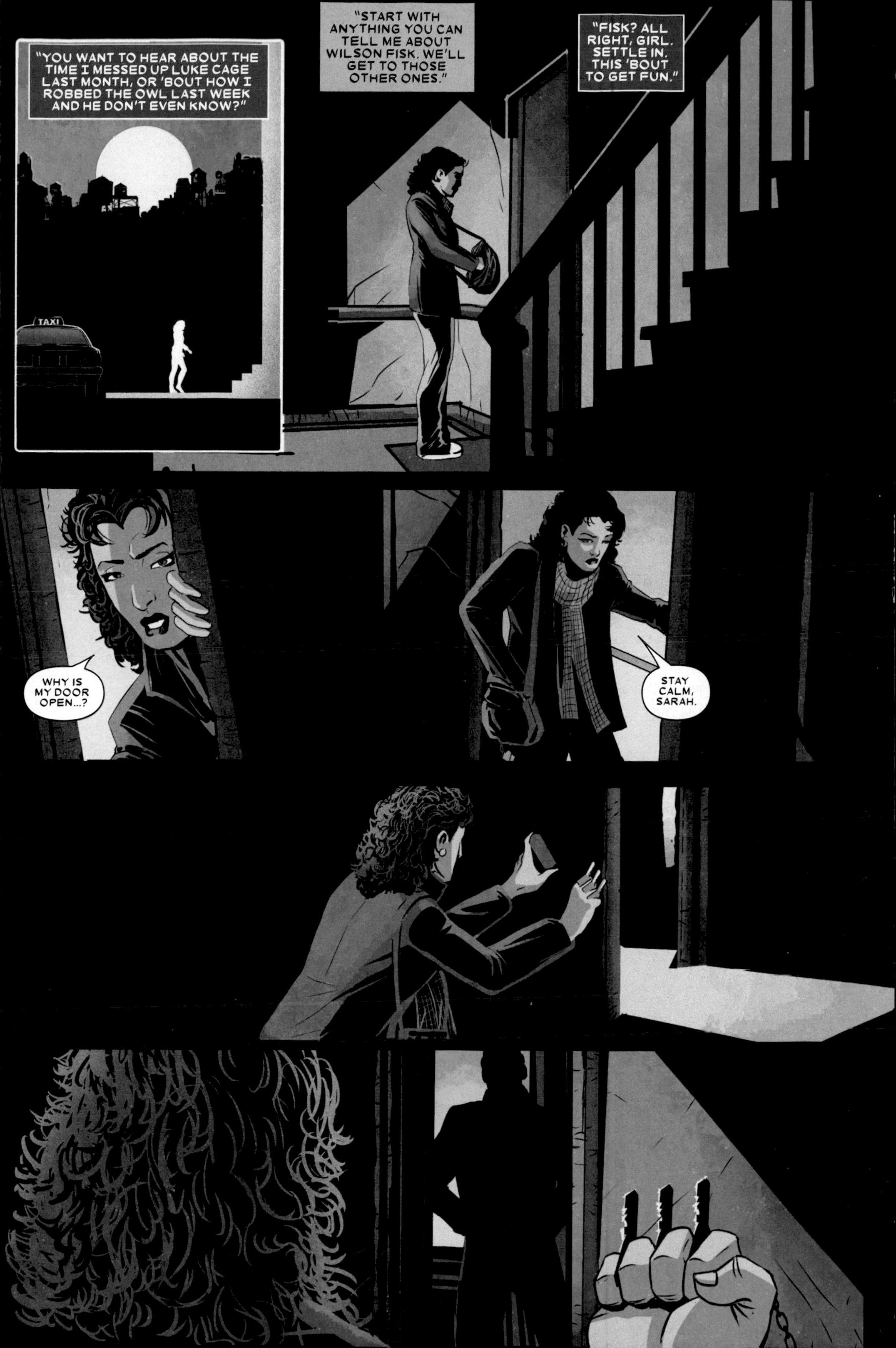
"YOU WANT TO HEAR ABOUT THE TIME I MESSED UP LUKE CAGE LAST MONTH, OR 'BOUT HOW I ROBBED THE OWL LAST WEEK AND HE DON'T EVEN KNOW?"
TAXI
"START WITH ANYTHING YOU CAN TELL ME ABOUT WILSON FISK. WE'LL GET TO THOSE OTHER ONES."
"FISK? ALL RIGHT, GIRL. SETTLE IN. THIS 'BOUT TO GET FUN."
WHY IS MY DOOR OPEN...?
STAY CALM, SARAH.

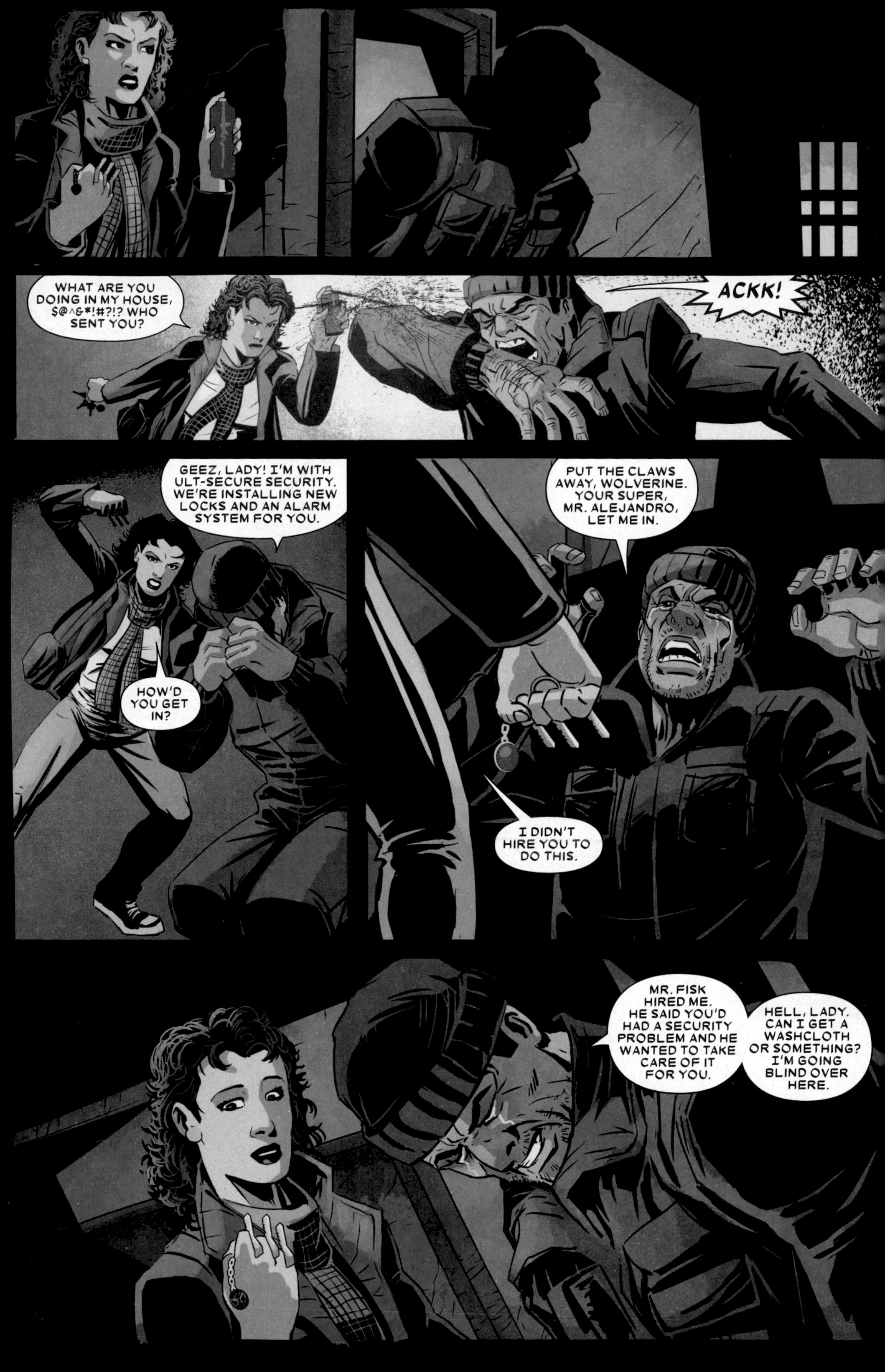

WHAT ARE YOU DOING IN MY HOUSE, $@^&*!#?!? WHO SENT YOU?
ACKK!
GEEZ, LADY! I'M WITH ULT-SECURE SECURITY. WE'RE INSTALLING NEW LOCKS AND AN ALARM SYSTEM FOR YOU.
HOW'D YOU GET IN?
PUT THE CLAWS AWAY, WOLVERINE. YOUR SUPER, MR. ALEJANDRO, LET ME IN.
I DIDN'T HIRE YOU TO DO THIS.
MR. FISK HIRED ME. HE SAID YOU'D HAD A SECURITY PROBLEM AND HE WANTED TO TAKE CARE OF IT FOR YOU.
HELL, LADY. CAN I GET A WASHCLOTH OR SOMETHING? I'M GOING BLIND OVER HERE.

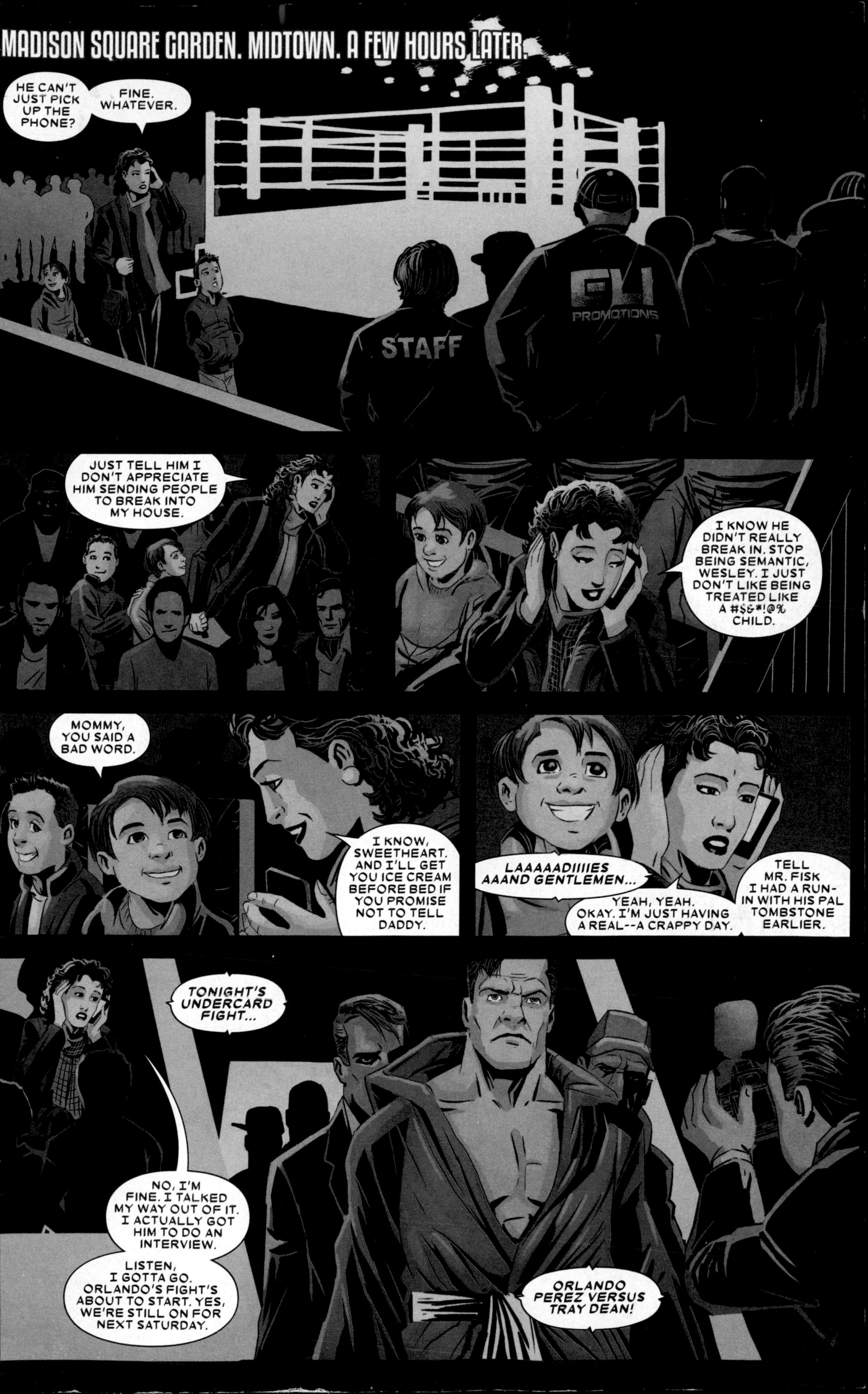
MADISON SQUARE GARDEN. MIDTOWN. A FEW HOURS LATER.
HE CAN'T JUST PICK UP THE PHONE?
FINE, WHATEVER.
STAFF
PROMOTIONS
JUST TELL HIM I DON'T APPRECIATE HIM SENDING PEOPLE TO BREAK INTO MY HOUSE.
I KNOW HE DIDN'T REALLY BREAK IN. STOP BEING SEMANTIC, WESLEY. I JUST DON'T LIKE BEING TREATED LIKE A #$&*!@% CHILD.
MOMMY, YOU SAID A BAD WORD.
I KNOW, SWEETHEART. AND I'LL GET YOU ICE CREAM BEFORE BED IF YOU PROMISE NOT TO TELL DADDY.
LAAAAADIIIIES AAAND GENTLEMEN...
YEAH, YEAH. OKAY. I'M JUST HAVING A REAL--A CRAPPY DAY.
TELL MR. FISK I HAD A RUN-IN WITH HIS PAL TOMBSTONE EARLIER.
TONIGHT'S UNDERCARD FIGHT...
NO, I'M FINE. I TALKED MY WAY OUT OF IT. I ACTUALLY GOT HIM TO DO AN INTERVIEW.
LISTEN, I GOTTA GO. ORLANDO'S FIGHT'S ABOUT TO START. YES, WE'RE STILL ON FOR NEXT SATURDAY.
ORLANDO PEREZ VERSUS TRAY DEAN!

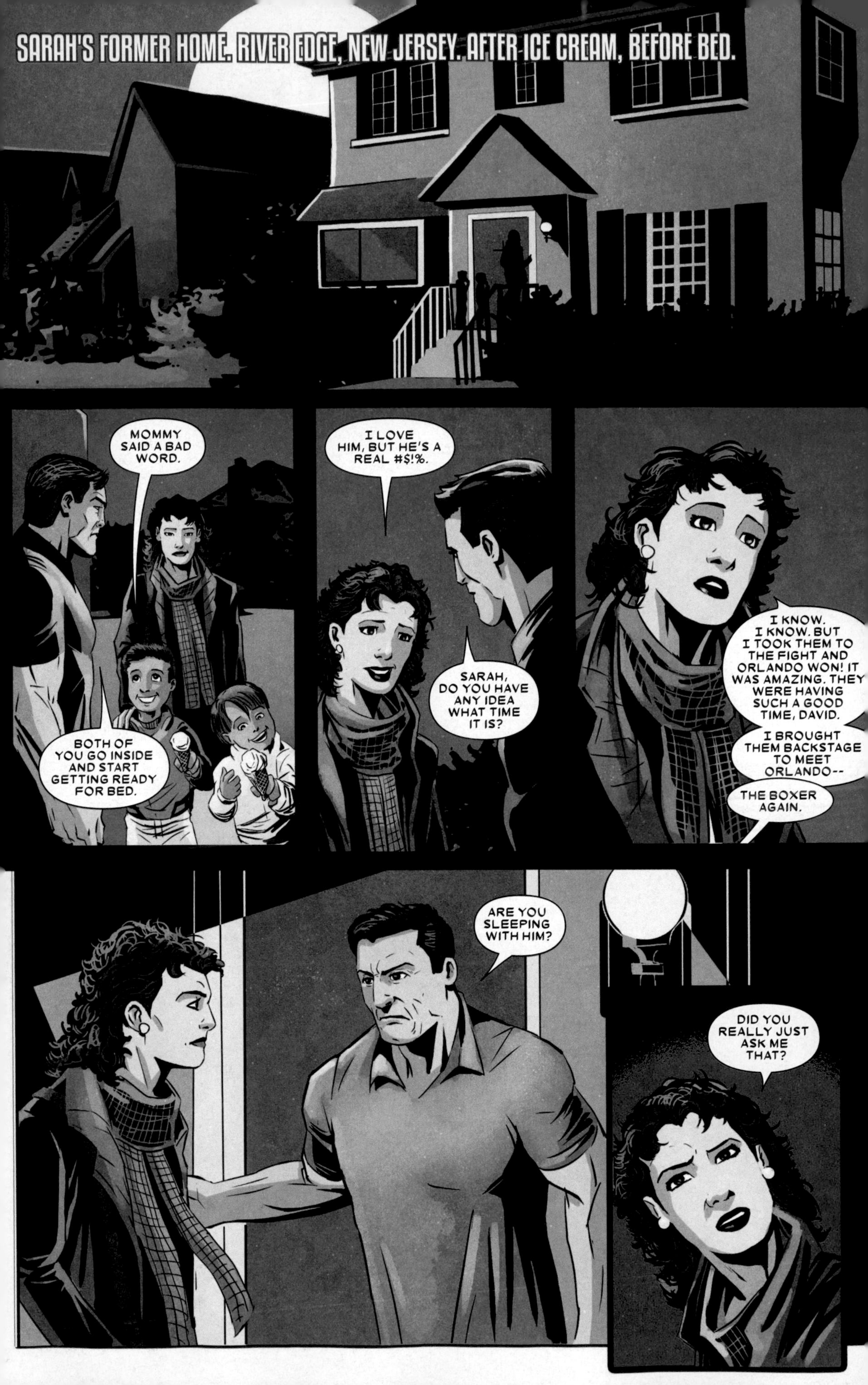
SARAH'S FORMER HOME. RIVER EDGE, NEW JERSEY. AFTER ICE CREAM, BEFORE BED.
MOMMY SAID A BAD WORD.
BOTH OF YOU GO INSIDE AND START GETTING READY FOR BED.
I LOVE HIM, BUT HE'S A REAL #$!%.
SARAH, DO YOU HAVE ANY IDEA WHAT TIME IT IS?
I KNOW. I KNOW. BUT I TOOK THEM TO THE FIGHT AND ORLANDO WON! IT WAS AMAZING. THEY WERE HAVING SUCH A GOOD TIME, DAVID.
I BROUGHT THEM BACKSTAGE TO MEET ORLANDO--
THE BOXER AGAIN.
ARE YOU SLEEPING WITH HIM?
DID YOU REALLY JUST ASK ME THAT?

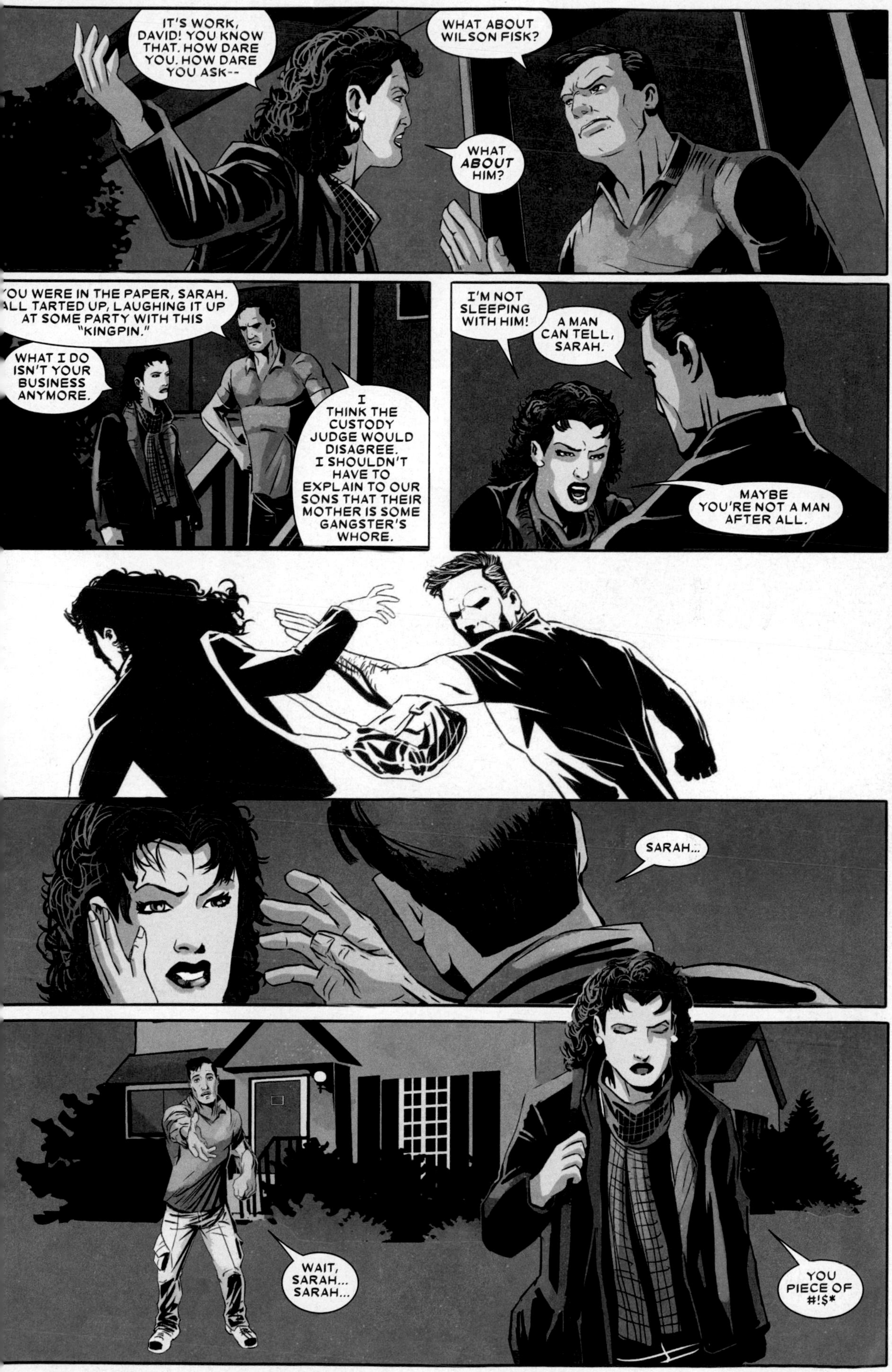

IT'S WORK, DAVID! YOU KNOW THAT. HOW DARE YOU. HOW DARE YOU ASK--
WHAT ABOUT WILSON FISK?
WHAT ABOUT HIM?
YOU WERE IN THE PAPER, SARAH. ALL TARTED UP, LAUGHING IT UP AT SOME PARTY WITH THIS "KINGPIN."
WHAT I DO ISN'T YOUR BUSINESS ANYMORE.
I THINK THE CUSTODY JUDGE WOULD DISAGREE. I SHOULDN'T HAVE TO EXPLAIN TO OUR SONS THAT THEIR MOTHER IS SOME GANGSTER'S WHORE.
I'M NOT SLEEPING WITH HIM!
A MAN CAN TELL, SARAH.
MAYBE YOU'RE NOT A MAN AFTER ALL.
SARAH...
WAIT, SARAH... SARAH...
YOU PIECE OF #!$*

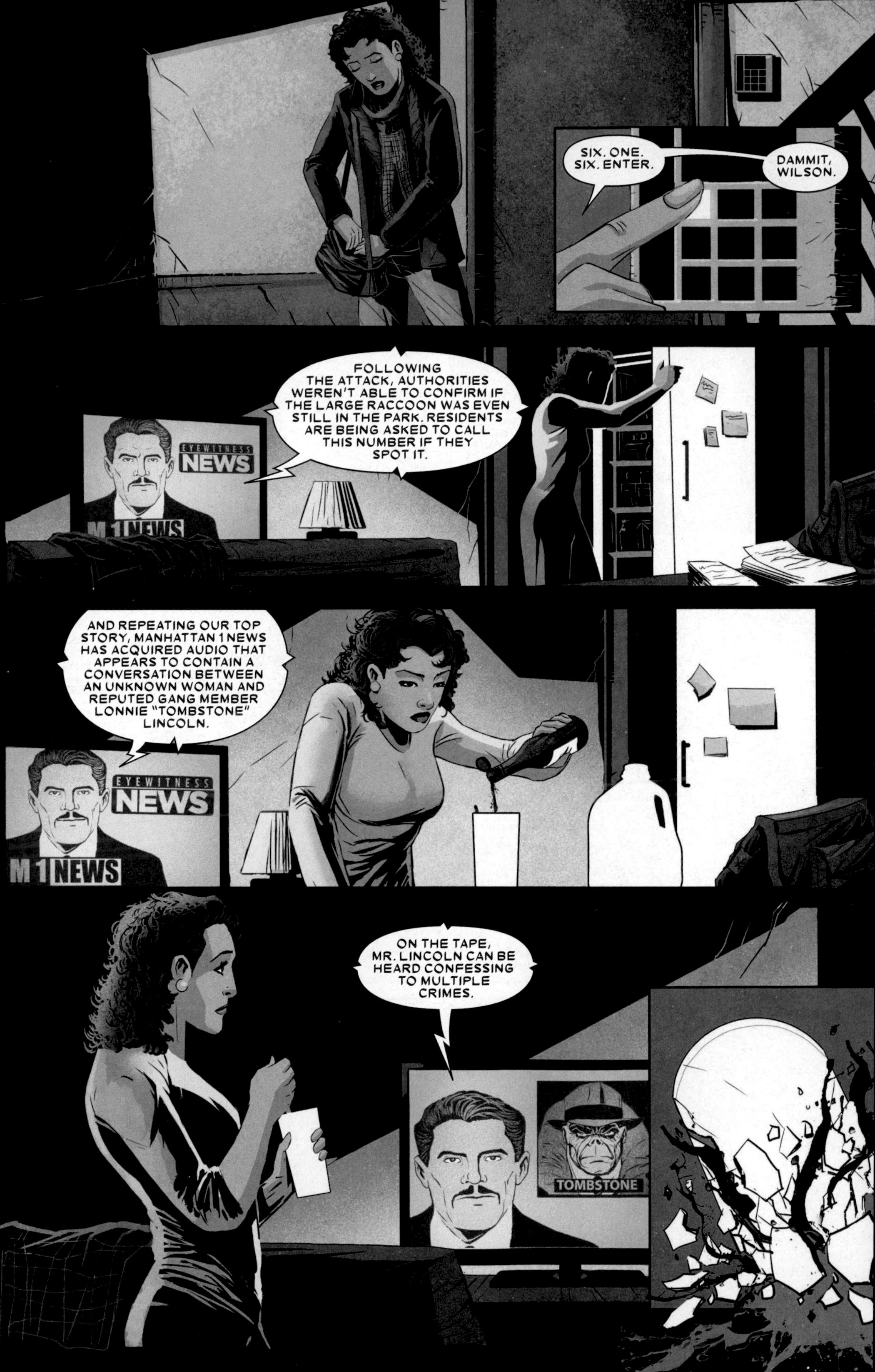
SIX. ONE. SIX. ENTER.
DAMMIT, WILSON.
FOLLOWING THE ATTACK, AUTHORITIES WEREN'T ABLE TO CONFIRM IF THE LARGE RACCOON WAS EVEN STILL IN THE PARK. RESIDENTS ARE BEING ASKED TO CALL THIS NUMBER IF THEY SPOT IT.
EYEWITNESS NEWS
M 1 NEWS
AND REPEATING OUR TOP STORY, MANHATTAN 1 NEWS HAS ACQUIRED AUDIO THAT APPEARS TO CONTAIN A CONVERSATION BETWEEN AN UNKNOWN WOMAN AND REPUTED GANG MEMBER LONNIE "TOMBSTONE" LINCOLN.
EYEWITNESS NEWS
M 1 NEWS
ON THE TAPE, MR. LINCOLN CAN BE HEARD CONFESSING TO MULTIPLE CRIMES.
TOMBSTONE

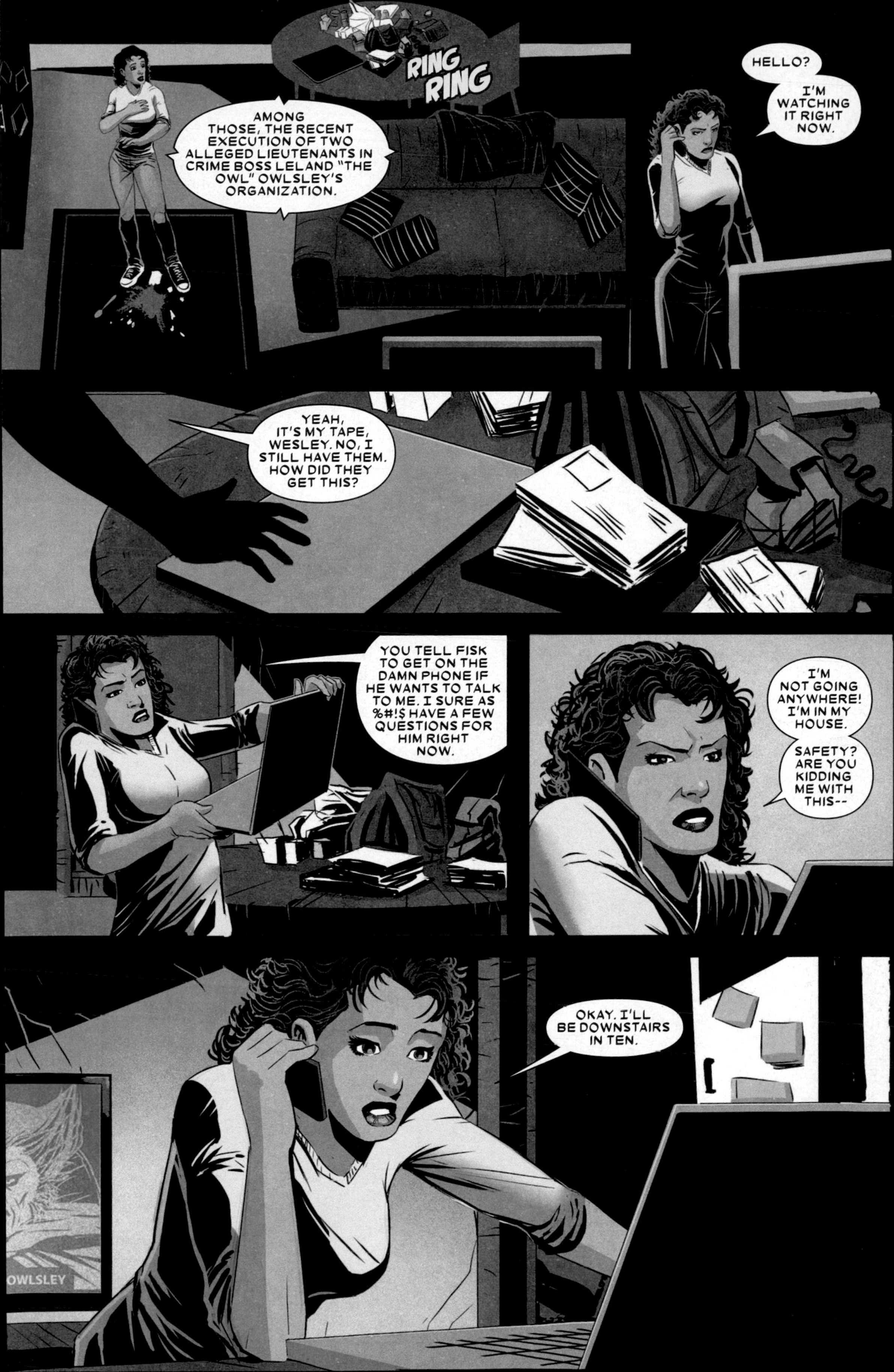
RING RING
AMONG THOSE, THE RECENT EXECUTION OF TWO ALLEGED LIEUTENANTS IN CRIME BOSS LELAND "THE OWL" OWLSLEY'S ORGANIZATION.
HELLO?
I'M WATCHING IT RIGHT NOW.
YEAH, IT'S MY TAPE, WESLEY. NO, I STILL HAVE THEM. HOW DID THEY GET THIS?
YOU TELL FISK TO GET ON THE DAMN PHONE IF HE WANTS TO TALK TO ME. I SURE AS %#!$ HAVE A FEW QUESTIONS FOR HIM RIGHT NOW.
I'M NOT GOING ANYWHERE! I'M IN MY HOUSE.
SAFETY? ARE YOU KIDDING ME WITH THIS--
OKAY. I'LL BE DOWNSTAIRS IN TEN.
OWLSLEY

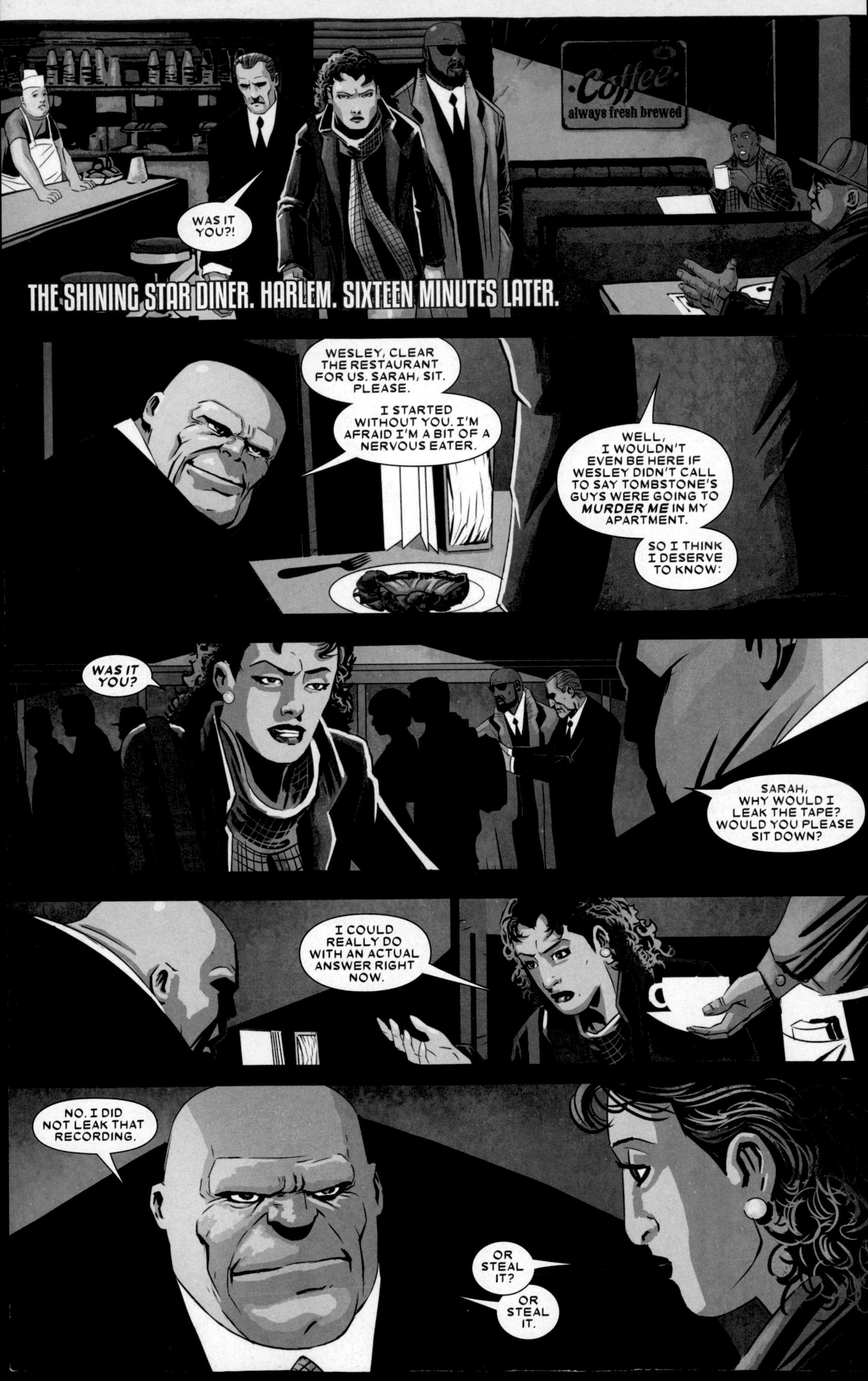
Coffee
always fresh brewed
WAS IT YOU?!
THE SHINING STAR DINER. HARLEM. SIXTEEN MINUTES LATER.
WESLEY, CLEAR THE RESTAURANT FOR US. SARAH, SIT. PLEASE.
I STARTED WITHOUT YOU. I'M AFRAID I'M A BIT OF A NERVOUS EATER.
WELL, I WOULDN'T EVEN BE HERE IF WESLEY DIDN'T CALL TO SAY TOMBSTONE'S GUYS WERE GOING TO *MURDER ME* IN MY APARTMENT.
SO I THINK I DESERVE TO KNOW:
WAS IT YOU?
SARAH, WHY WOULD I LEAK THE TAPE? WOULD YOU PLEASE SIT DOWN?
I COULD REALLY DO WITH AN ACTUAL ANSWER RIGHT NOW.
NO. I DID NOT LEAK THAT RECORDING.
OR STEAL IT?
OR STEAL IT.

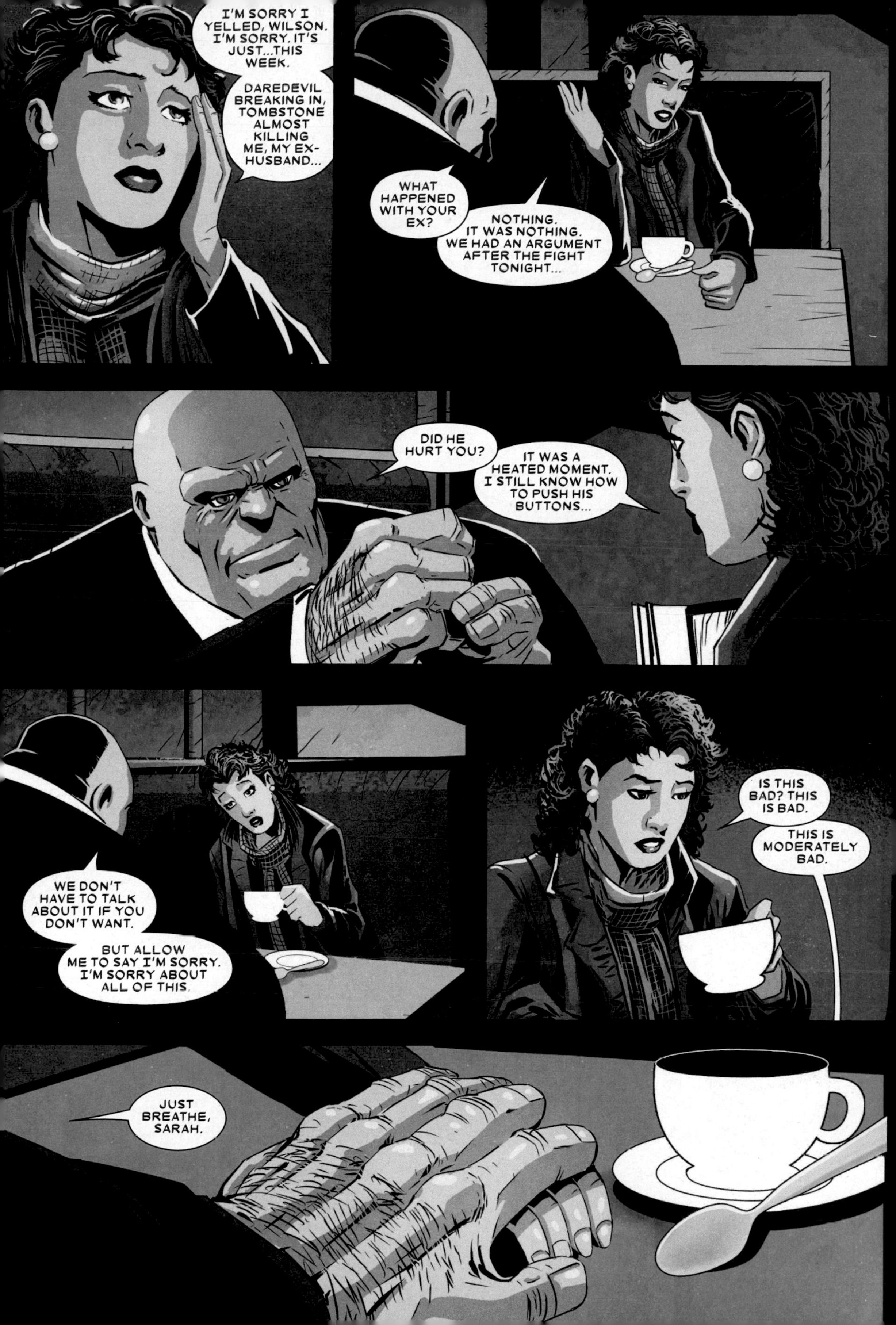

I'M SORRY I YELLED, WILSON. I'M SORRY. IT'S JUST...THIS WEEK.
DAREDEVIL BREAKING IN, TOMBSTONE ALMOST KILLING ME, MY EX-HUSBAND...
WHAT HAPPENED WITH YOUR EX?
NOTHING. IT WAS NOTHING. WE HAD AN ARGUMENT AFTER THE FIGHT TONIGHT...
DID HE HURT YOU?
IT WAS A HEATED MOMENT. I STILL KNOW HOW TO PUSH HIS BUTTONS...
WE DON'T HAVE TO TALK ABOUT IT IF YOU DON'T WANT.
BUT ALLOW ME TO SAY I'M SORRY. I'M SORRY ABOUT ALL OF THIS.
IS THIS BAD? THIS IS BAD.
THIS IS MODERATELY BAD.
JUST BREATHE, SARAH.

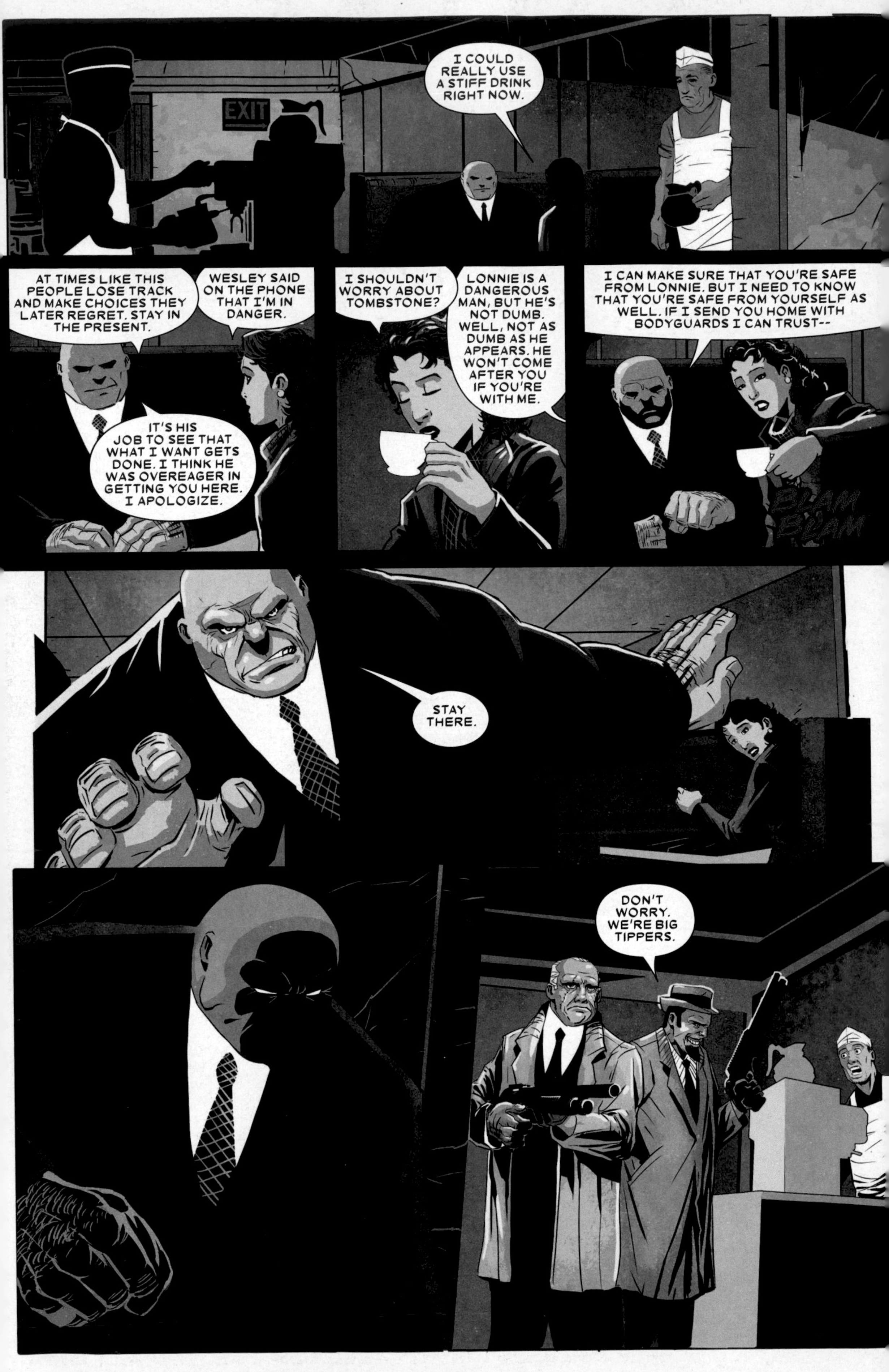

EXIT
I COULD REALLY USE A STIFF DRINK RIGHT NOW.
AT TIMES LIKE THIS PEOPLE LOSE TRACK AND MAKE CHOICES THEY LATER REGRET. STAY IN THE PRESENT.
WESLEY SAID ON THE PHONE THAT I'M IN DANGER.
IT'S HIS JOB TO SEE THAT WHAT I WANT GETS DONE. I THINK HE WAS OVEREAGER IN GETTING YOU HERE. I APOLOGIZE.
I SHOULDN'T WORRY ABOUT TOMBSTONE?
LONNIE IS A DANGEROUS MAN, BUT HE'S NOT DUMB. WELL, NOT AS DUMB AS HE APPEARS. HE WON'T COME AFTER YOU IF YOU'RE WITH ME.
I CAN MAKE SURE THAT YOU'RE SAFE FROM LONNIE. BUT I NEED TO KNOW THAT YOU'RE SAFE FROM YOURSELF AS WELL. IF I SEND YOU HOME WITH BODYGUARDS I CAN TRUST--
BLAM BLAM
STAY THERE.
DON'T WORRY. WE'RE BIG TIPPERS.

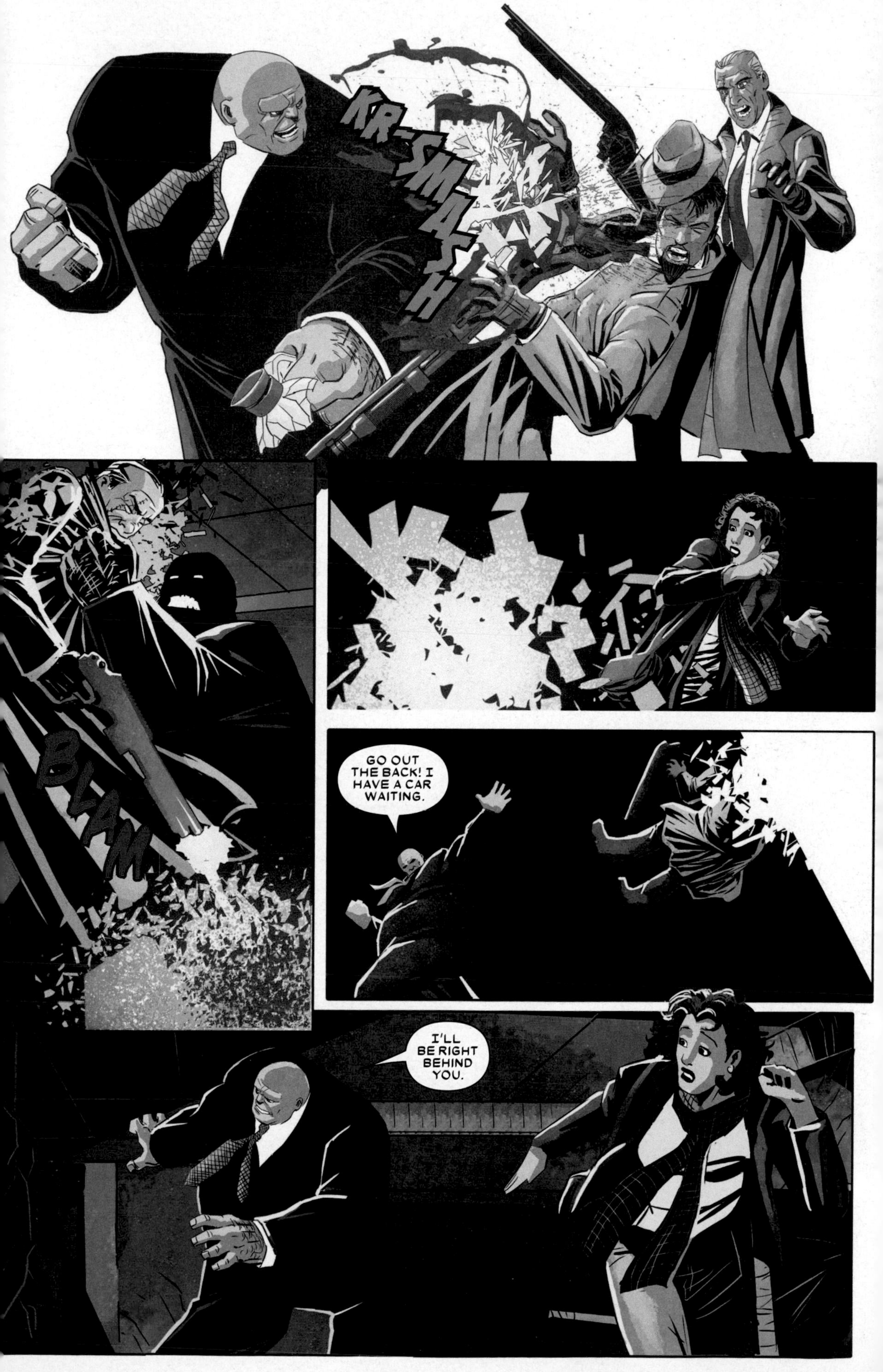
KR-SMASH
BLAM
GO OUT THE BACK! I HAVE A CAR WAITING.
I'LL BE RIGHT BEHIND YOU.

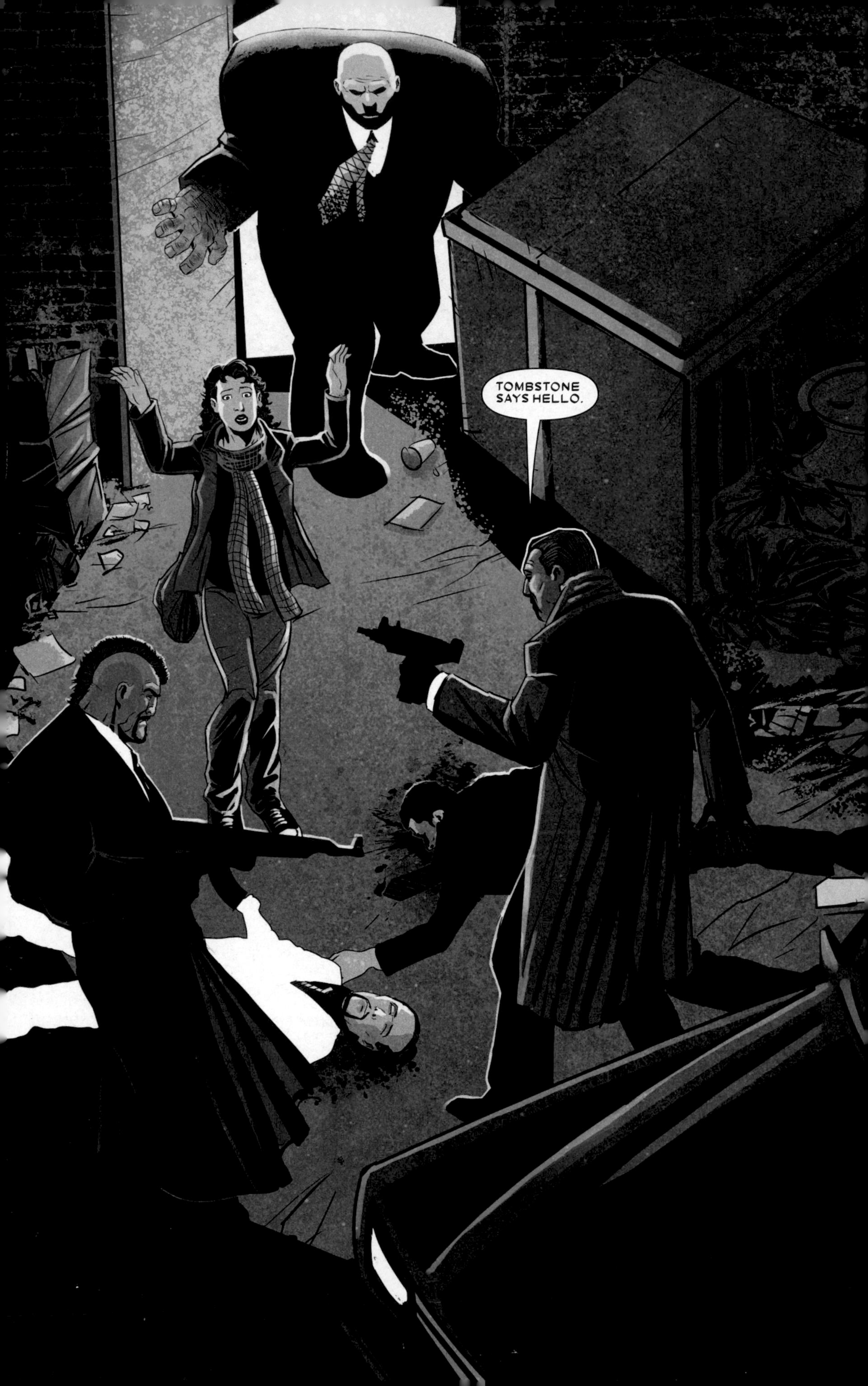
TOMBSTONE SAYS HELLO.

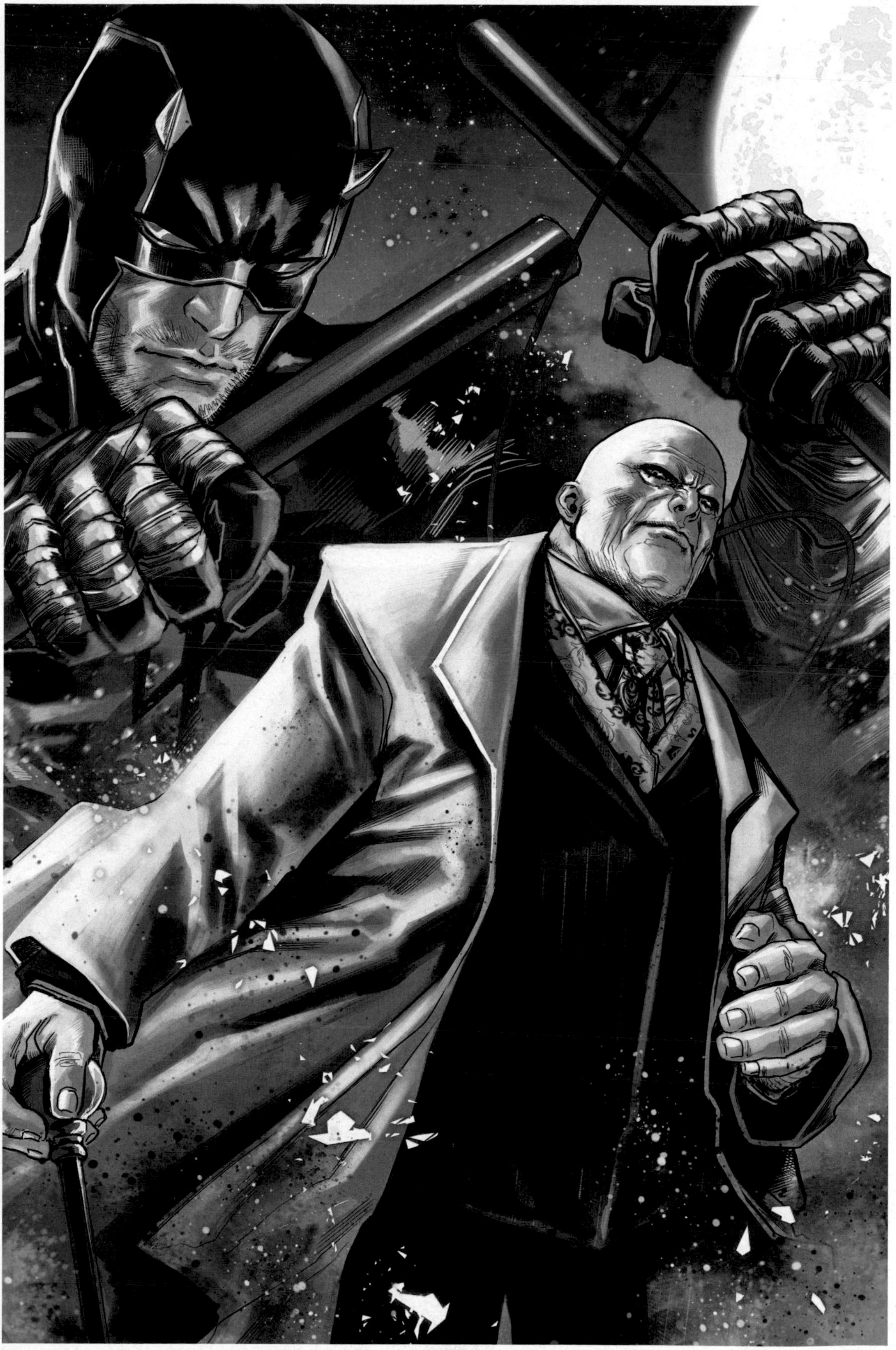

MARCO CHECCHETTO

1 VARIANT

FOUR

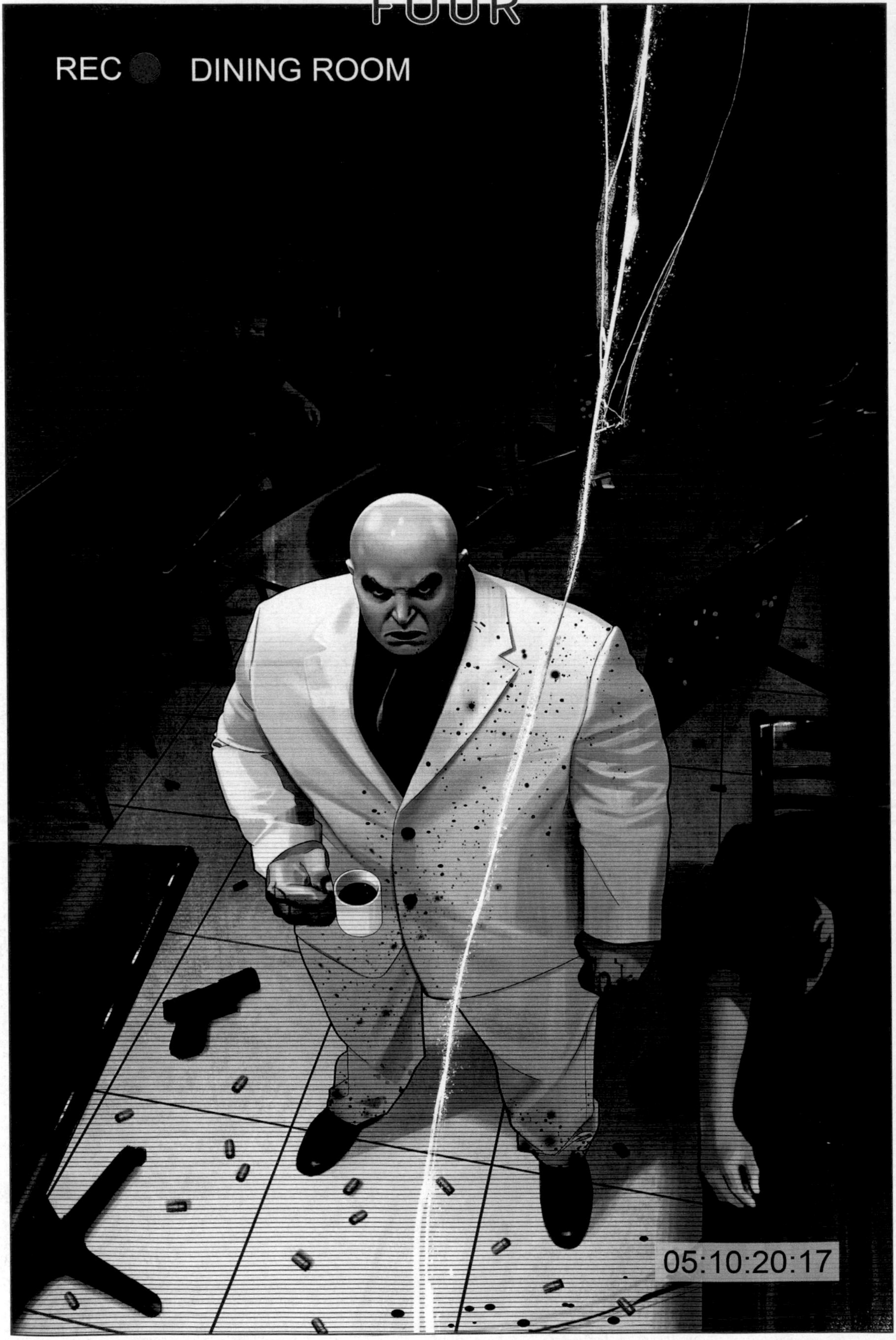
REC
DINING ROOM
05:10:20:17

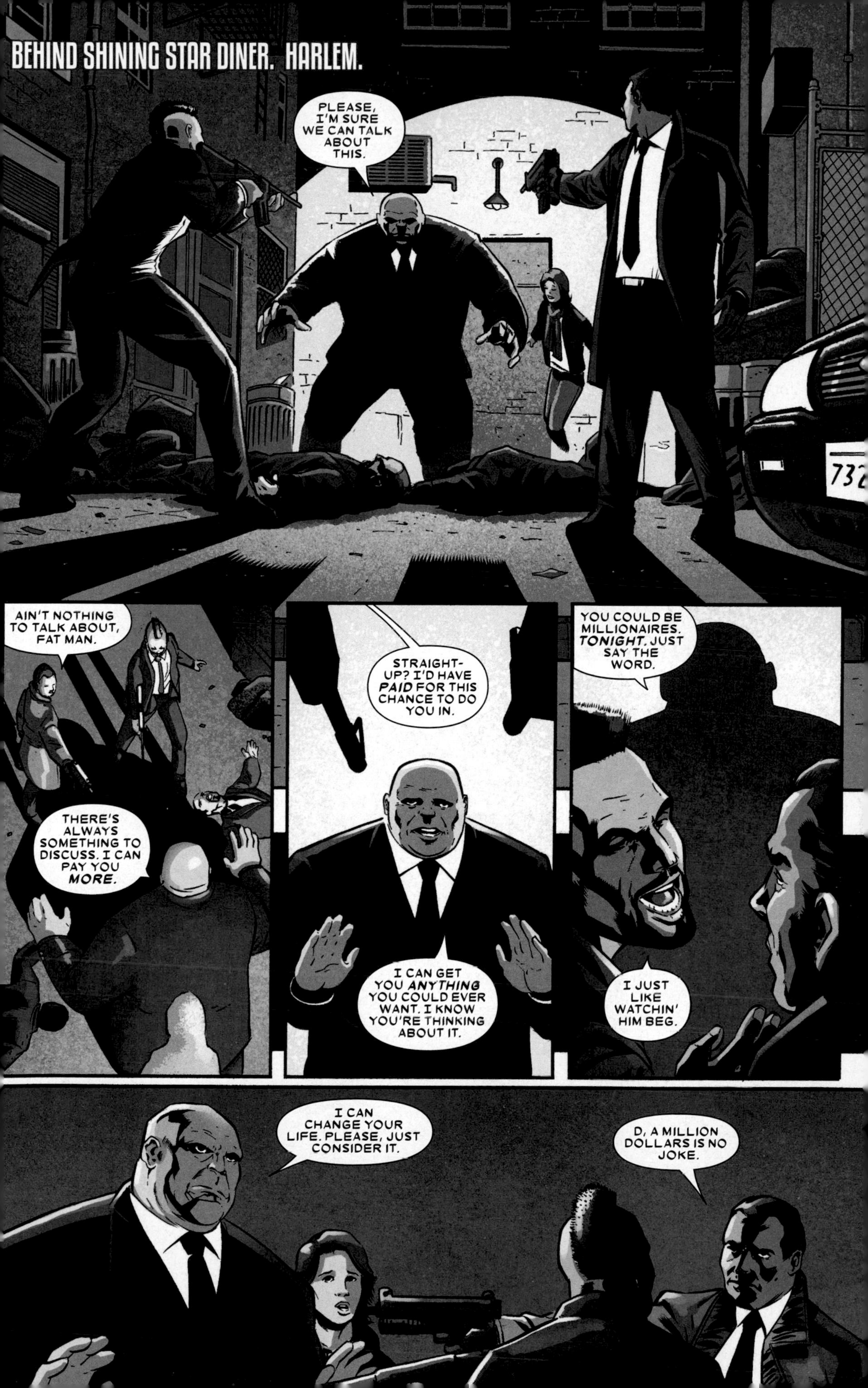
BEHIND SHINING STAR DINER. HARLEM.
PLEASE, I'M SURE WE CAN TALK ABOUT THIS.
732
AIN'T NOTHING TO TALK ABOUT, FAT MAN.
THERE'S ALWAYS SOMETHING TO DISCUSS. I CAN PAY YOU MORE.
STRAIGHT-UP? I'D HAVE PAID FOR THIS CHANCE TO DO YOU IN.
I CAN GET YOU ANYTHING YOU COULD EVER WANT. I KNOW YOU'RE THINKING ABOUT IT.
YOU COULD BE MILLIONAIRES. TONIGHT. JUST SAY THE WORD.
I JUST LIKE WATCHIN' HIM BEG.
I CAN CHANGE YOUR LIFE. PLEASE, JUST CONSIDER IT.
D, A MILLION DOLLARS IS NO JOKE.

IF WE DON'T OFF THE GIRL, TOMBSTONE'LL OFF US. DON'T MATTER HOW MUCH MONEY WE HAVE IN OUR BANK ACCOUNTS, CHRIS.

YOU'RE RIGHT. PLUS WE'RE GONNA GET A LOTTA LOVE BEING THE $%!@*&#?!@S WHO ENDED THE KINGPIN.

YOU WANT TO GO FIRST OR SECOND, FAT MAN?

PLEASE...

FIRST OR SECOND?

SECOND.

LADIES FIRST, THEN.

ARRGH!!

SNAP

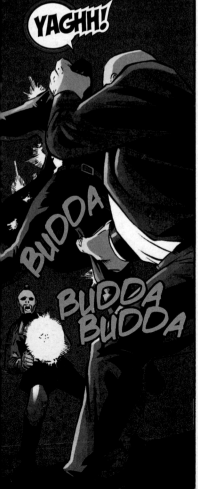

YAGHH!

BUDDA

BUDDA

BUDDA BUDDA

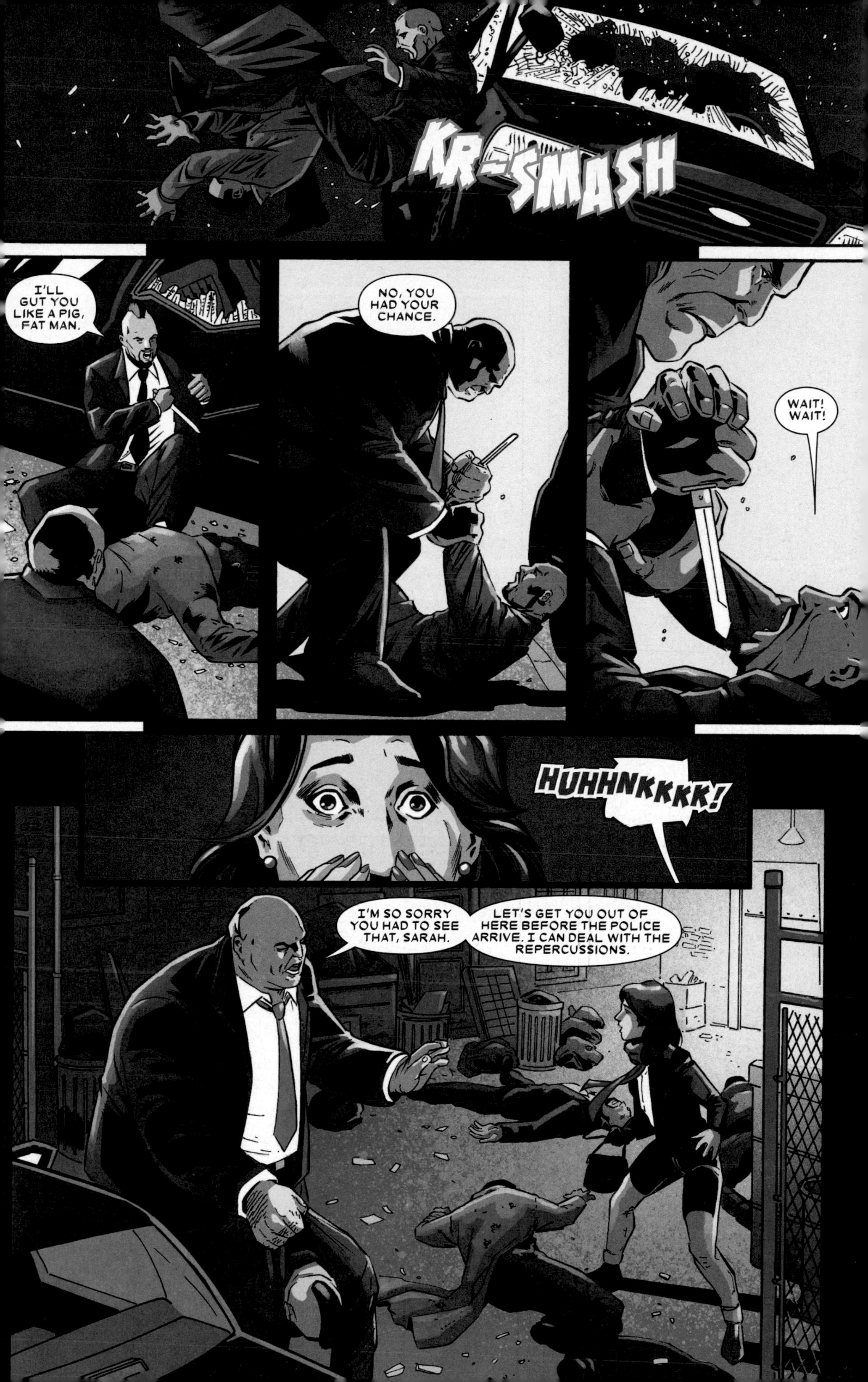
KR-SMASH
I'LL GUT YOU LIKE A PIG, FAT MAN.
NO, YOU HAD YOUR CHANCE.
WAIT! WAIT!
HUHHNKKKK!
I'M SO SORRY YOU HAD TO SEE THAT, SARAH.
LET'S GET YOU OUT OF HERE BEFORE THE POLICE ARRIVE. I CAN DEAL WITH THE REPERCUSSIONS.

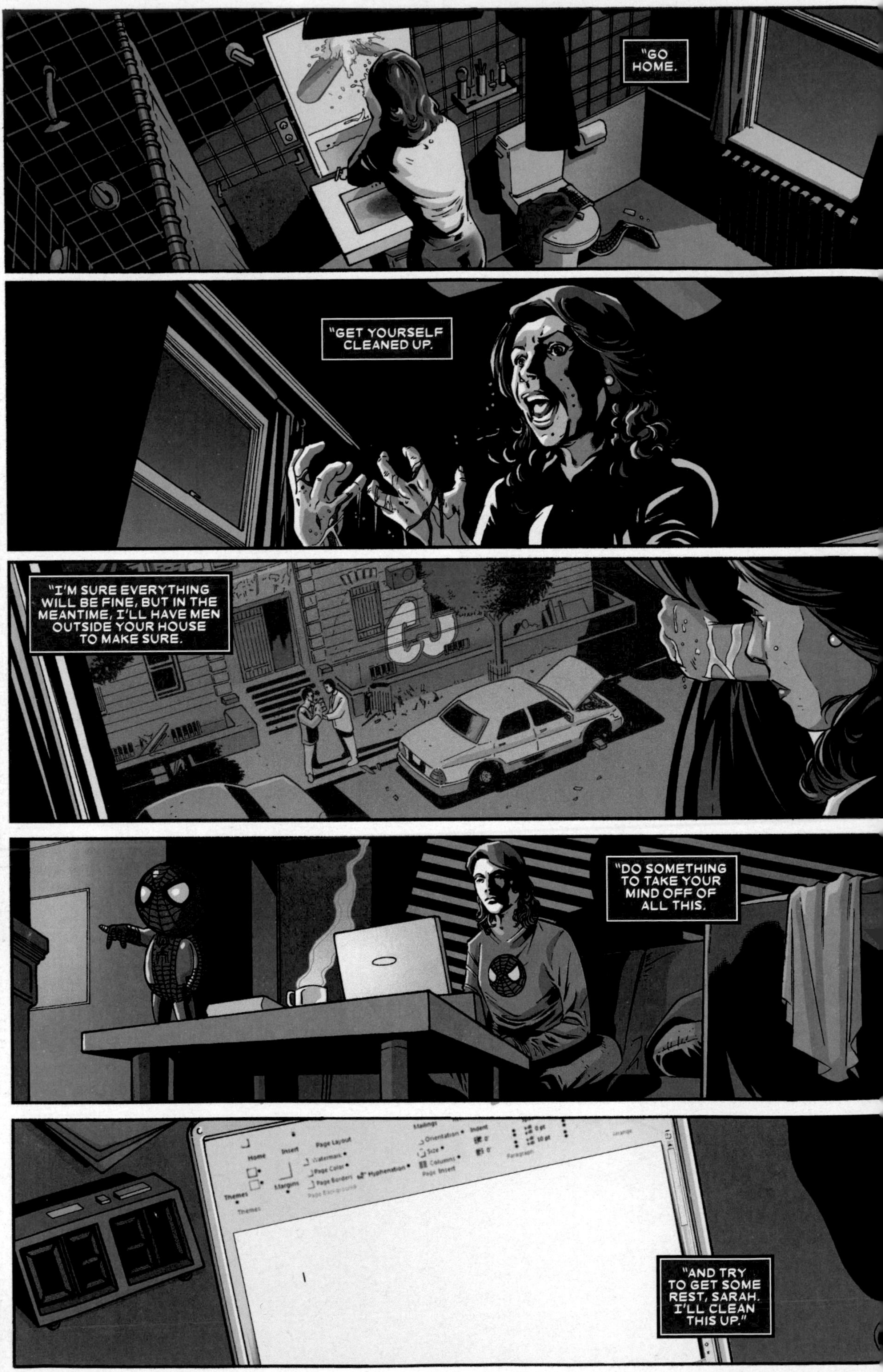
"GO HOME.
"GET YOURSELF CLEANED UP.
"I'M SURE EVERYTHING WILL BE FINE, BUT IN THE MEANTIME, I'LL HAVE MEN OUTSIDE YOUR HOUSE TO MAKE SURE.
"DO SOMETHING TO TAKE YOUR MIND OFF OF ALL THIS.
"AND TRY TO GET SOME REST, SARAH. I'LL CLEAN THIS UP."

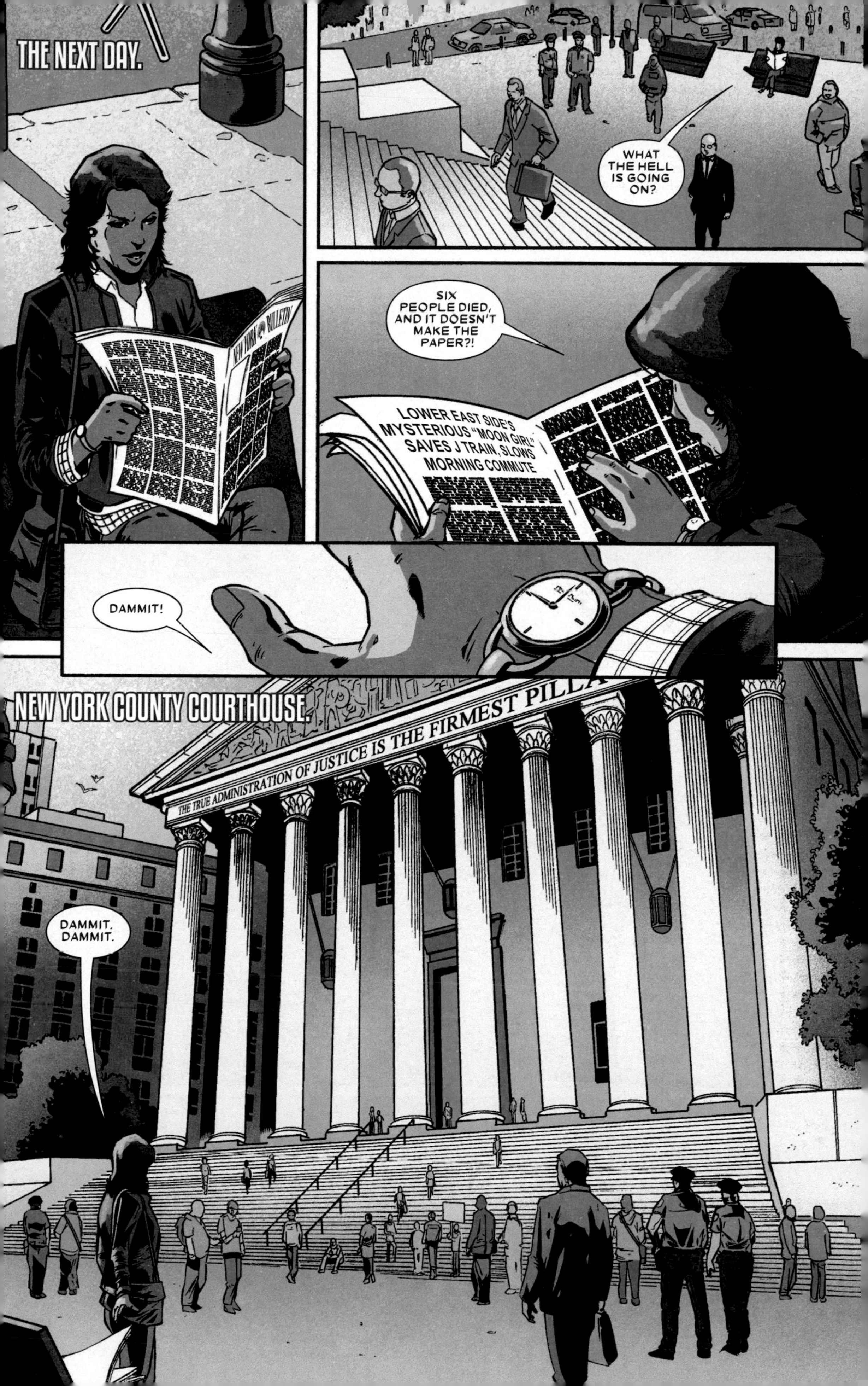
THE NEXT DAY.
NEW YORK BULLETIN
WHAT THE HELL IS GOING ON?
SIX PEOPLE DIED, AND IT DOESN'T MAKE THE PAPER?!
LOWER EAST SIDE'S MYSTERIOUS "MOON GIRL" SAVES J TRAIN, SLOWS MORNING COMMUTE
DAMMIT!
NEW YORK COUNTY COURTHOUSE.
THE TRUE ADMINISTRATION OF JUSTICE IS THE FIRMEST PILLA
DAMMIT. DAMMIT.

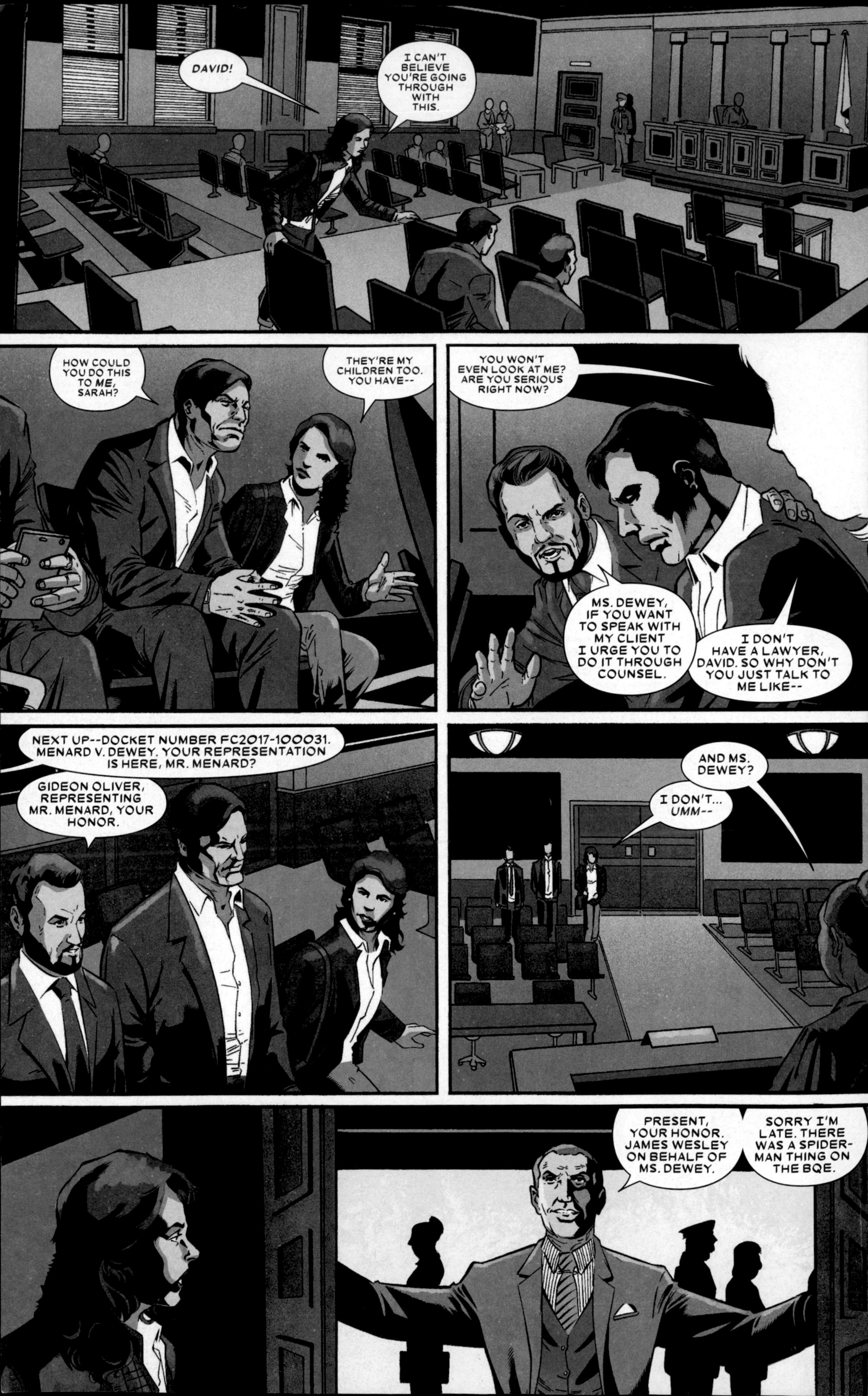
DAVID!
I CAN'T BELIEVE YOU'RE GOING THROUGH WITH THIS.
HOW COULD YOU DO THIS TO ME, SARAH?
THEY'RE MY CHILDREN TOO. YOU HAVE--
YOU WON'T EVEN LOOK AT ME? ARE YOU SERIOUS RIGHT NOW?
MS. DEWEY, IF YOU WANT TO SPEAK WITH MY CLIENT I URGE YOU TO DO IT THROUGH COUNSEL.
I DON'T HAVE A LAWYER, DAVID. SO WHY DON'T YOU JUST TALK TO ME LIKE--
NEXT UP--DOCKET NUMBER FC2017-100031. MENARD V. DEWEY. YOUR REPRESENTATION IS HERE, MR. MENARD?
GIDEON OLIVER, REPRESENTING MR. MENARD, YOUR HONOR.
AND MS. DEWEY?
I DON'T... UMM--
PRESENT, YOUR HONOR, JAMES WESLEY ON BEHALF OF MS. DEWEY.
SORRY I'M LATE. THERE WAS A SPIDER-MAN THING ON THE BQE.

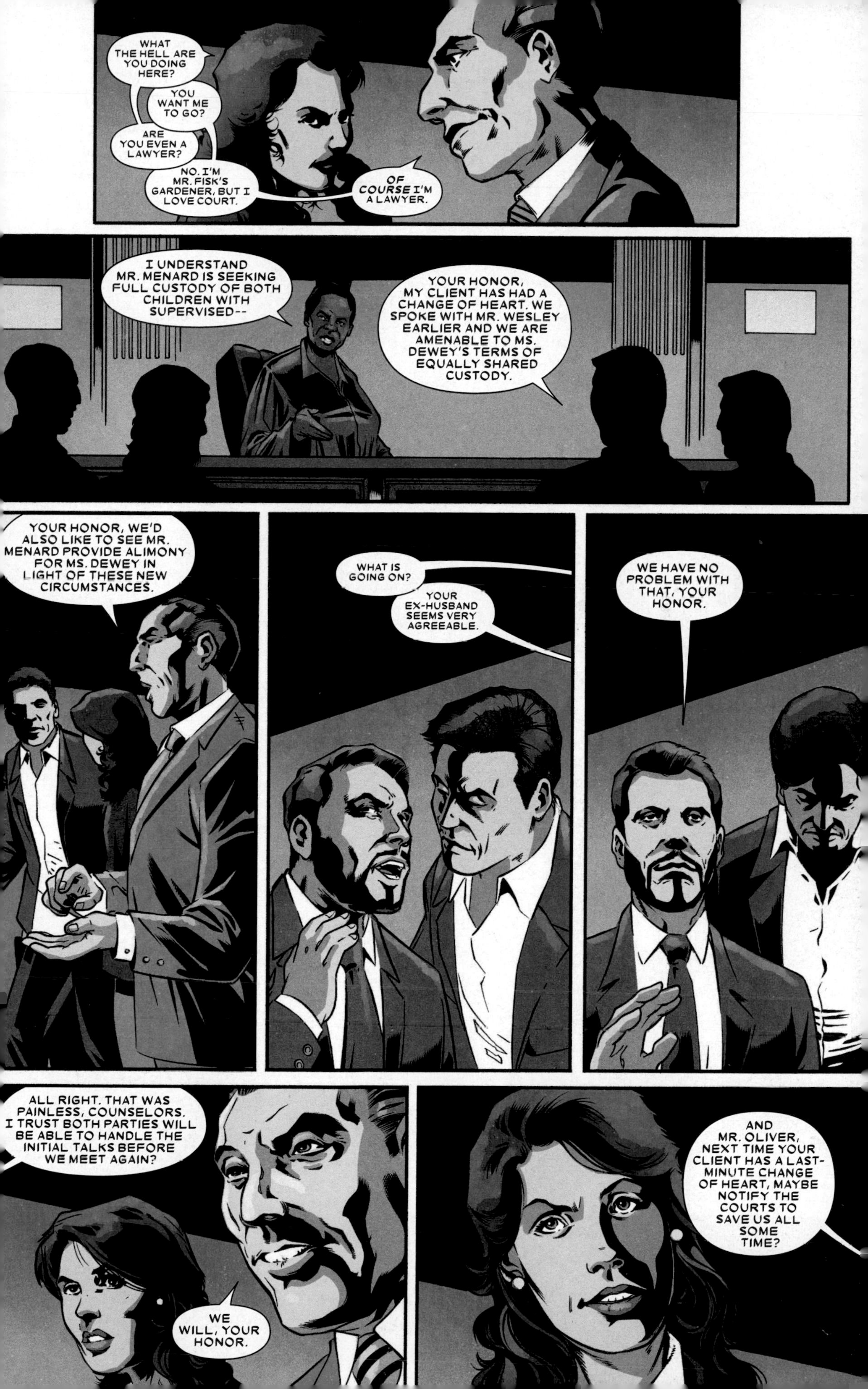
WHAT THE HELL ARE YOU DOING HERE?
YOU WANT ME TO GO?
ARE YOU EVEN A LAWYER?
OF COURSE I'M A LAWYER.
NO. I'M MR. FISK'S GARDENER, BUT I LOVE COURT.
I UNDERSTAND MR. MENARD IS SEEKING FULL CUSTODY OF BOTH CHILDREN WITH SUPERVISED--
YOUR HONOR, MY CLIENT HAS HAD A CHANGE OF HEART. WE SPOKE WITH MR. WESLEY EARLIER AND WE ARE AMENABLE TO MS. DEWEY'S TERMS OF EQUALLY SHARED CUSTODY.
YOUR HONOR, WE'D ALSO LIKE TO SEE MR. MENARD PROVIDE ALIMONY FOR MS. DEWEY IN LIGHT OF THESE NEW CIRCUMSTANCES.
WHAT IS GOING ON?
YOUR EX-HUSBAND SEEMS VERY AGREEABLE.
WE HAVE NO PROBLEM WITH THAT, YOUR HONOR.
ALL RIGHT. THAT WAS PAINLESS, COUNSELORS. I TRUST BOTH PARTIES WILL BE ABLE TO HANDLE THE INITIAL TALKS BEFORE WE MEET AGAIN?
WE WILL, YOUR HONOR.
AND MR. OLIVER, NEXT TIME YOUR CLIENT HAS A LAST-MINUTE CHANGE OF HEART, MAYBE NOTIFY THE COURTS TO SAVE US ALL SOME TIME?

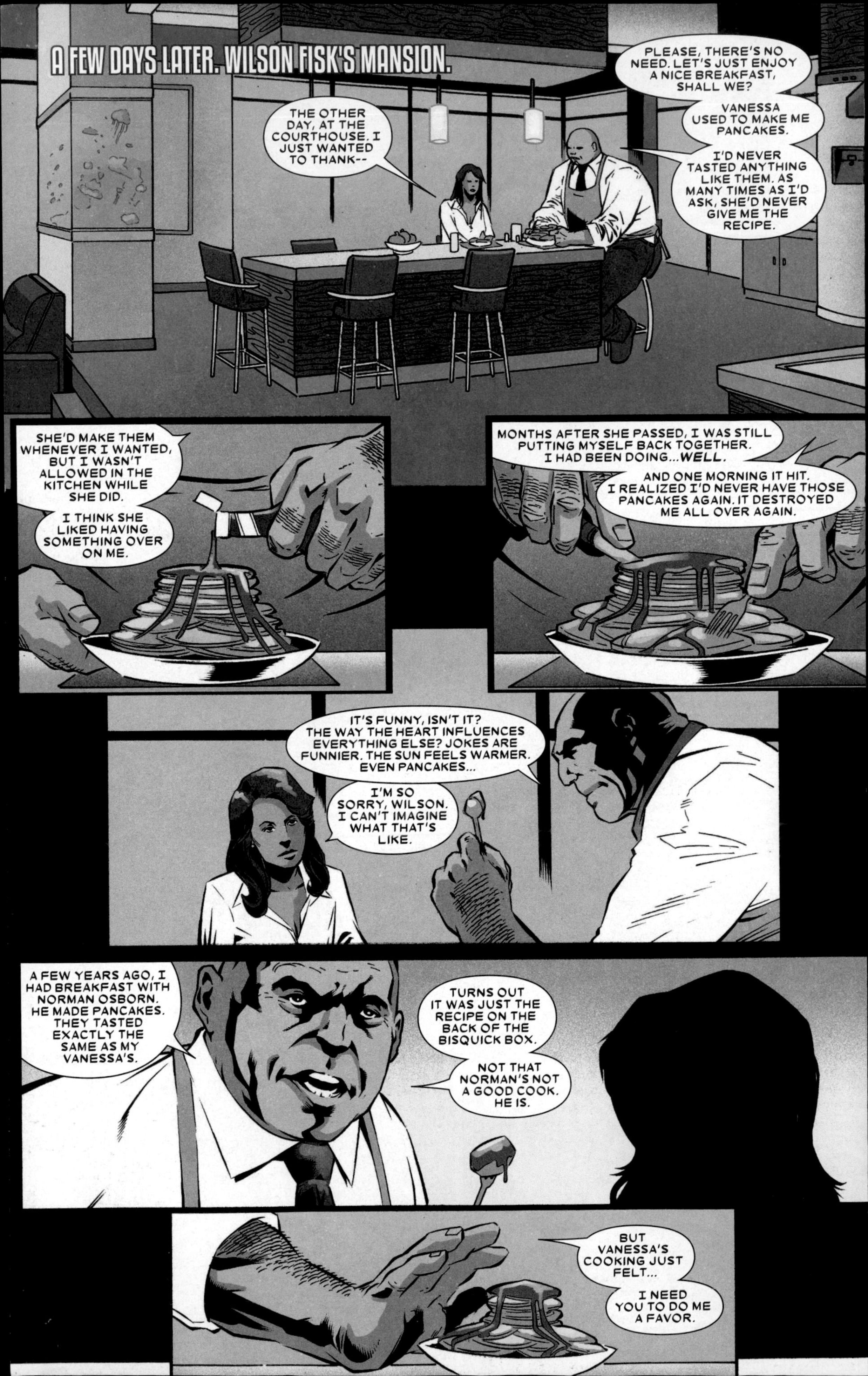

A FEW DAYS LATER. WILSON FISK'S MANSION.
THE OTHER DAY, AT THE COURTHOUSE. I JUST WANTED TO THANK--
PLEASE, THERE'S NO NEED. LET'S JUST ENJOY A NICE BREAKFAST, SHALL WE?
VANESSA USED TO MAKE ME PANCAKES.
I'D NEVER TASTED ANYTHING LIKE THEM. AS MANY TIMES AS I'D ASK, SHE'D NEVER GIVE ME THE RECIPE.
SHE'D MAKE THEM WHENEVER I WANTED, BUT I WASN'T ALLOWED IN THE KITCHEN WHILE SHE DID.
I THINK SHE LIKED HAVING SOMETHING OVER ON ME.
MONTHS AFTER SHE PASSED, I WAS STILL PUTTING MYSELF BACK TOGETHER. I HAD BEEN DOING...*WELL.*
AND ONE MORNING IT HIT. I REALIZED I'D NEVER HAVE THOSE PANCAKES AGAIN. IT DESTROYED ME ALL OVER AGAIN.
IT'S FUNNY, ISN'T IT? THE WAY THE HEART INFLUENCES EVERYTHING ELSE? JOKES ARE FUNNIER. THE SUN FEELS WARMER. EVEN PANCAKES...
I'M SO SORRY, WILSON. I CAN'T IMAGINE WHAT THAT'S LIKE.
A FEW YEARS AGO, I HAD BREAKFAST WITH NORMAN OSBORN. HE MADE PANCAKES. THEY TASTED EXACTLY THE SAME AS MY VANESSA'S.
TURNS OUT IT WAS JUST THE RECIPE ON THE BACK OF THE BISQUICK BOX.
NOT THAT NORMAN'S NOT A GOOD COOK. HE IS.
BUT VANESSA'S COOKING JUST FELT...
I NEED YOU TO DO ME A FAVOR.

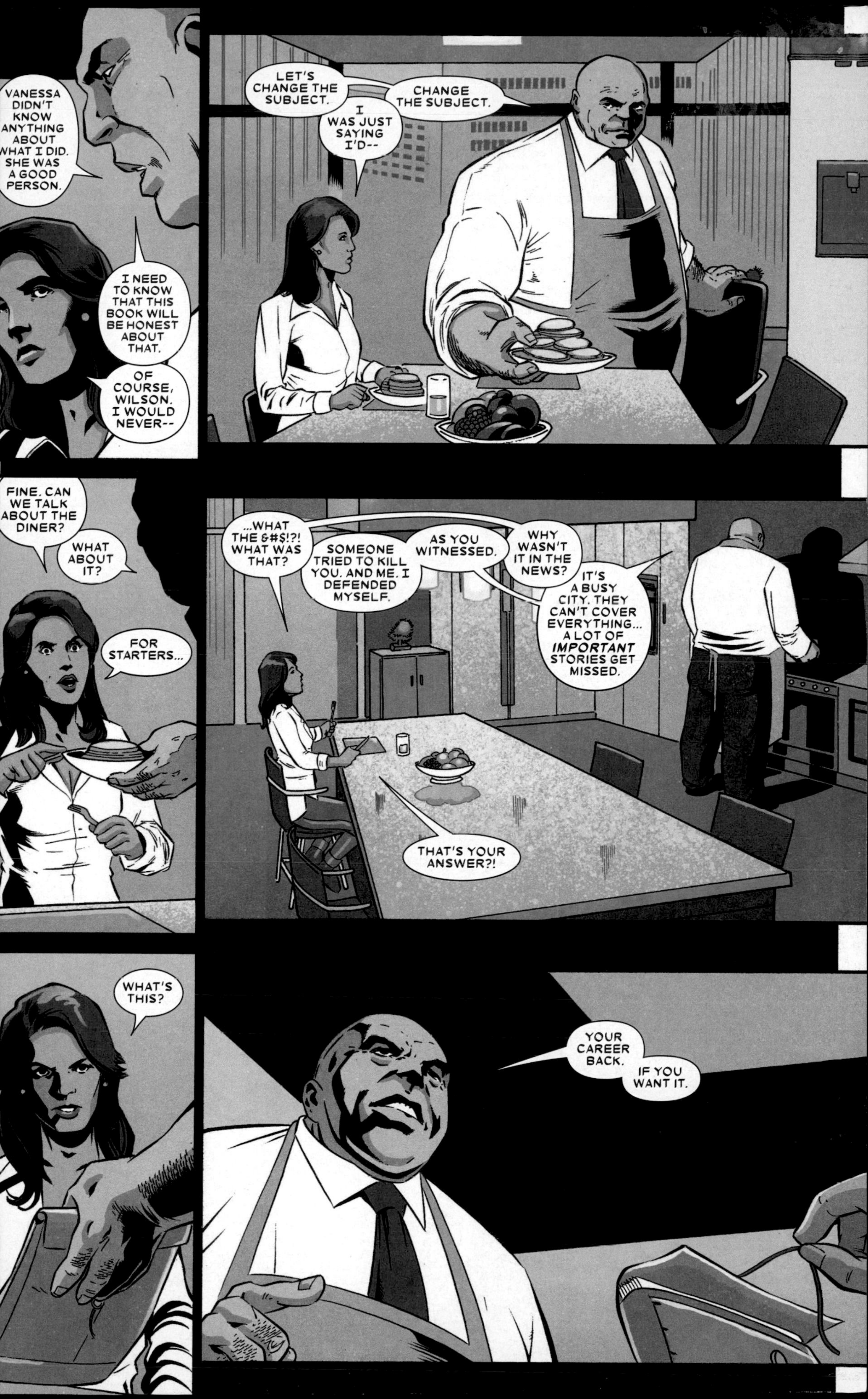
VANESSA DIDN'T KNOW ANYTHING ABOUT WHAT I DID. SHE WAS A GOOD PERSON.
I NEED TO KNOW THAT THIS BOOK WILL BE HONEST ABOUT THAT.
OF COURSE, WILSON. I WOULD NEVER--
LET'S CHANGE THE SUBJECT.
I WAS JUST SAYING I'D--
CHANGE THE SUBJECT.
FINE. CAN WE TALK ABOUT THE DINER?
WHAT ABOUT IT?
FOR STARTERS...
...WHAT THE &#$!?! WHAT WAS THAT?
SOMEONE TRIED TO KILL YOU. AND ME. I DEFENDED MYSELF.
AS YOU WITNESSED.
WHY WASN'T IT IN THE NEWS?
IT'S A BUSY CITY. THEY CAN'T COVER EVERYTHING... A LOT OF IMPORTANT STORIES GET MISSED.
THAT'S YOUR ANSWER?!
WHAT'S THIS?
YOUR CAREER BACK.
IF YOU WANT IT.

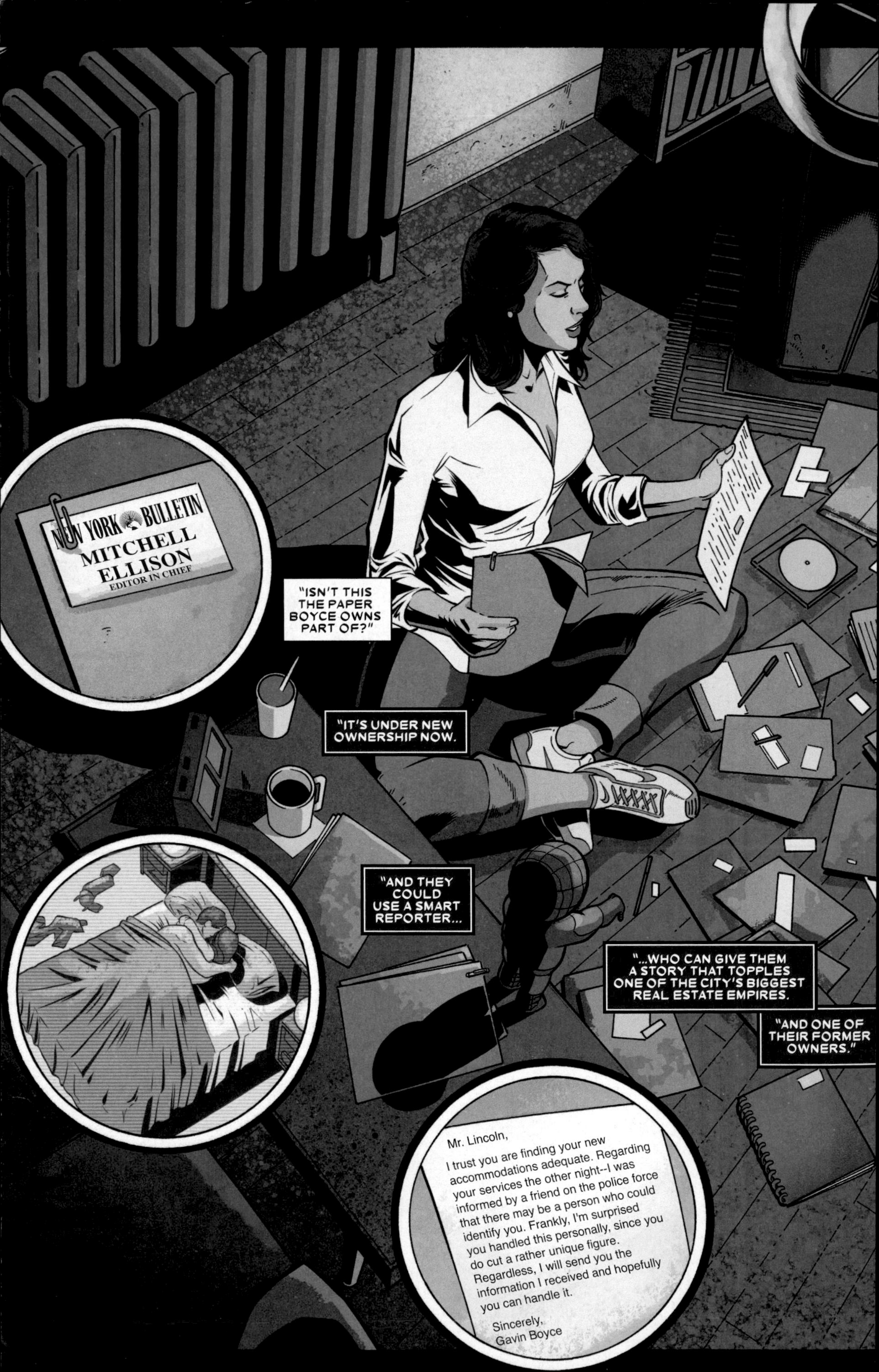
NEW YORK BULLETIN
MITCHELL ELLISON
EDITOR IN CHIEF
"ISN'T THIS THE PAPER BOYCE OWNS PART OF?"
"IT'S UNDER NEW OWNERSHIP NOW.
"AND THEY COULD USE A SMART REPORTER...
"...WHO CAN GIVE THEM A STORY THAT TOPPLES ONE OF THE CITY'S BIGGEST REAL ESTATE EMPIRES.
"AND ONE OF THEIR FORMER OWNERS."
Mr. Lincoln,
I trust you are finding your new accommodations adequate. Regarding your services the other night--I was informed by a friend on the police force that there may be a person who could identify you. Frankly, I'm surprised you handled this personally, since you do cut a rather unique figure. Regardless, I will send you the information I received and hopefully you can handle it.
Sincerely,
Gavin Boyce

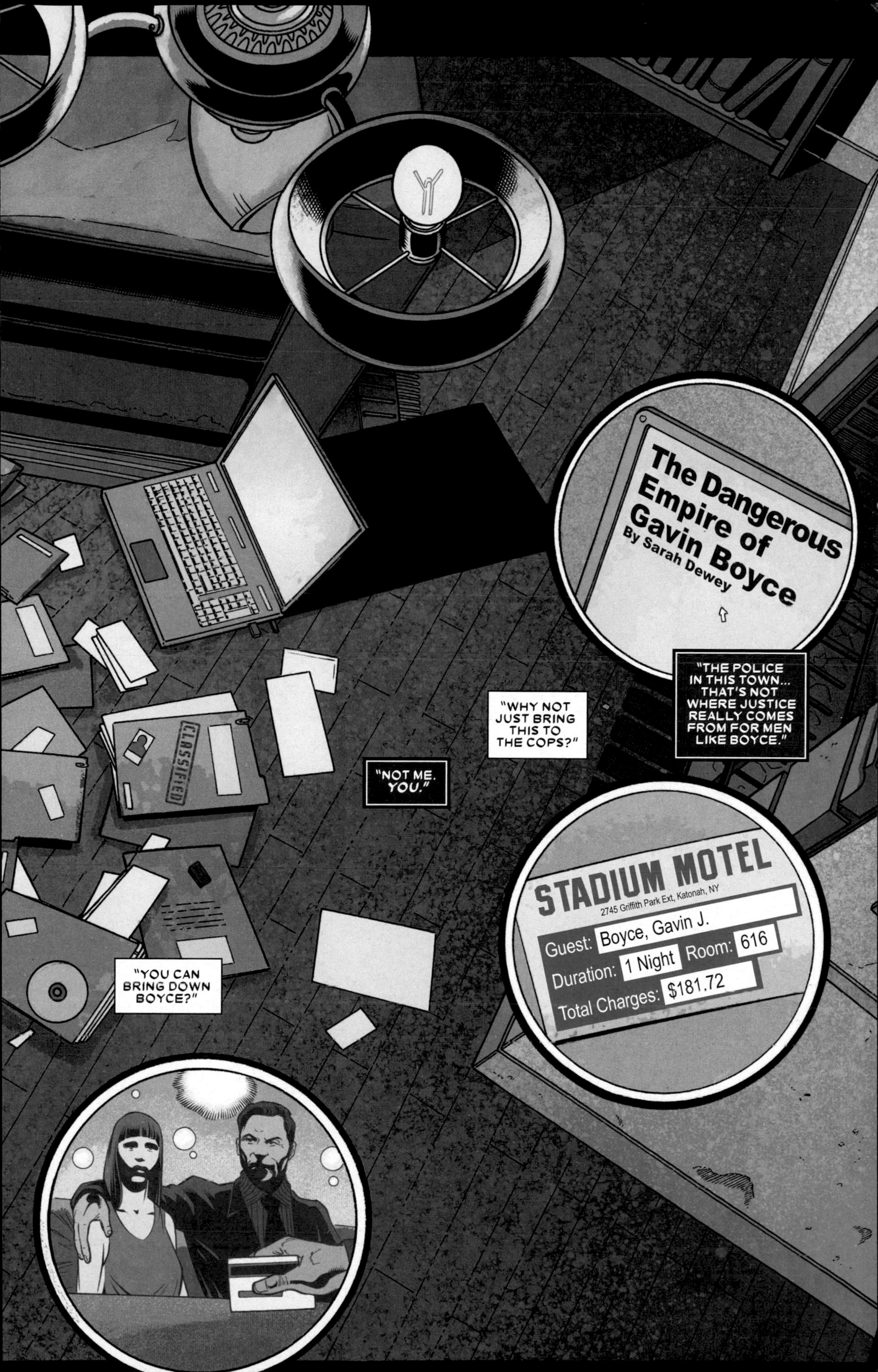

The Dangerous Empire of Gavin Boyce
By Sarah Dewey
"THE POLICE IN THIS TOWN... THAT'S NOT WHERE JUSTICE REALLY COMES FROM FOR MEN LIKE BOYCE."
"WHY NOT JUST BRING THIS TO THE COPS?"
"NOT ME. YOU."
CLASSIFIED
STADIUM MOTEL
2745 Griffith Park Ext, Katonah, NY
Guest: Boyce, Gavin J.
Room: 616
Duration: 1 Night
Total Charges: $181.72
"YOU CAN BRING DOWN BOYCE?"

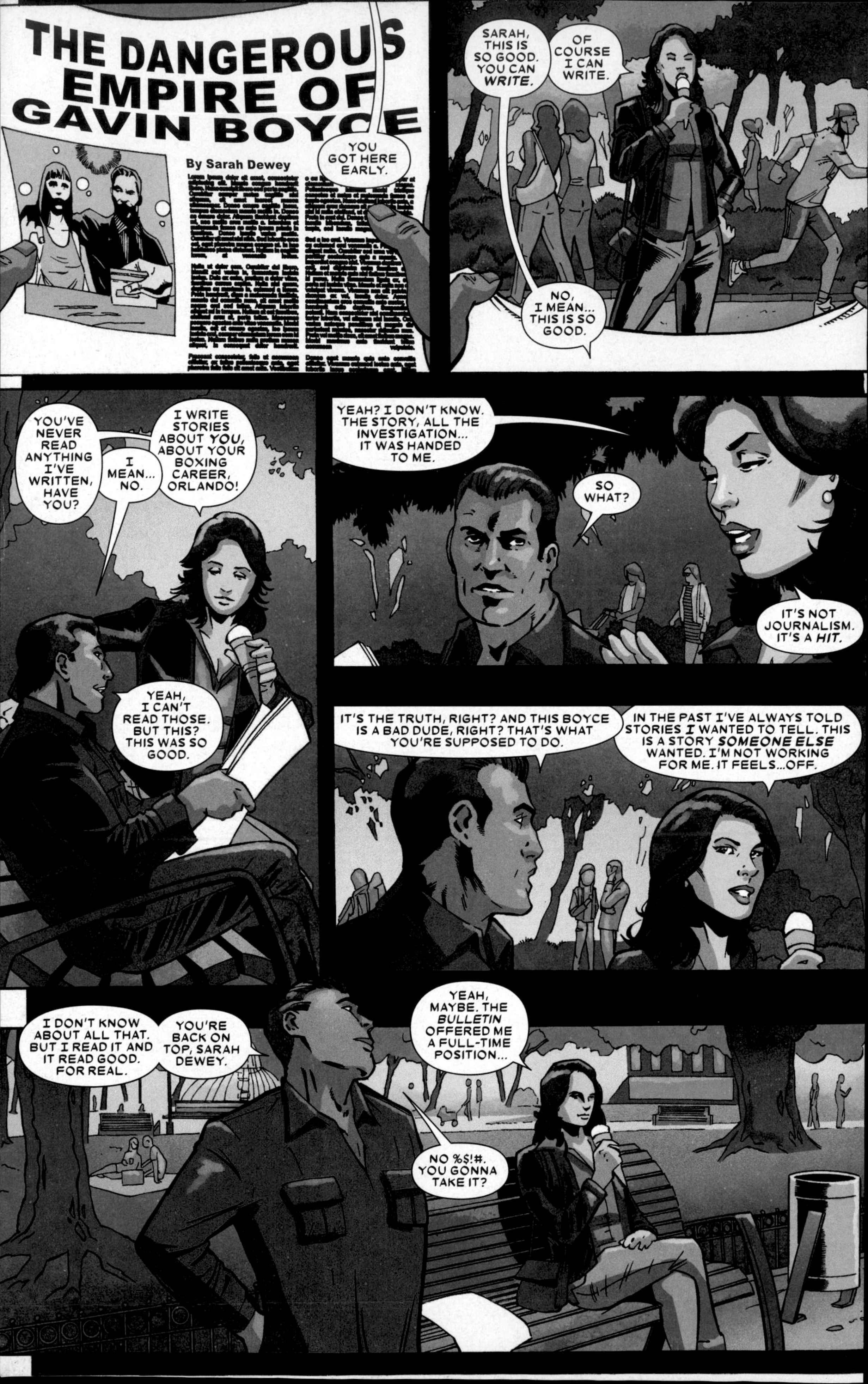
THE DANGEROUS EMPIRE OF GAVIN BOYCE
By Sarah Dewey
YOU GOT HERE EARLY.
SARAH, THIS IS SO GOOD. YOU CAN *WRITE.*
OF COURSE I CAN WRITE.
NO, I MEAN... THIS IS SO GOOD.
YOU'VE NEVER READ ANYTHING I'VE WRITTEN, HAVE YOU?
I MEAN... NO.
I WRITE STORIES ABOUT *YOU*, ABOUT YOUR BOXING CAREER, ORLANDO!
YEAH, I CAN'T READ THOSE. BUT THIS? THIS WAS SO GOOD.
YEAH? I DON'T KNOW. THE STORY, ALL THE INVESTIGATION... IT WAS HANDED TO ME.
SO WHAT?
IT'S NOT JOURNALISM. IT'S A *HIT.*
IT'S THE TRUTH, RIGHT? AND THIS BOYCE IS A BAD DUDE, RIGHT? THAT'S WHAT YOU'RE SUPPOSED TO DO.
IN THE PAST I'VE ALWAYS TOLD STORIES *I* WANTED TO TELL. THIS IS A STORY *SOMEONE ELSE* WANTED. I'M NOT WORKING FOR ME. IT FEELS...OFF.
I DON'T KNOW ABOUT ALL THAT. BUT I READ IT AND IT READ GOOD. FOR REAL.
YOU'RE BACK ON TOP, SARAH DEWEY.
YEAH, MAYBE. THE *BULLETIN* OFFERED ME A FULL-TIME POSITION...
NO %$!#. YOU GONNA TAKE IT?

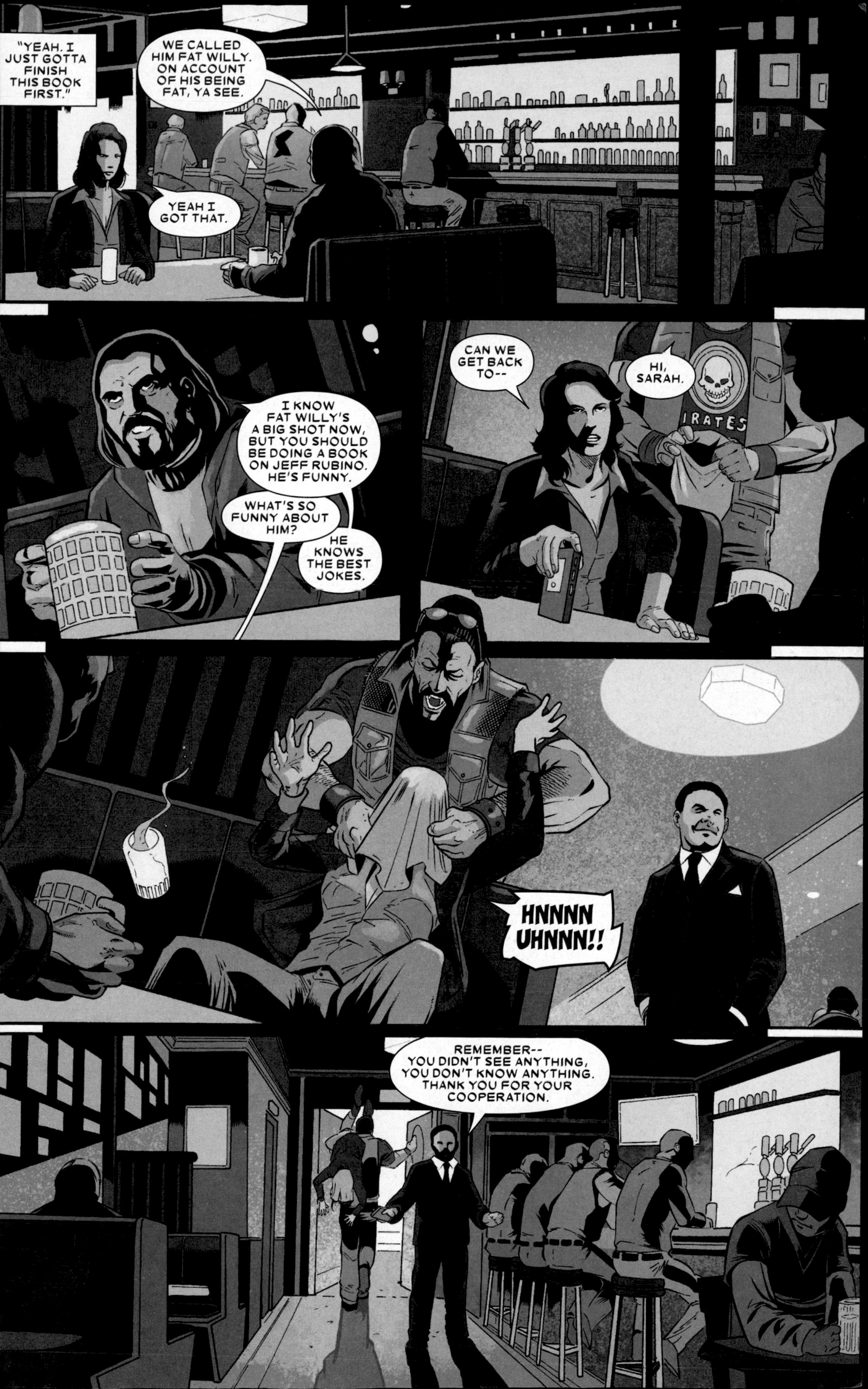

"YEAH. I JUST GOTTA FINISH THIS BOOK FIRST."
WE CALLED HIM FAT WILLY. ON ACCOUNT OF HIS BEING FAT, YA SEE.
YEAH I GOT THAT.
I KNOW FAT WILLY'S A BIG SHOT NOW, BUT YOU SHOULD BE DOING A BOOK ON JEFF RUBINO. HE'S FUNNY.
WHAT'S SO FUNNY ABOUT HIM?
HE KNOWS THE BEST JOKES.
CAN WE GET BACK TO--
HI, SARAH.
IRATES
HNNNN UHNNN!!
REMEMBER-- YOU DIDN'T SEE ANYTHING, YOU DON'T KNOW ANYTHING. THANK YOU FOR YOUR COOPERATION.

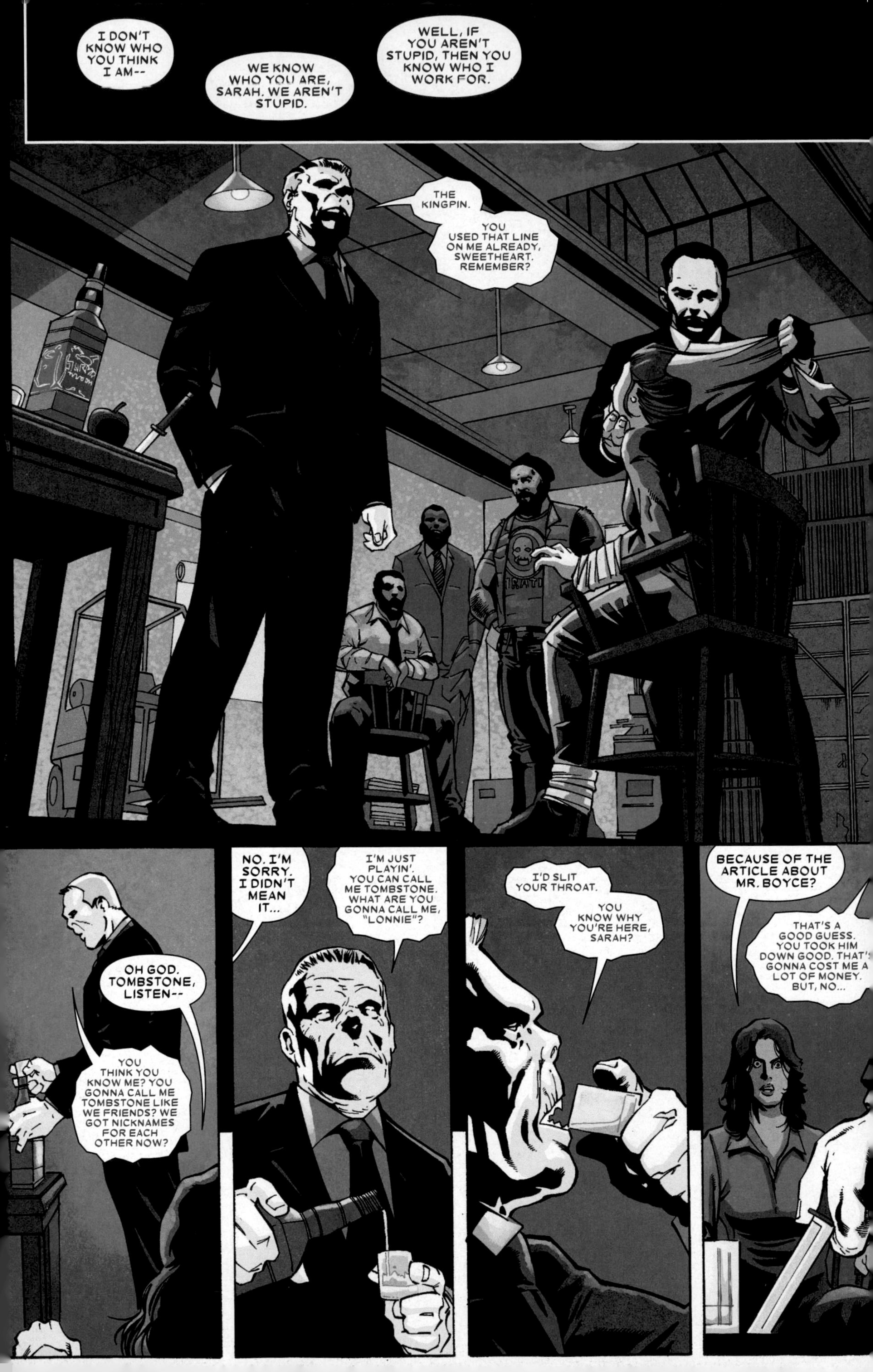

I DON'T KNOW WHO YOU THINK I AM--
WE KNOW WHO YOU ARE, SARAH. WE AREN'T STUPID.
WELL, IF YOU AREN'T STUPID, THEN YOU KNOW WHO I WORK FOR.
THE KINGPIN.
YOU USED THAT LINE ON ME ALREADY, SWEETHEART. REMEMBER?
OH GOD. TOMBSTONE, LISTEN--
YOU THINK YOU KNOW ME? YOU GONNA CALL ME TOMBSTONE LIKE WE FRIENDS? WE GOT NICKNAMES FOR EACH OTHER NOW?
NO. I'M SORRY. I DIDN'T MEAN IT...
I'M JUST PLAYIN'. YOU CAN CALL ME TOMBSTONE. WHAT ARE YOU GONNA CALL ME, "LONNIE"?
I'D SLIT YOUR THROAT.
YOU KNOW WHY YOU'RE HERE, SARAH?
BECAUSE OF THE ARTICLE ABOUT MR. BOYCE?
THAT'S A GOOD GUESS. YOU TOOK HIM DOWN GOOD. THAT'S GONNA COST ME A LOT OF MONEY. BUT, NO...

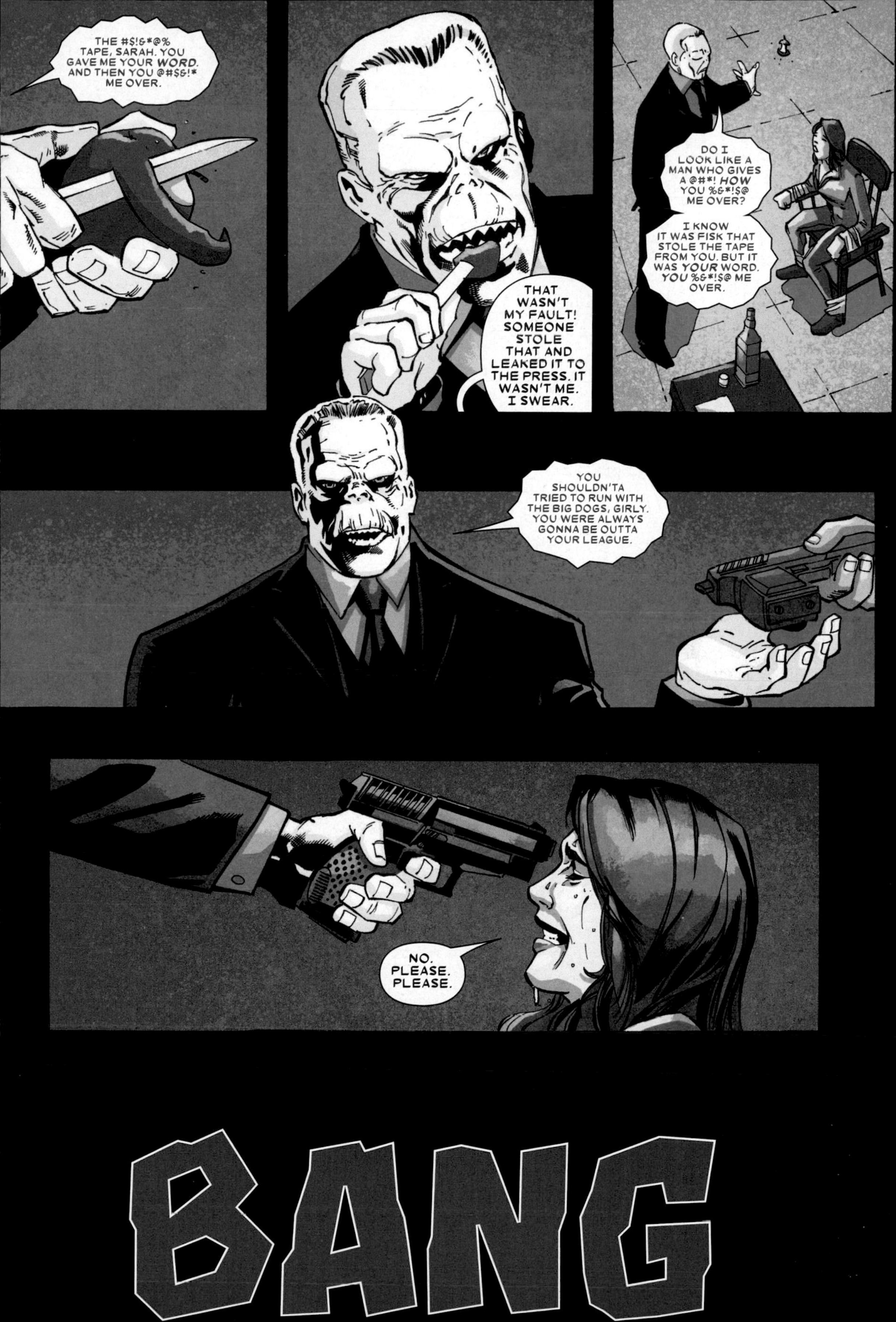

THE #$!&*@% TAPE, SARAH. YOU GAVE ME YOUR WORD. AND THEN YOU @#$&!* ME OVER.
THAT WASN'T MY FAULT! SOMEONE STOLE THAT AND LEAKED IT TO THE PRESS. IT WASN'T ME. I SWEAR.
DO I LOOK LIKE A MAN WHO GIVES A @#*! HOW YOU %&*!$@ ME OVER?
I KNOW IT WAS FISK THAT STOLE THE TAPE FROM YOU. BUT IT WAS YOUR WORD. YOU %&*!$@ ME OVER.
YOU SHOULDN'TA TRIED TO RUN WITH THE BIG DOGS, GIRLY. YOU WERE ALWAYS GONNA BE OUTTA YOUR LEAGUE.
NO. PLEASE. PLEASE.
BANG

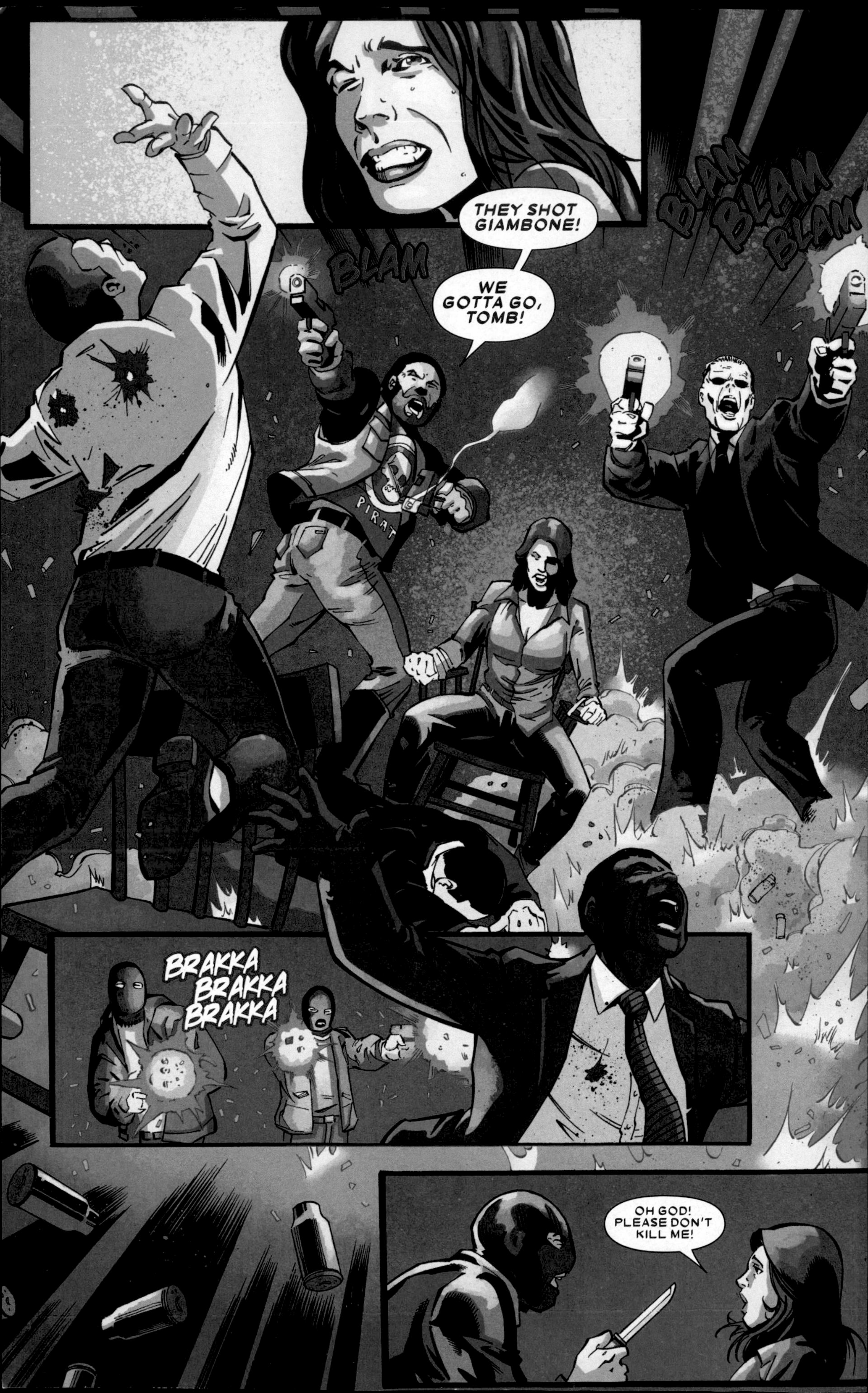
THEY SHOT GIAMBONE!
WE GOTTA GO, TOMB!
BLAM
BLAM BLAM BLAM
PIRAT
BRAKKA BRAKKA BRAKKA
OH GOD! PLEASE DON'T KILL ME!

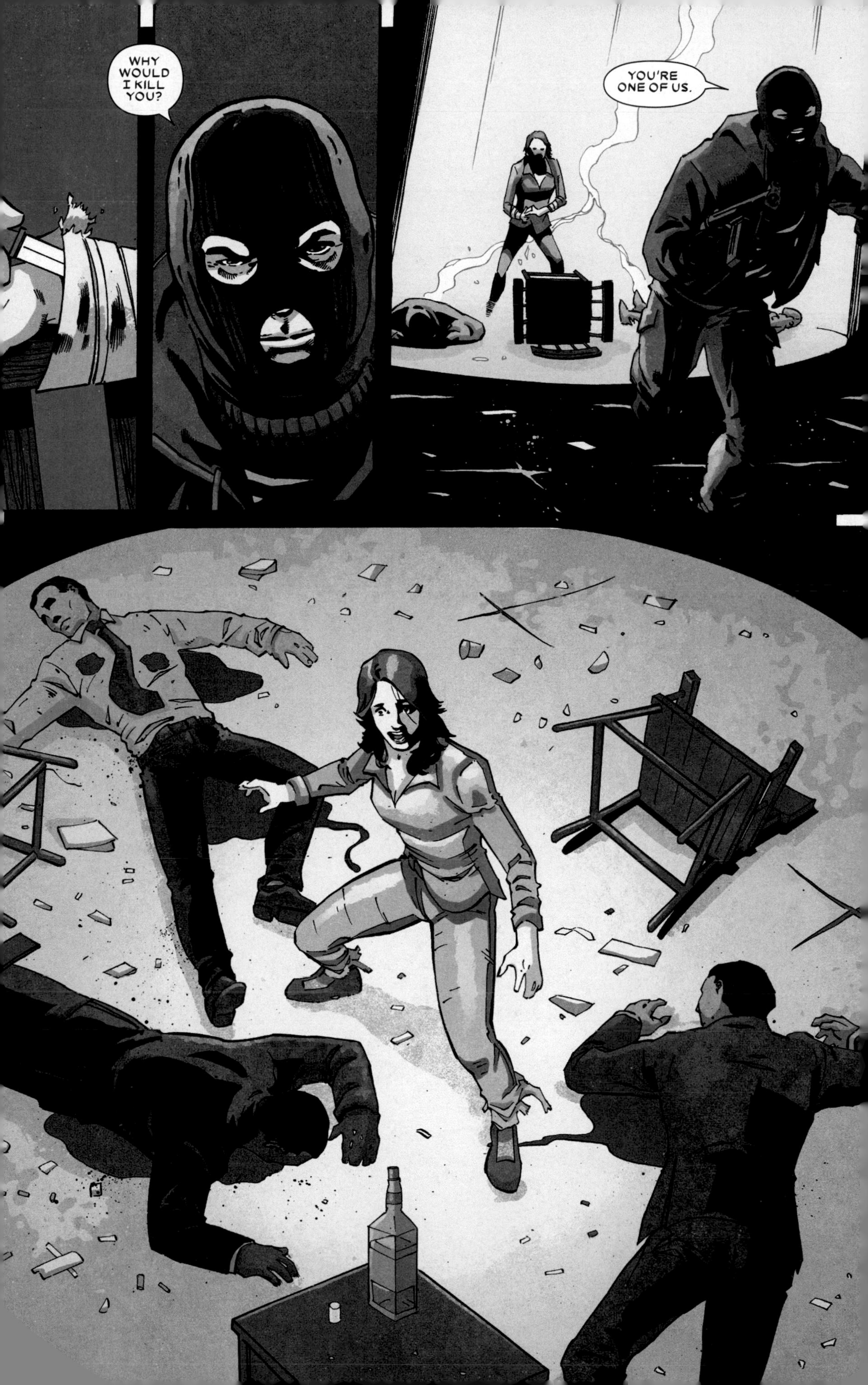
WHY WOULD I KILL YOU?
YOU'RE ONE OF US.

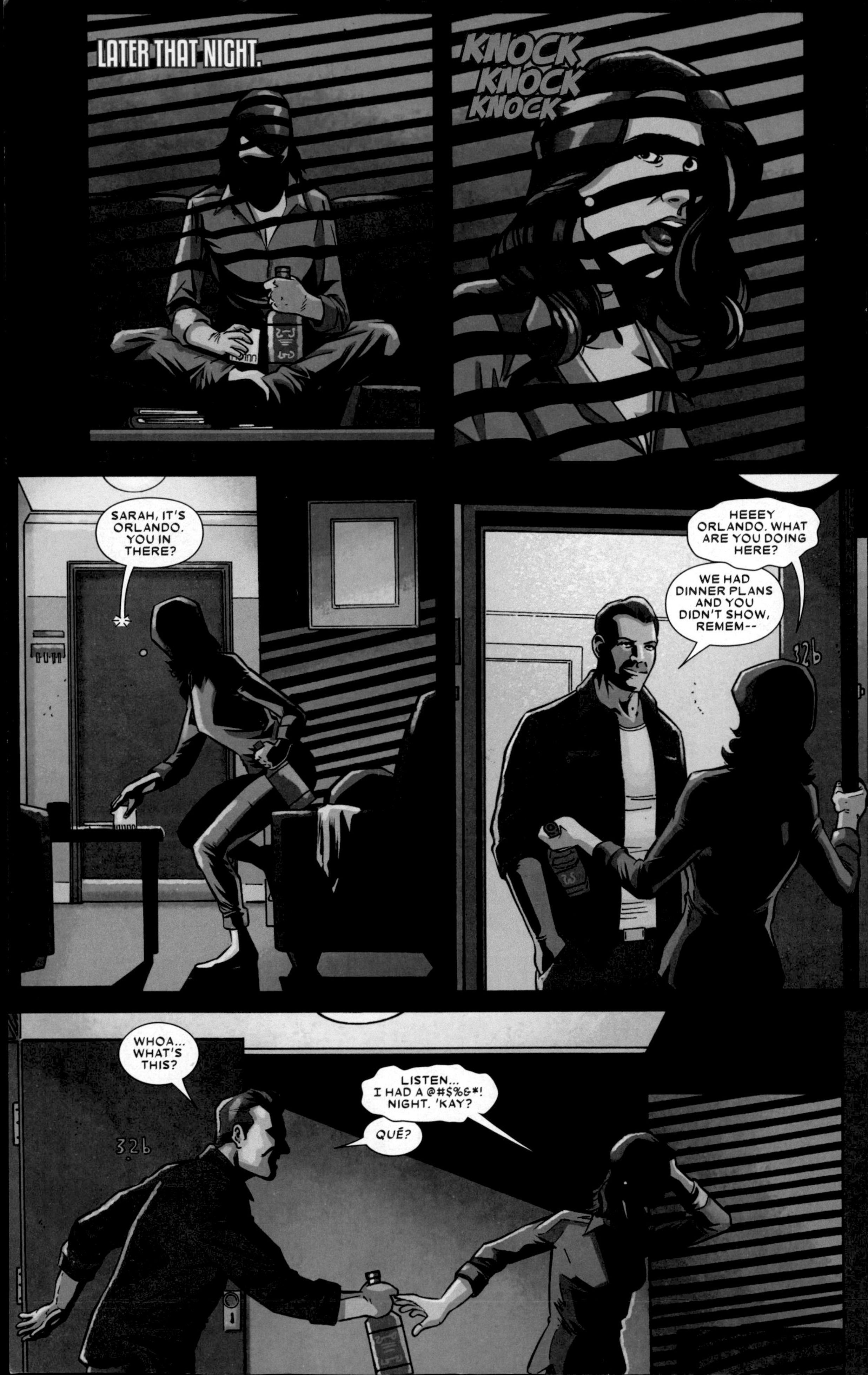
LATER THAT NIGHT.
KNOCK KNOCK KNOCK
SARAH, IT'S ORLANDO. YOU IN THERE?
HEEEY ORLANDO. WHAT ARE YOU DOING HERE?
WE HAD DINNER PLANS AND YOU DIDN'T SHOW, REMEM--
326
WHOA... WHAT'S THIS?
LISTEN... I HAD A @#$%&*! NIGHT. 'KAY?
QUÉ?
326

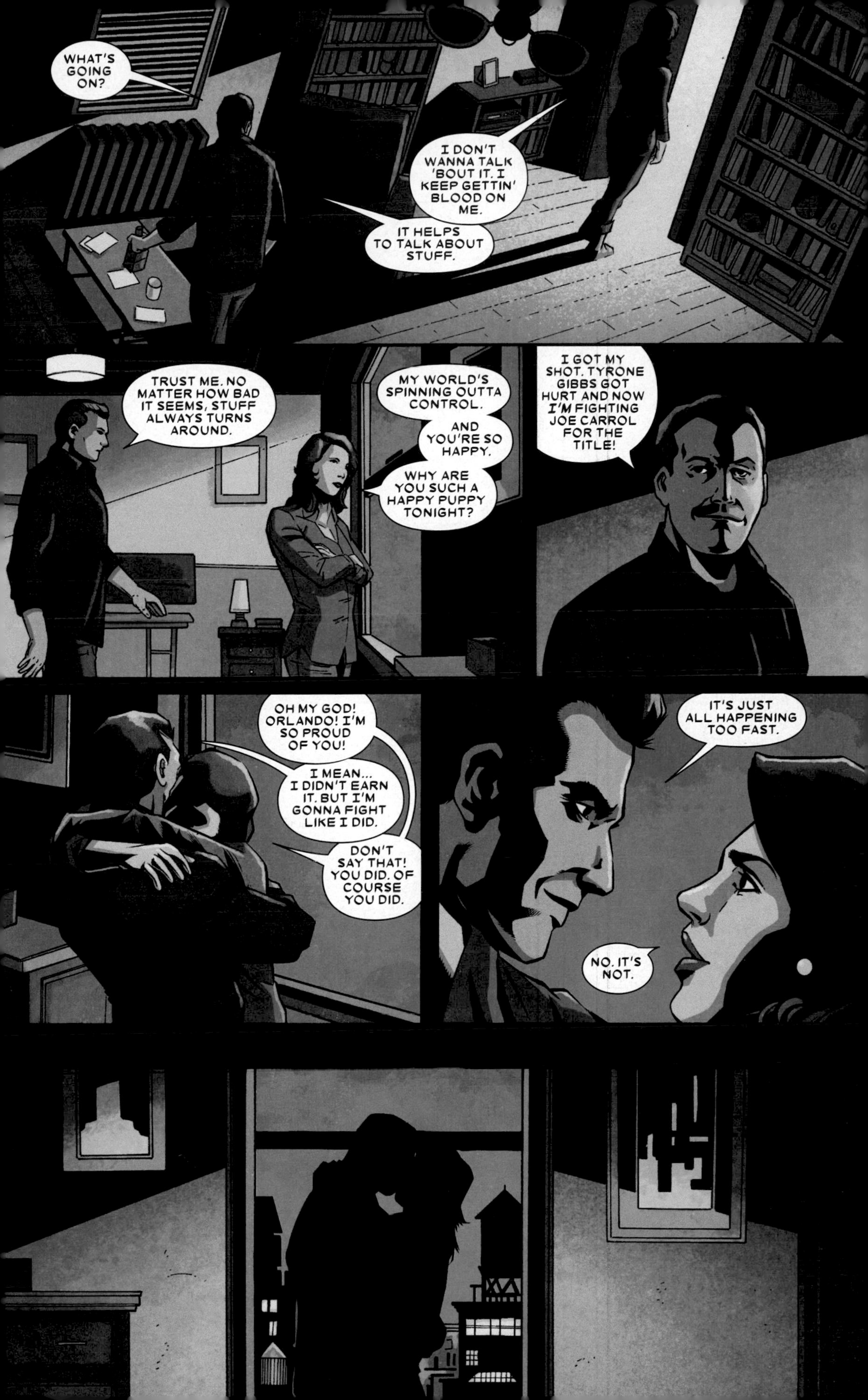
WHAT'S GOING ON?
I DON'T WANNA TALK 'BOUT IT. I KEEP GETTIN' BLOOD ON ME.
IT HELPS TO TALK ABOUT STUFF.
TRUST ME. NO MATTER HOW BAD IT SEEMS, STUFF ALWAYS TURNS AROUND.
MY WORLD'S SPINNING OUTTA CONTROL.
AND YOU'RE SO HAPPY.
WHY ARE YOU SUCH A HAPPY PUPPY TONIGHT?
I GOT MY SHOT. TYRONE GIBBS GOT HURT AND NOW I'M FIGHTING JOE CARROL FOR THE TITLE!
OH MY GOD! ORLANDO! I'M SO PROUD OF YOU!
I MEAN... I DIDN'T EARN IT. BUT I'M GONNA FIGHT LIKE I DID.
DON'T SAY THAT! YOU DID. OF COURSE YOU DID.
IT'S JUST ALL HAPPENING TOO FAST.
NO. IT'S NOT.

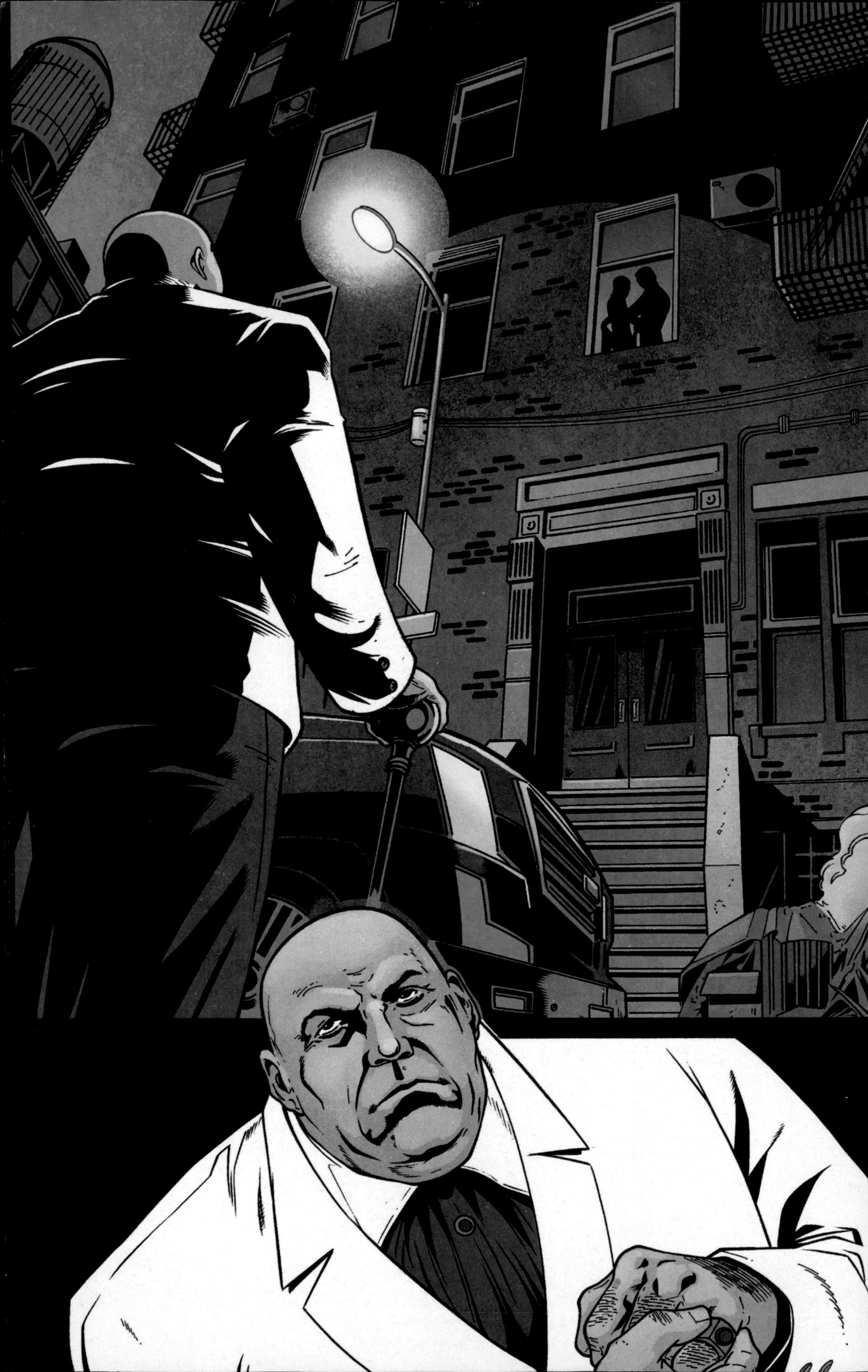

FIVE

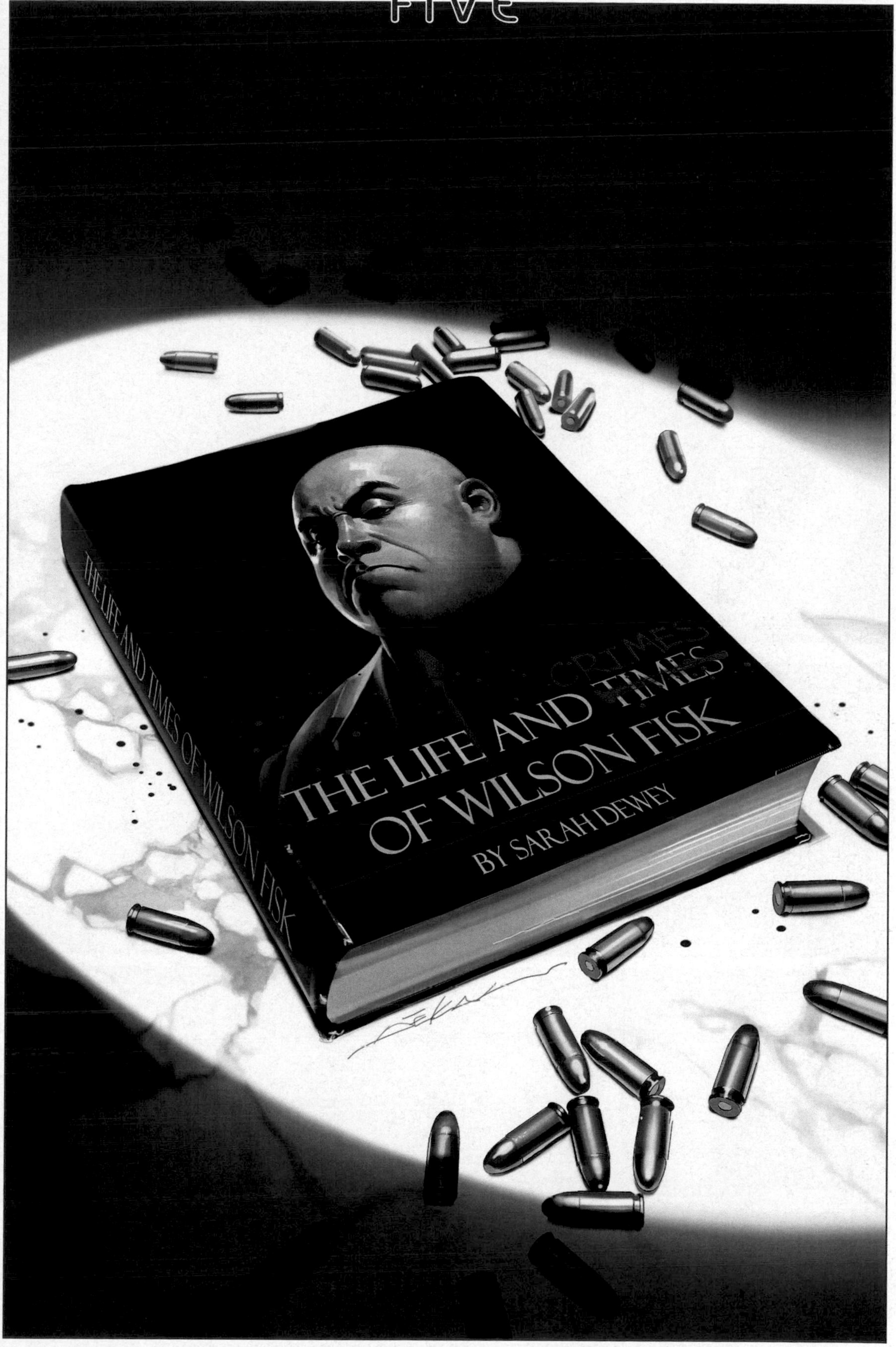

CRIMES
THE LIFE AND TIMES
OF WILSON FISK
BY SARAH DEWEY
THE LIFE AND TIMES OF WILSON FISK

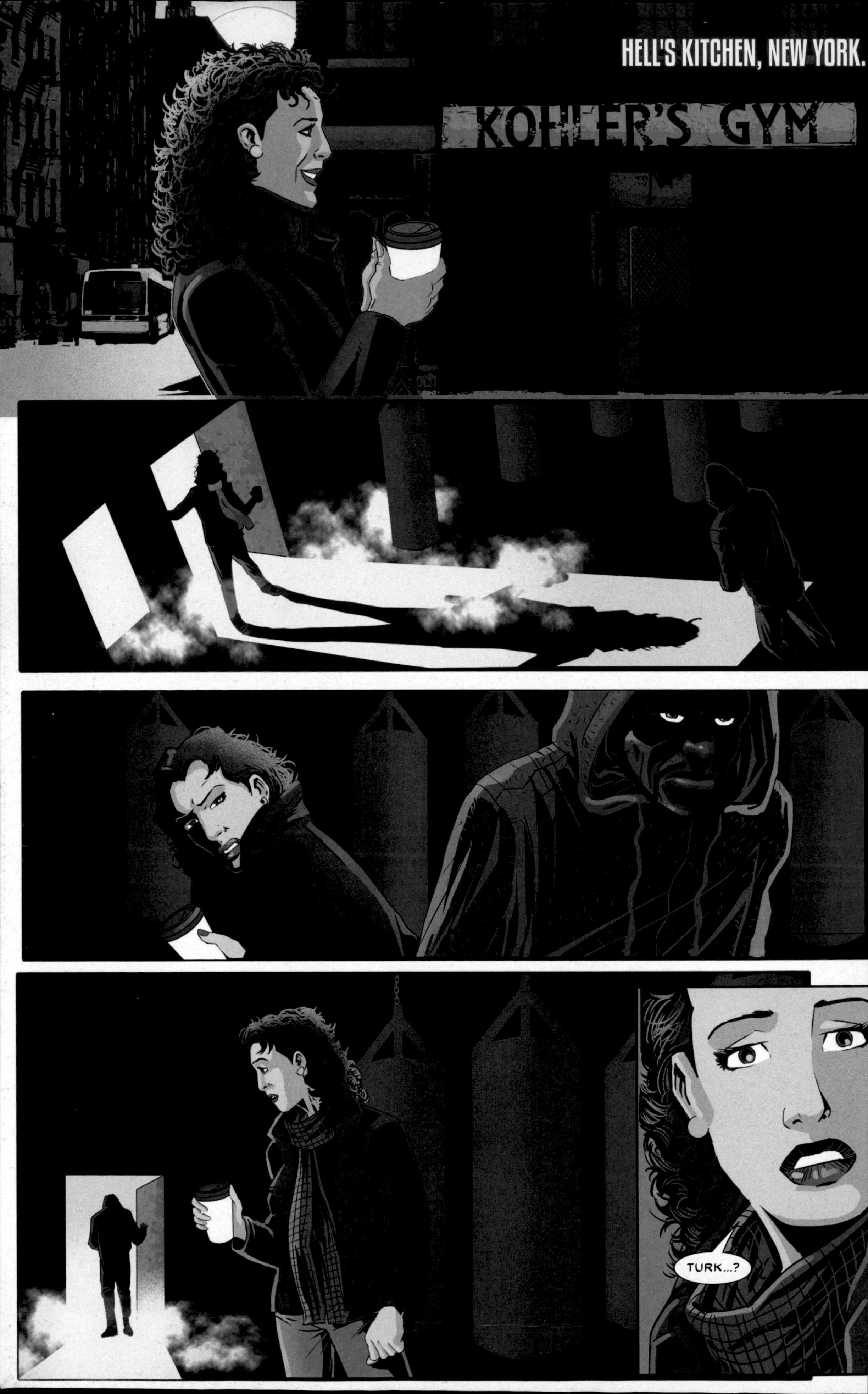
HELL'S KITCHEN, NEW YORK.
KOHLER'S GYM
TURK...?

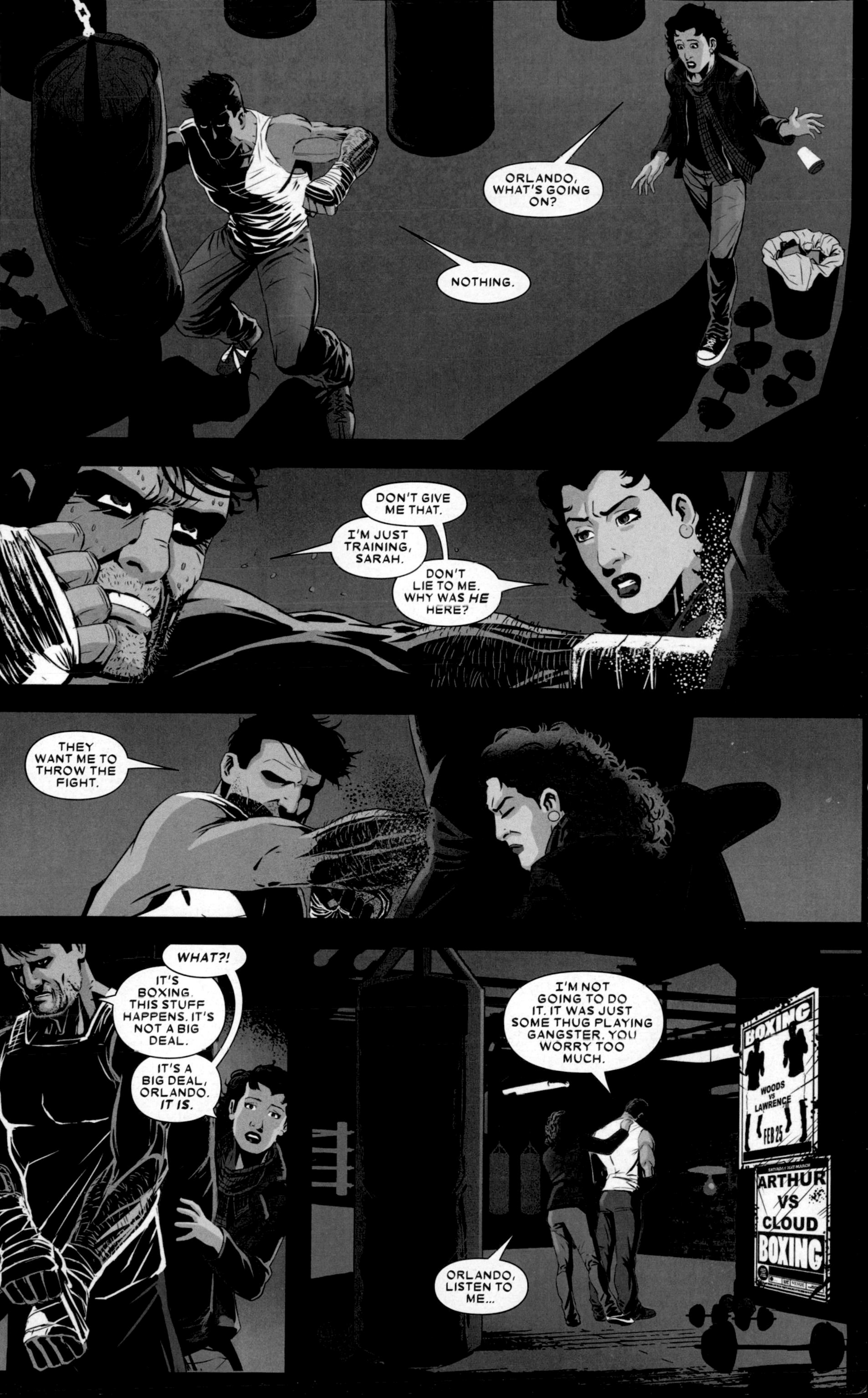
ORLANDO, WHAT'S GOING ON?
NOTHING.
DON'T GIVE ME THAT.
I'M JUST TRAINING, SARAH.
DON'T LIE TO ME. WHY WAS HE HERE?
THEY WANT ME TO THROW THE FIGHT.
WHAT?!
IT'S BOXING. THIS STUFF HAPPENS. IT'S NOT A BIG DEAL.
IT'S A BIG DEAL, ORLANDO. IT IS.
I'M NOT GOING TO DO IT. IT WAS JUST SOME THUG PLAYING GANGSTER. YOU WORRY TOO MUCH.
BOXING
WOODS VS LAWRENCE
FEB 25
ARTHUR VS CLOUD
BOXING
ORLANDO, LISTEN TO ME...

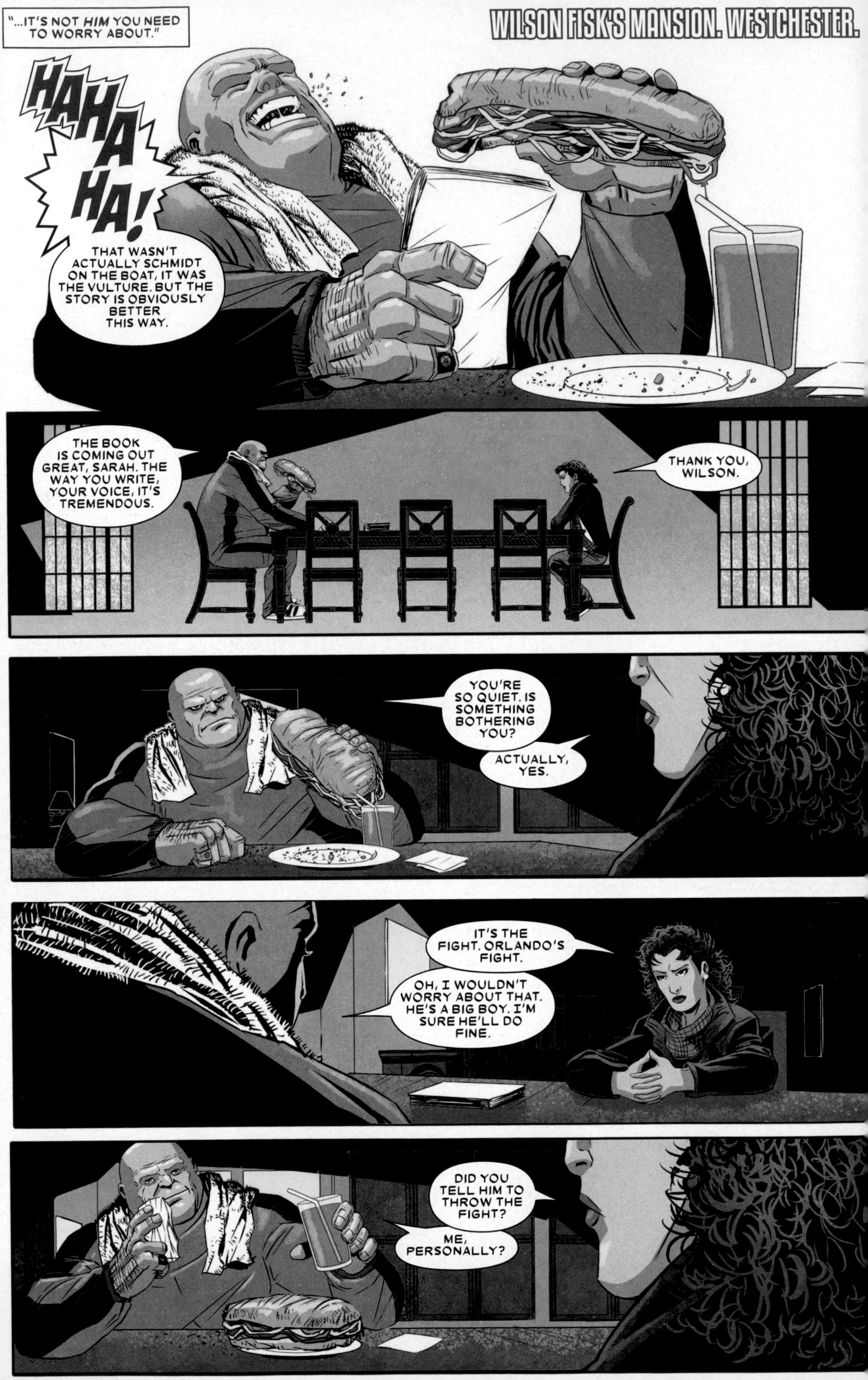
"...IT'S NOT *HIM* YOU NEED TO WORRY ABOUT."
WILSON FISK'S MANSION. WESTCHESTER.
HAHAHA HA!
THAT WASN'T ACTUALLY SCHMIDT ON THE BOAT, IT WAS THE VULTURE. BUT THE STORY IS OBVIOUSLY BETTER THIS WAY.
THE BOOK IS COMING OUT GREAT, SARAH. THE WAY YOU WRITE, YOUR VOICE, IT'S TREMENDOUS.
THANK YOU, WILSON.
YOU'RE SO QUIET. IS SOMETHING BOTHERING YOU?
ACTUALLY, YES.
IT'S THE FIGHT. ORLANDO'S FIGHT.
OH, I WOULDN'T WORRY ABOUT THAT. HE'S A BIG BOY. I'M SURE HE'LL DO FINE.
DID YOU TELL HIM TO THROW THE FIGHT?
ME, PERSONALLY?

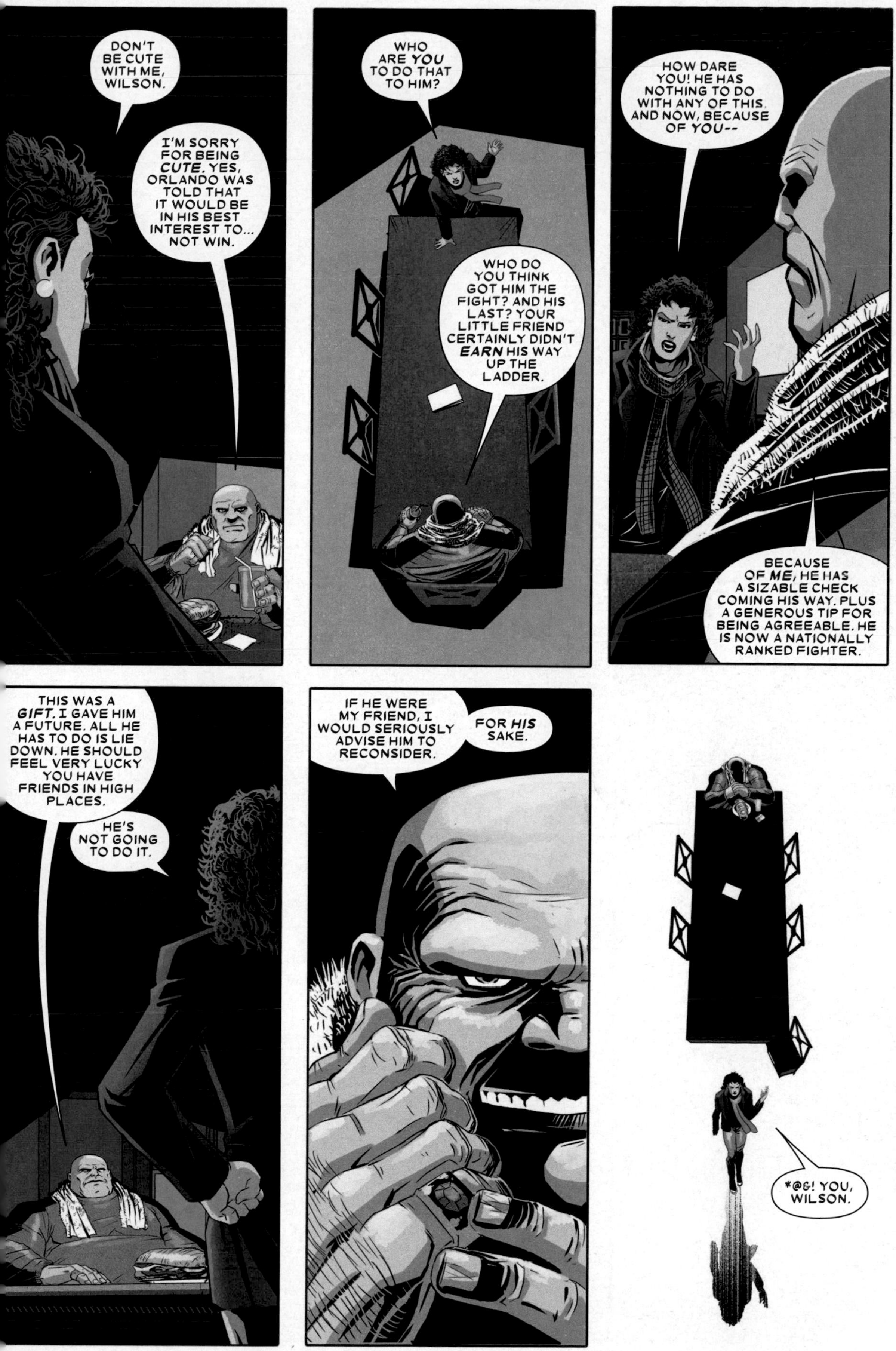
DON'T BE CUTE WITH ME, WILSON.
I'M SORRY FOR BEING CUTE. YES, ORLANDO WAS TOLD THAT IT WOULD BE IN HIS BEST INTEREST TO... NOT WIN.
WHO ARE YOU TO DO THAT TO HIM?
WHO DO YOU THINK GOT HIM THE FIGHT? AND HIS LAST? YOUR LITTLE FRIEND CERTAINLY DIDN'T EARN HIS WAY UP THE LADDER.
HOW DARE YOU! HE HAS NOTHING TO DO WITH ANY OF THIS. AND NOW, BECAUSE OF YOU--
BECAUSE OF ME, HE HAS A SIZABLE CHECK COMING HIS WAY. PLUS A GENEROUS TIP FOR BEING AGREEABLE. HE IS NOW A NATIONALLY RANKED FIGHTER.
THIS WAS A GIFT. I GAVE HIM A FUTURE. ALL HE HAS TO DO IS LIE DOWN. HE SHOULD FEEL VERY LUCKY YOU HAVE FRIENDS IN HIGH PLACES.
HE'S NOT GOING TO DO IT.
IF HE WERE MY FRIEND, I WOULD SERIOUSLY ADVISE HIM TO RECONSIDER.
FOR HIS SAKE.
*@&! YOU, WILSON.

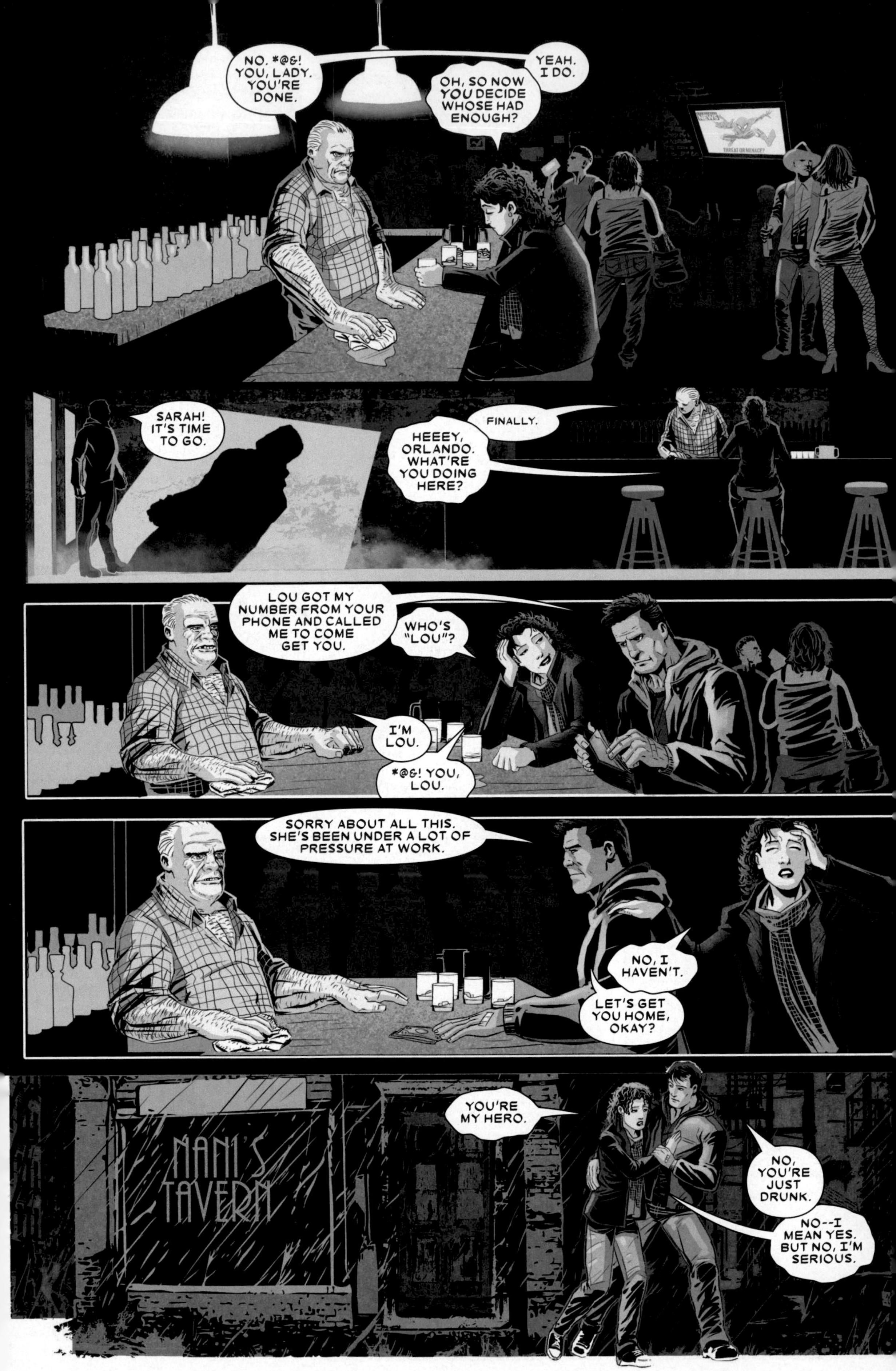
NO. *@&! YOU, LADY. YOU'RE DONE.
OH, SO NOW YOU DECIDE WHOSE HAD ENOUGH?
YEAH. I DO.
NEWS
THREAT OR MENACE?
SARAH! IT'S TIME TO GO.
HEEEY, ORLANDO. WHAT'RE YOU DOING HERE?
FINALLY.
LOU GOT MY NUMBER FROM YOUR PHONE AND CALLED ME TO COME GET YOU.
WHO'S "LOU"?
I'M LOU.
*@&! YOU, LOU.
SORRY ABOUT ALL THIS. SHE'S BEEN UNDER A LOT OF PRESSURE AT WORK.
NO, I HAVEN'T.
LET'S GET YOU HOME, OKAY?
NANI'S TAVERN
YOU'RE MY HERO.
NO, YOU'RE JUST DRUNK.
NO--I MEAN YES. BUT NO, I'M SERIOUS.

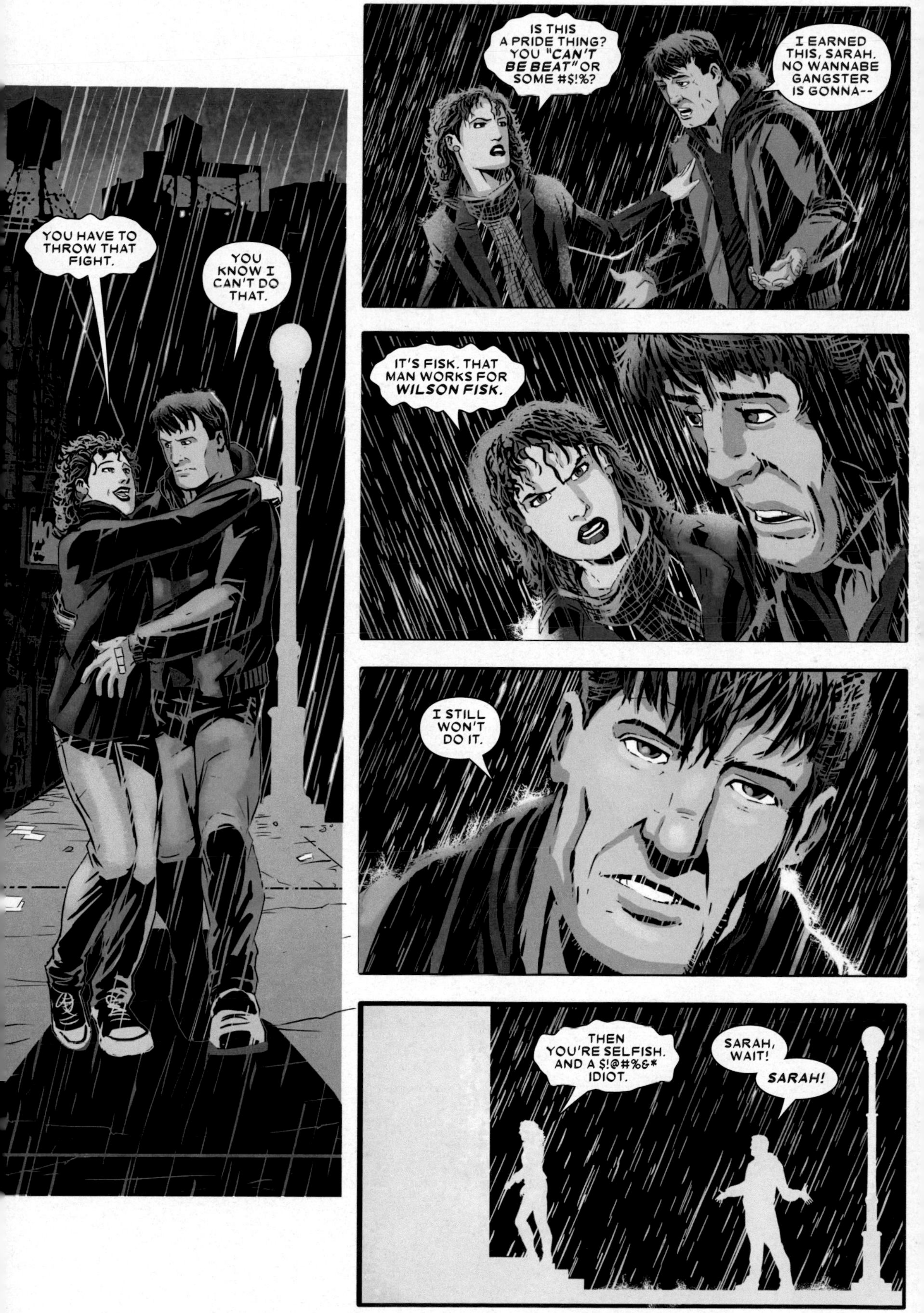
YOU HAVE TO THROW THAT FIGHT.
YOU KNOW I CAN'T DO THAT.
IS THIS A PRIDE THING? YOU *"CAN'T BE BEAT"* OR SOME #$!%?
I EARNED THIS, SARAH. NO WANNABE GANGSTER IS GONNA--
IT'S FISK. THAT MAN WORKS FOR ***WILSON FISK.***
I STILL WON'T DO IT.
THEN YOU'RE SELFISH. AND A $!@#%&* IDIOT.
SARAH, WAIT!
SARAH!

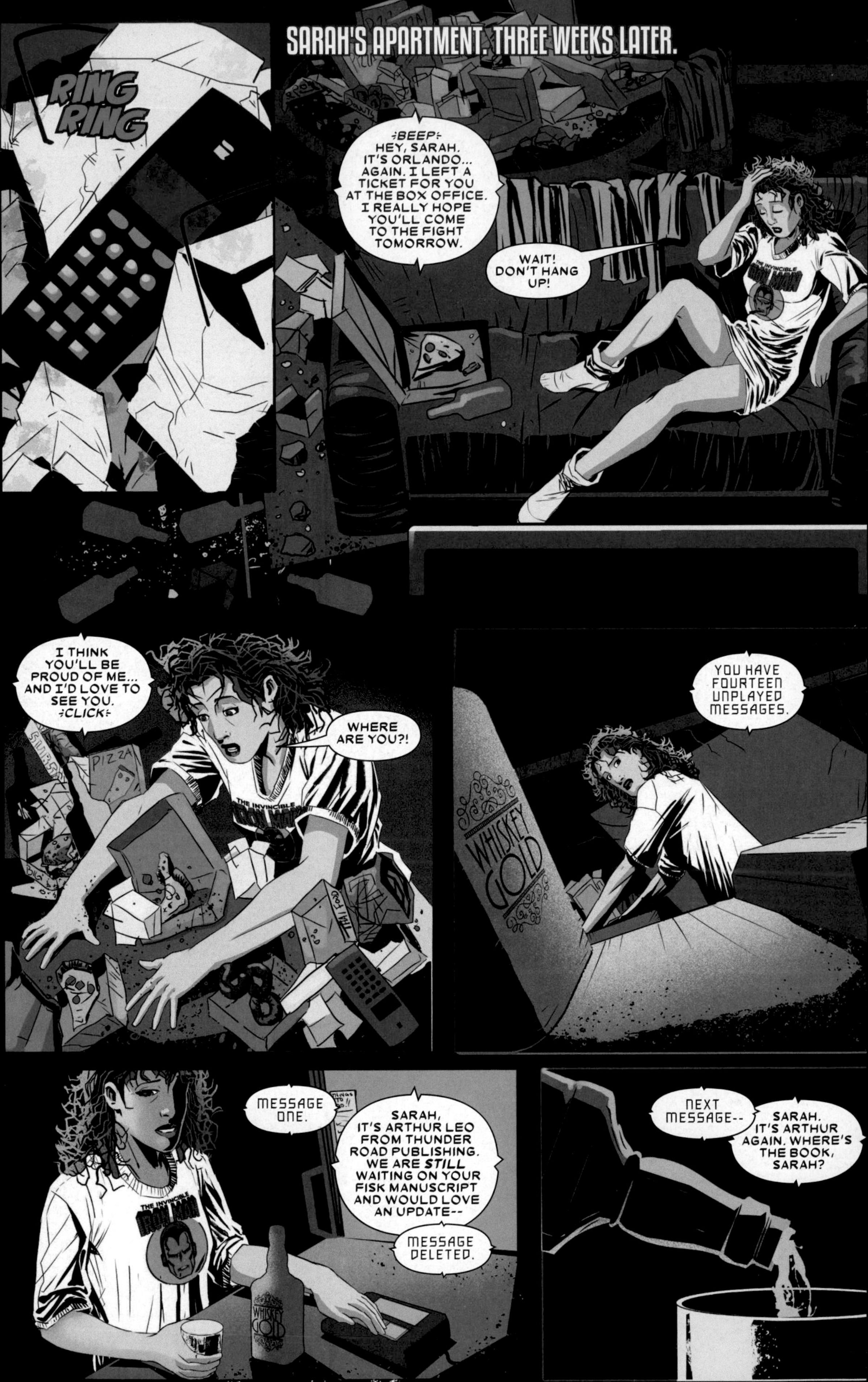
SARAH'S APARTMENT. THREE WEEKS LATER.
RING RING
BEEP HEY, SARAH. IT'S ORLANDO... AGAIN. I LEFT A TICKET FOR YOU AT THE BOX OFFICE. I REALLY HOPE YOU'LL COME TO THE FIGHT TOMORROW.
WAIT! DON'T HANG UP!
I THINK YOU'LL BE PROUD OF ME... AND I'D LOVE TO SEE YOU. *CLICK*
WHERE ARE YOU?!
PIZZA
YOU HAVE FOURTEEN UNPLAYED MESSAGES.
WHISKEY GOLD
MESSAGE ONE.
SARAH, IT'S ARTHUR LEO FROM THUNDER ROAD PUBLISHING. WE ARE STILL WAITING ON YOUR FISK MANUSCRIPT AND WOULD LOVE AN UPDATE--
MESSAGE DELETED.
NEXT MESSAGE--
SARAH. IT'S ARTHUR AGAIN. WHERE'S THE BOOK, SARAH?

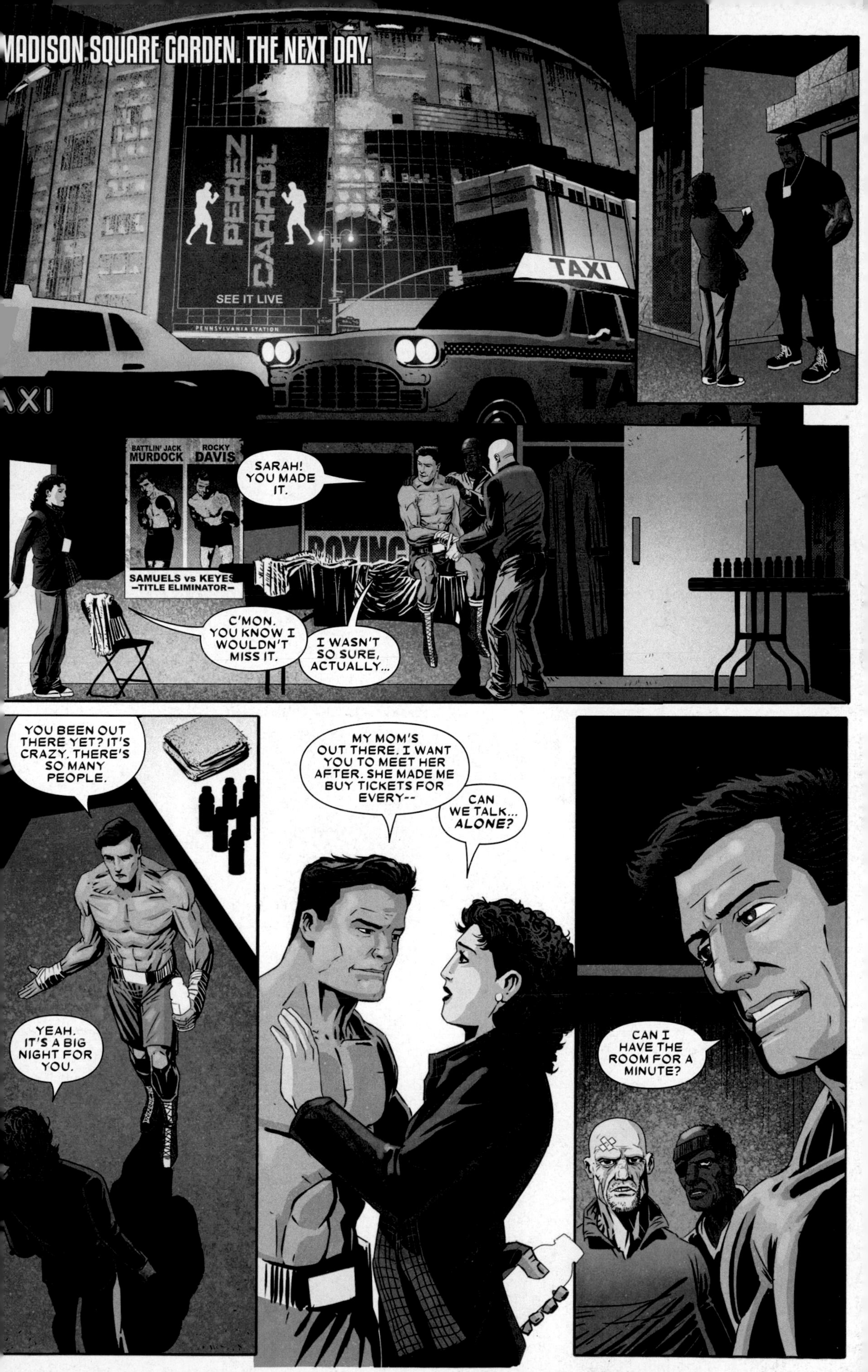

MADISON SQUARE GARDEN. THE NEXT DAY.
PEREZ
CARROL
SEE IT LIVE
PENNSYLVANIA STATION
TAXI
BATTLIN' JACK MURDOCK
ROCKY DAVIS
SAMUELS vs KEYES
—TITLE ELIMINATOR—
BOXING
SARAH! YOU MADE IT.
C'MON. YOU KNOW I WOULDN'T MISS IT.
I WASN'T SO SURE, ACTUALLY...
YOU BEEN OUT THERE YET? IT'S CRAZY. THERE'S SO MANY PEOPLE.
YEAH. IT'S A BIG NIGHT FOR YOU.
MY MOM'S OUT THERE. I WANT YOU TO MEET HER AFTER. SHE MADE ME BUY TICKETS FOR EVERY--
CAN WE TALK... ALONE?
CAN I HAVE THE ROOM FOR A MINUTE?

YOU HAVE TO LOSE TONIGHT.

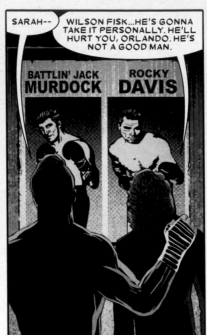

SARAH--

WILSON FISK...HE'S GONNA TAKE IT PERSONALLY. HE'LL HURT YOU, ORLANDO. HE'S NOT A GOOD MAN.

BATTLIN' JACK MURDOCK

ROCKY DAVIS

YOU WORK FOR HIM.

AND I WISH I DIDN'T.

YOU KNOW WHAT YOU'RE ASKING ME, RIGHT? I EARNED THIS. I WOULDN'T BE HERE IF THEY DIDN'T THINK I STOOD A CHANCE.

THAT'S NOT--

I COULD WIN THIS. I NEED TO KNOW THAT YOU BELIEVE THAT.

I DO.

OKAY. I'LL DO IT.

AT 2:40 IN THE FIRST ROUND, I'LL GO DOWN.

BECAUSE I LOVE YOU.

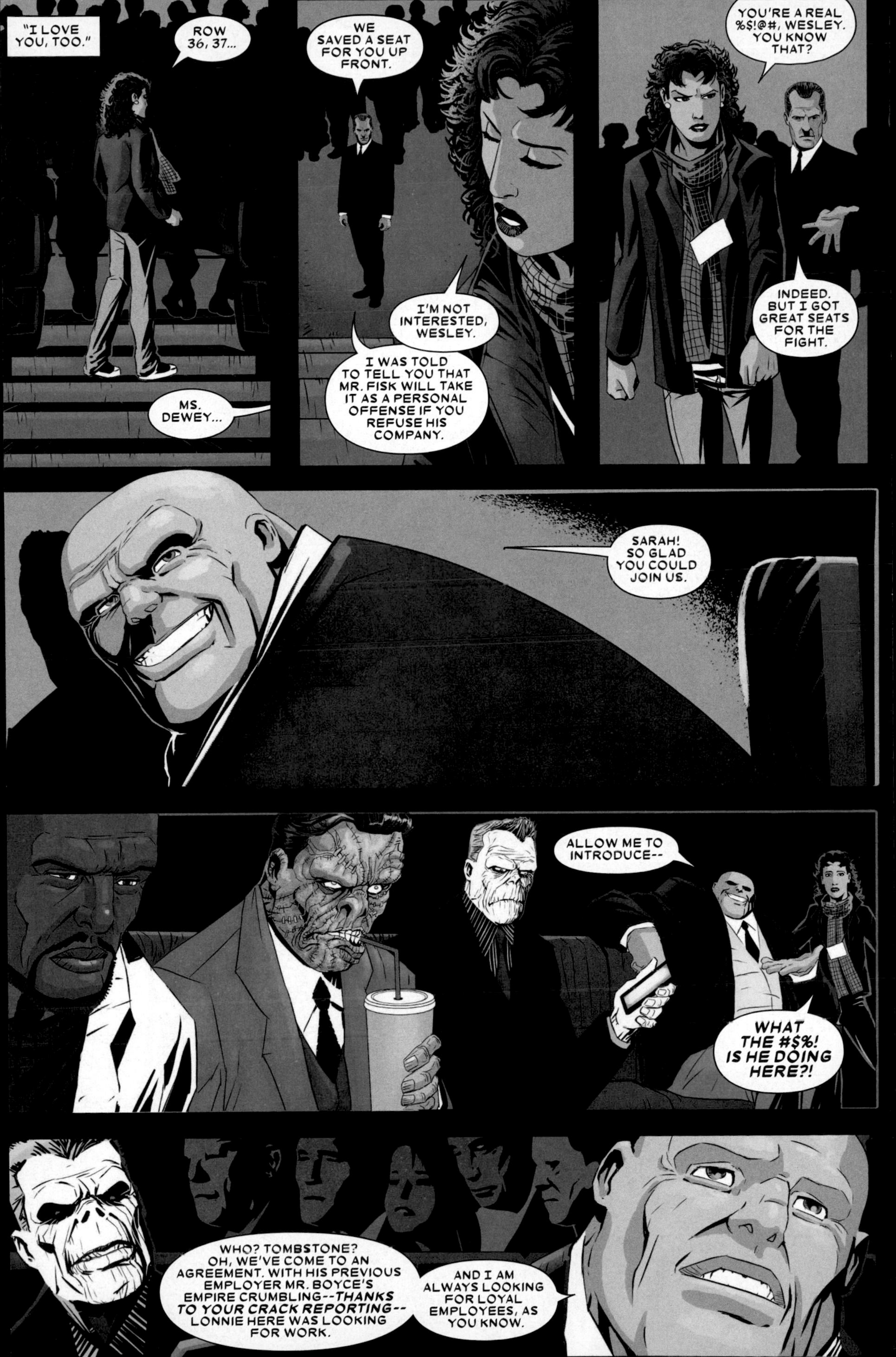
"I LOVE YOU, TOO."
ROW 36, 37...
MS. DEWEY...
WE SAVED A SEAT FOR YOU UP FRONT.
I'M NOT INTERESTED, WESLEY.
I WAS TOLD TO TELL YOU THAT MR. FISK WILL TAKE IT AS A PERSONAL OFFENSE IF YOU REFUSE HIS COMPANY.
YOU'RE A REAL %$!@#, WESLEY. YOU KNOW THAT?
INDEED. BUT I GOT GREAT SEATS FOR THE FIGHT.
SARAH! SO GLAD YOU COULD JOIN US.
ALLOW ME TO INTRODUCE--
WHAT THE #$%! IS HE DOING HERE?!
WHO? TOMBSTONE? OH, WE'VE COME TO AN AGREEMENT. WITH HIS PREVIOUS EMPLOYER MR. BOYCE'S EMPIRE CRUMBLING--THANKS TO YOUR CRACK REPORTING--LONNIE HERE WAS LOOKING FOR WORK.
AND I AM ALWAYS LOOKING FOR LOYAL EMPLOYEES, AS YOU KNOW.

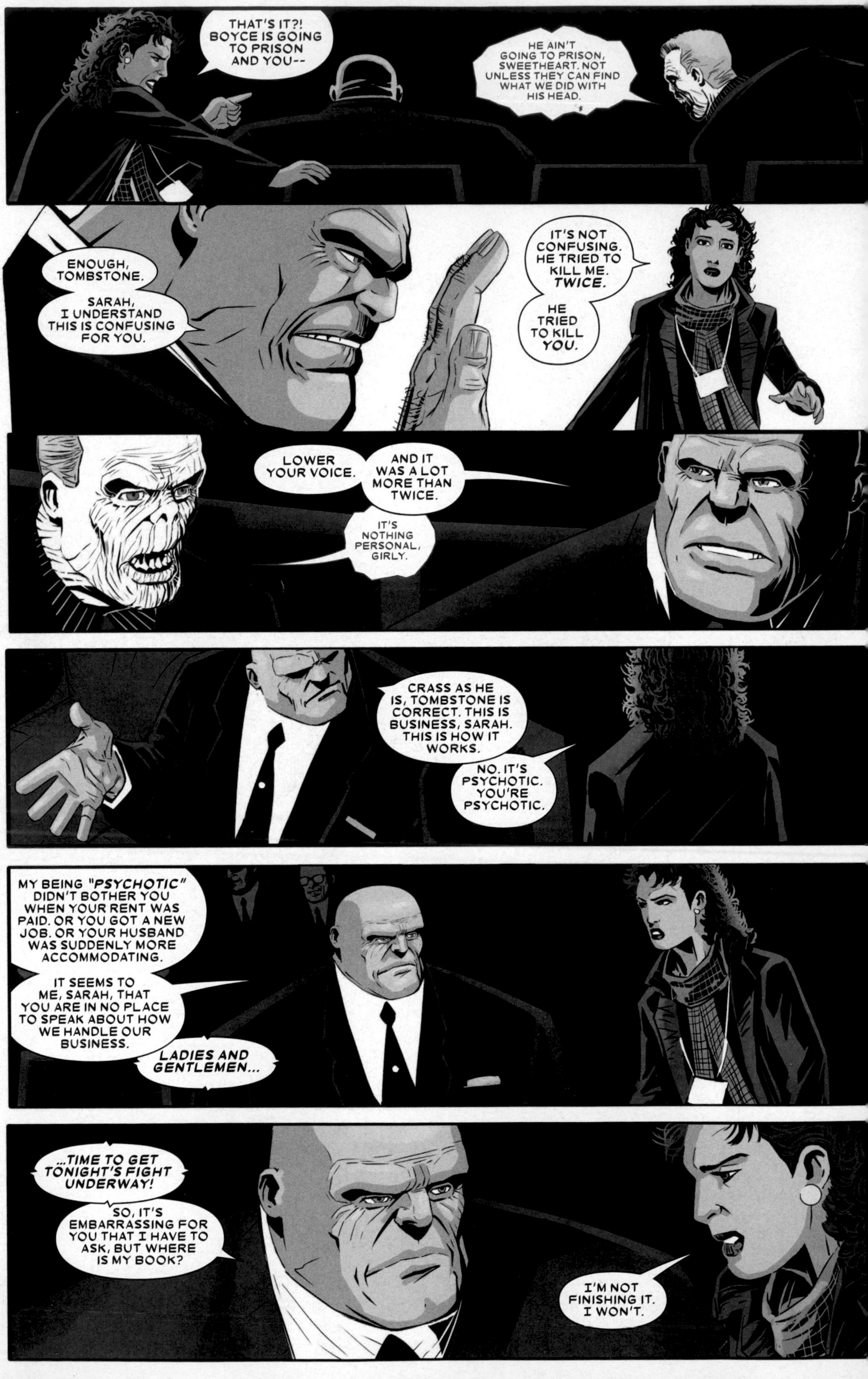
THAT'S IT?! BOYCE IS GOING TO PRISON AND YOU--
HE AIN'T GOING TO PRISON, SWEETHEART. NOT UNLESS THEY CAN FIND WHAT WE DID WITH HIS HEAD.
ENOUGH, TOMBSTONE.
SARAH, I UNDERSTAND THIS IS CONFUSING FOR YOU.
IT'S NOT CONFUSING. HE TRIED TO KILL ME. *TWICE.*
HE TRIED TO KILL *YOU.*
LOWER YOUR VOICE.
AND IT WAS A LOT MORE THAN TWICE.
IT'S NOTHING PERSONAL, GIRLY.
CRASS AS HE IS, TOMBSTONE IS CORRECT. THIS IS BUSINESS, SARAH. THIS IS HOW IT WORKS.
NO. IT'S PSYCHOTIC. YOU'RE PSYCHOTIC.
MY BEING "*PSYCHOTIC*" DIDN'T BOTHER YOU WHEN YOUR RENT WAS PAID. OR YOU GOT A NEW JOB. OR YOUR HUSBAND WAS SUDDENLY MORE ACCOMMODATING.
IT SEEMS TO ME, SARAH, THAT YOU ARE IN NO PLACE TO SPEAK ABOUT HOW WE HANDLE OUR BUSINESS.
LADIES AND GENTLEMEN...
...TIME TO GET TONIGHT'S FIGHT UNDERWAY!
SO, IT'S EMBARRASSING FOR YOU THAT I HAVE TO ASK, BUT WHERE IS MY BOOK?
I'M NOT FINISHING IT. I WON'T.

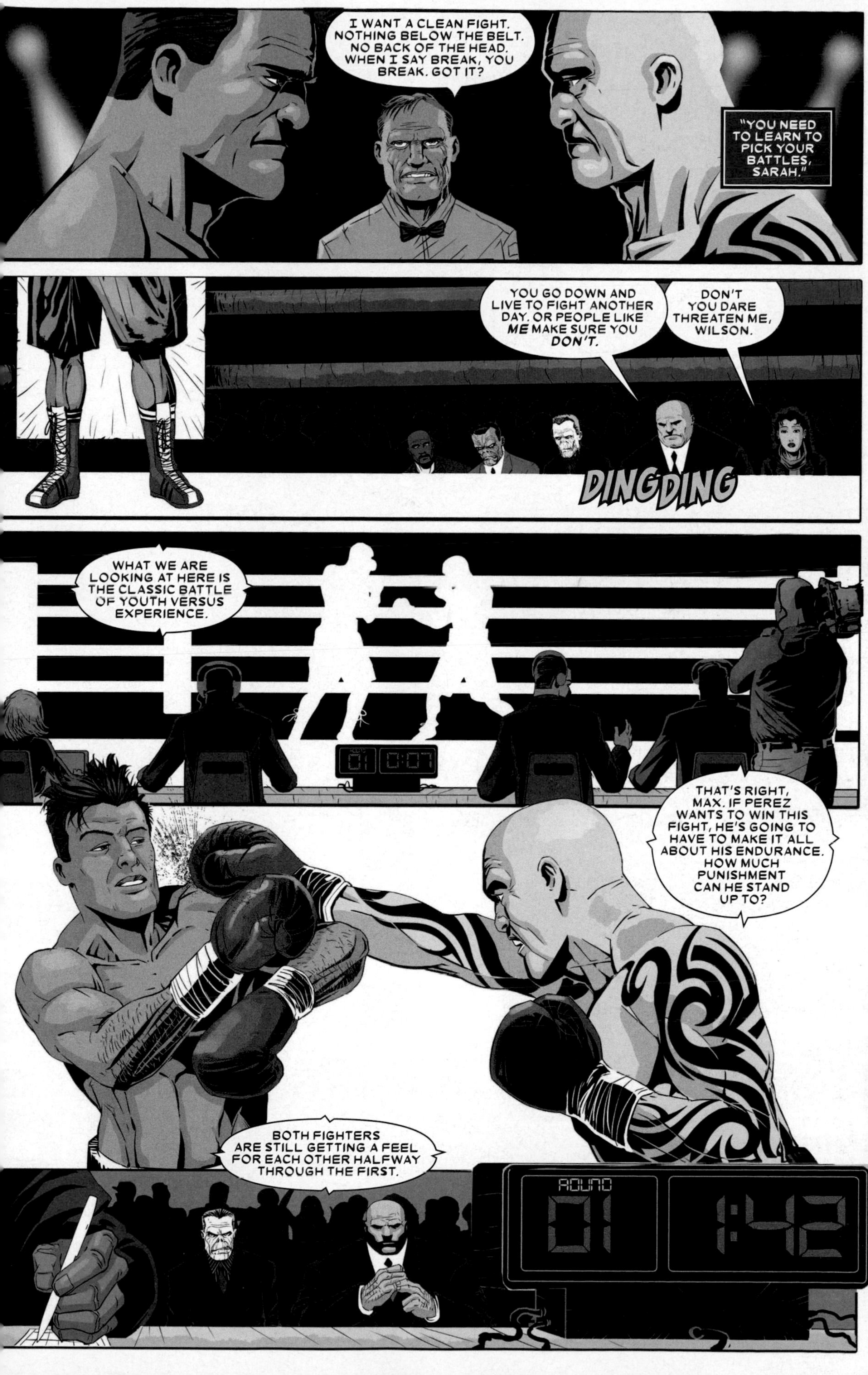
I WANT A CLEAN FIGHT. NOTHING BELOW THE BELT. NO BACK OF THE HEAD. WHEN I SAY BREAK, YOU BREAK. GOT IT?
"YOU NEED TO LEARN TO PICK YOUR BATTLES, SARAH."
YOU GO DOWN AND LIVE TO FIGHT ANOTHER DAY. OR PEOPLE LIKE ME MAKE SURE YOU DON'T.
DON'T YOU DARE THREATEN ME, WILSON.
DING DING
WHAT WE ARE LOOKING AT HERE IS THE CLASSIC BATTLE OF YOUTH VERSUS EXPERIENCE.
THAT'S RIGHT, MAX. IF PEREZ WANTS TO WIN THIS FIGHT, HE'S GOING TO HAVE TO MAKE IT ALL ABOUT HIS ENDURANCE. HOW MUCH PUNISHMENT CAN HE STAND UP TO?
BOTH FIGHTERS ARE STILL GETTING A FEEL FOR EACH OTHER HALFWAY THROUGH THE FIRST.
ROUND
01 1:42

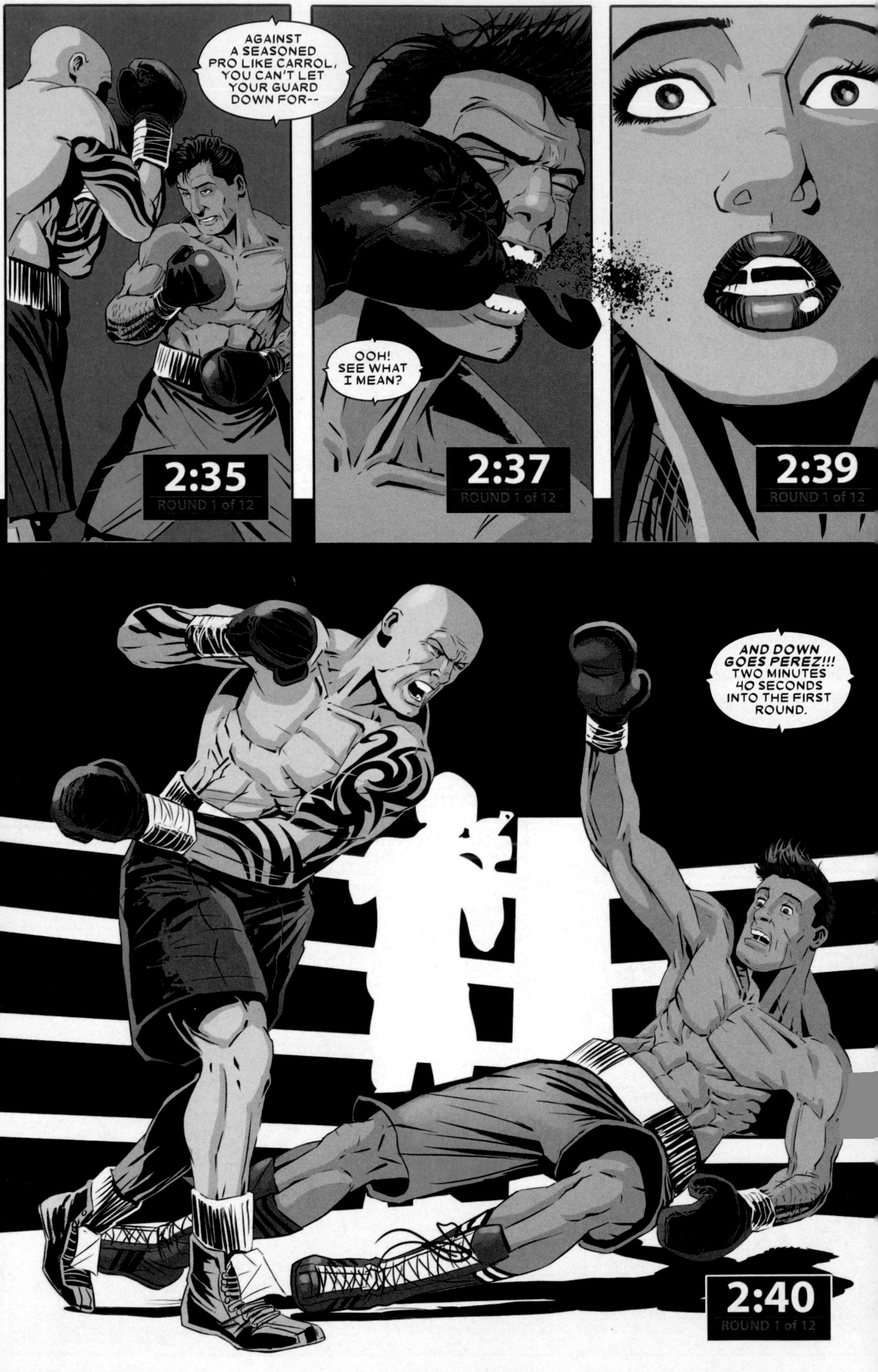
AGAINST A SEASONED PRO LIKE CARROL, YOU CAN'T LET YOUR GUARD DOWN FOR--
2:35
ROUND 1 of 12
OOH! SEE WHAT I MEAN?
2:37
ROUND 1 of 12
2:39
ROUND 1 of 12
AND DOWN GOES PEREZ!!! TWO MINUTES 40 SECONDS INTO THE FIRST ROUND.
2:40
ROUND 1 of 12

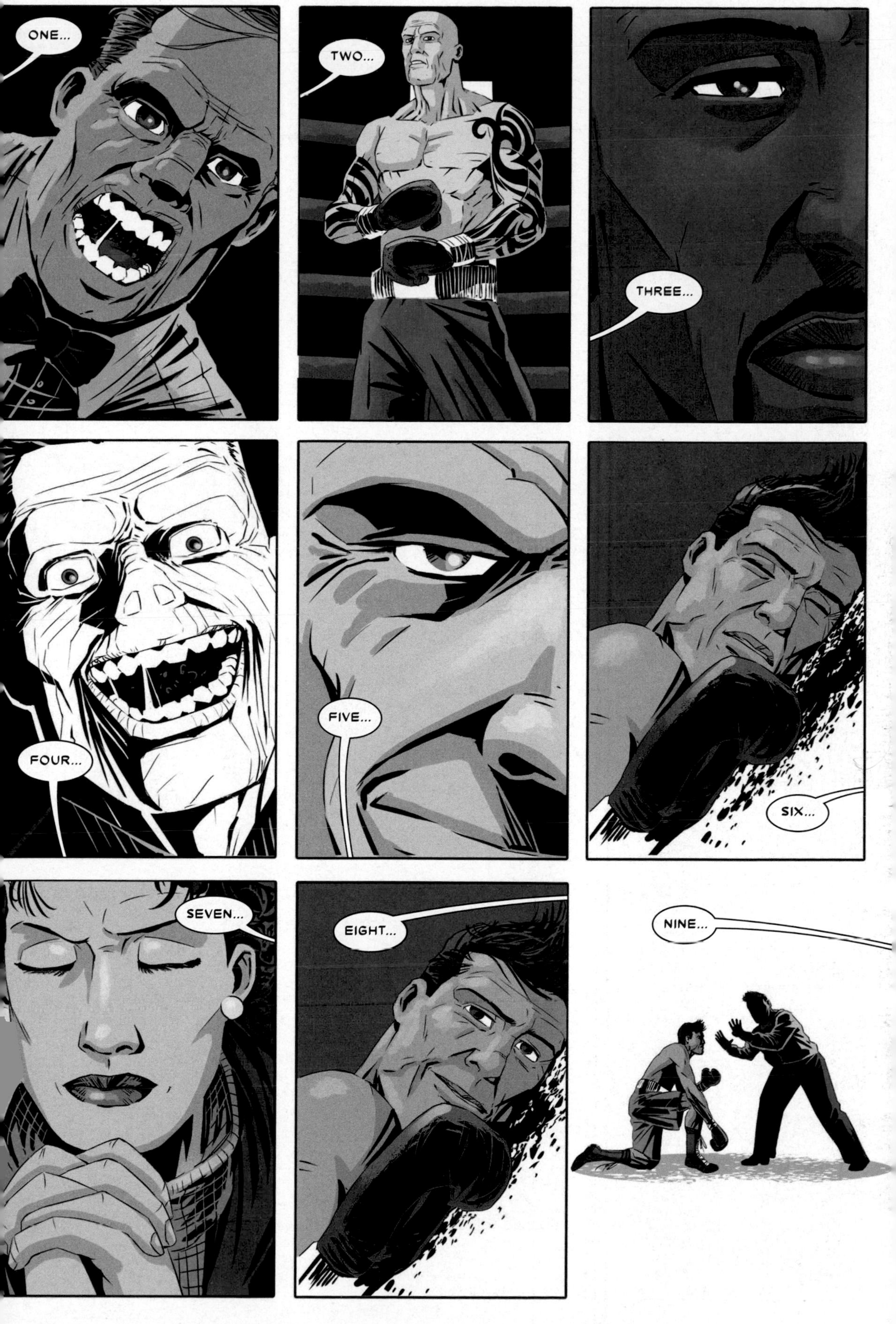
ONE...
TWO...
THREE...
FOUR...
FIVE...
SIX...
SEVEN...
EIGHT...
NINE...

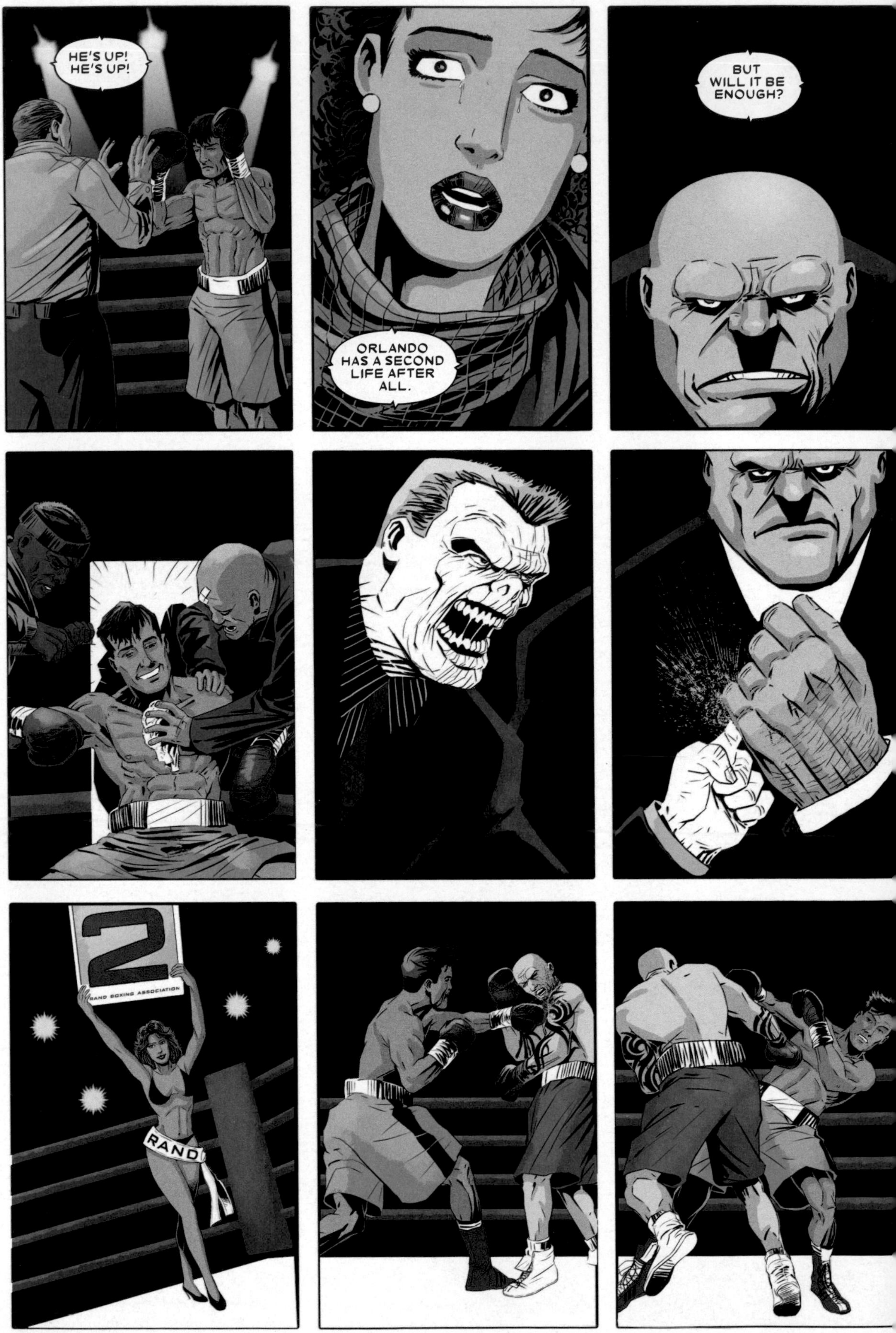
HE'S UP! HE'S UP!
ORLANDO HAS A SECOND LIFE AFTER ALL.
BUT WILL IT BE ENOUGH?
2
RAND BOXING ASSOCIATION
RAND

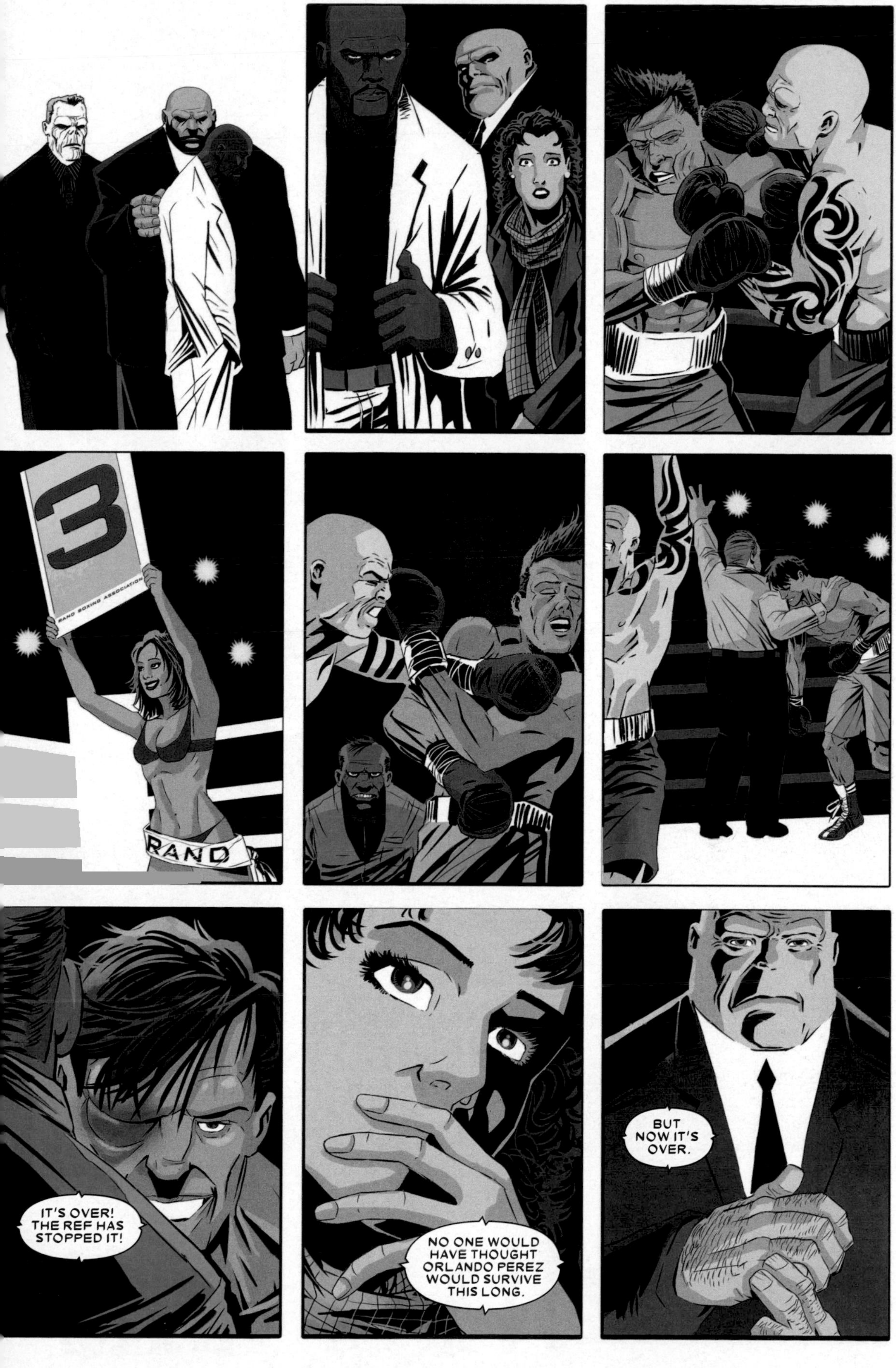
3
RAND BOXING ASSOCIATION
RAND
IT'S OVER! THE REF HAS STOPPED IT!
NO ONE WOULD HAVE THOUGHT ORLANDO PEREZ WOULD SURVIVE THIS LONG.
BUT NOW IT'S OVER.

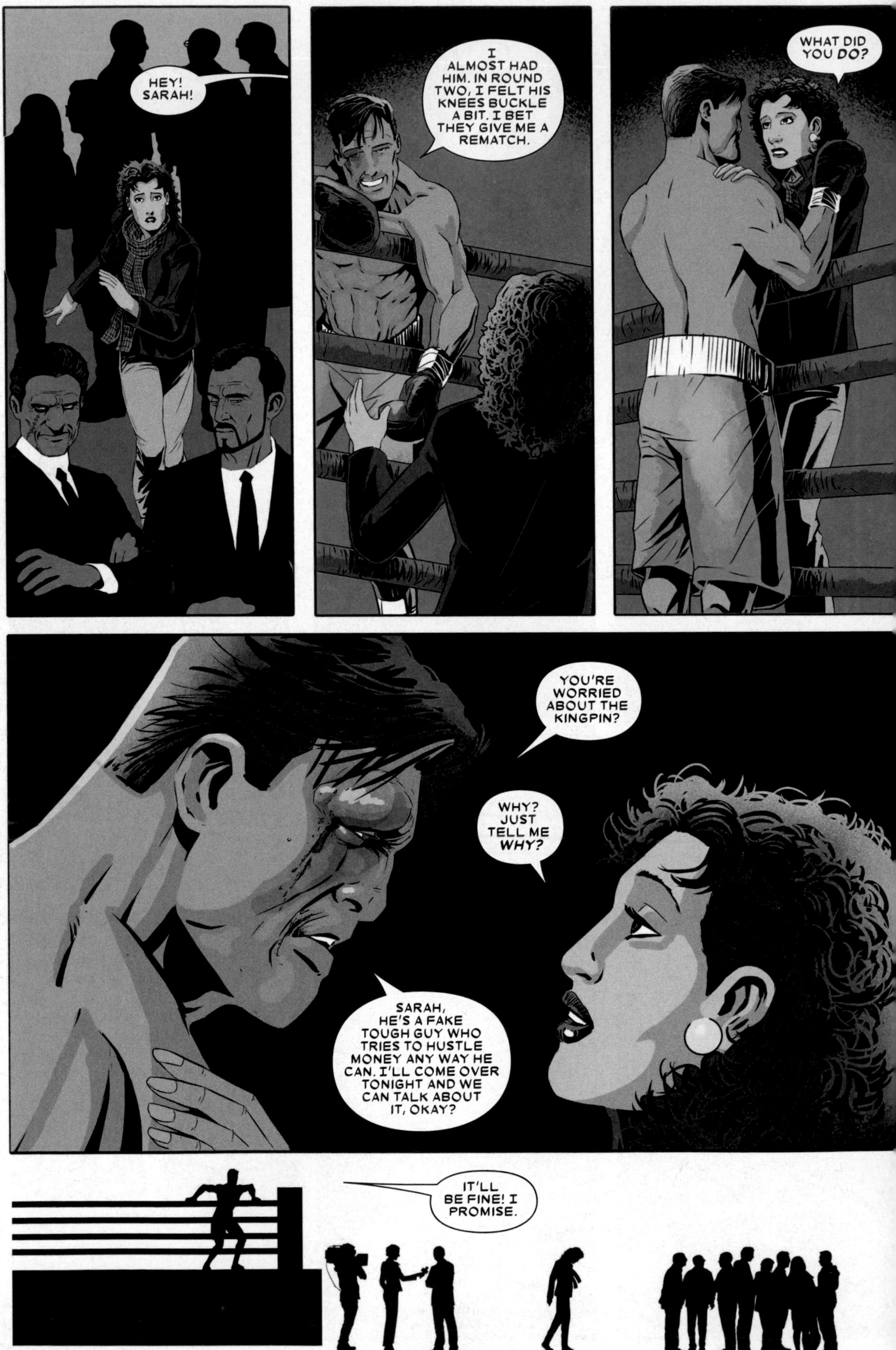
HEY! SARAH!
I ALMOST HAD HIM. IN ROUND TWO, I FELT HIS KNEES BUCKLE A BIT. I BET THEY GIVE ME A REMATCH.
WHAT DID YOU DO?
YOU'RE WORRIED ABOUT THE KINGPIN?
WHY? JUST TELL ME WHY?
SARAH, HE'S A FAKE TOUGH GUY WHO TRIES TO HUSTLE MONEY ANY WAY HE CAN. I'LL COME OVER TONIGHT AND WE CAN TALK ABOUT IT, OKAY?
IT'LL BE FINE! I PROMISE.

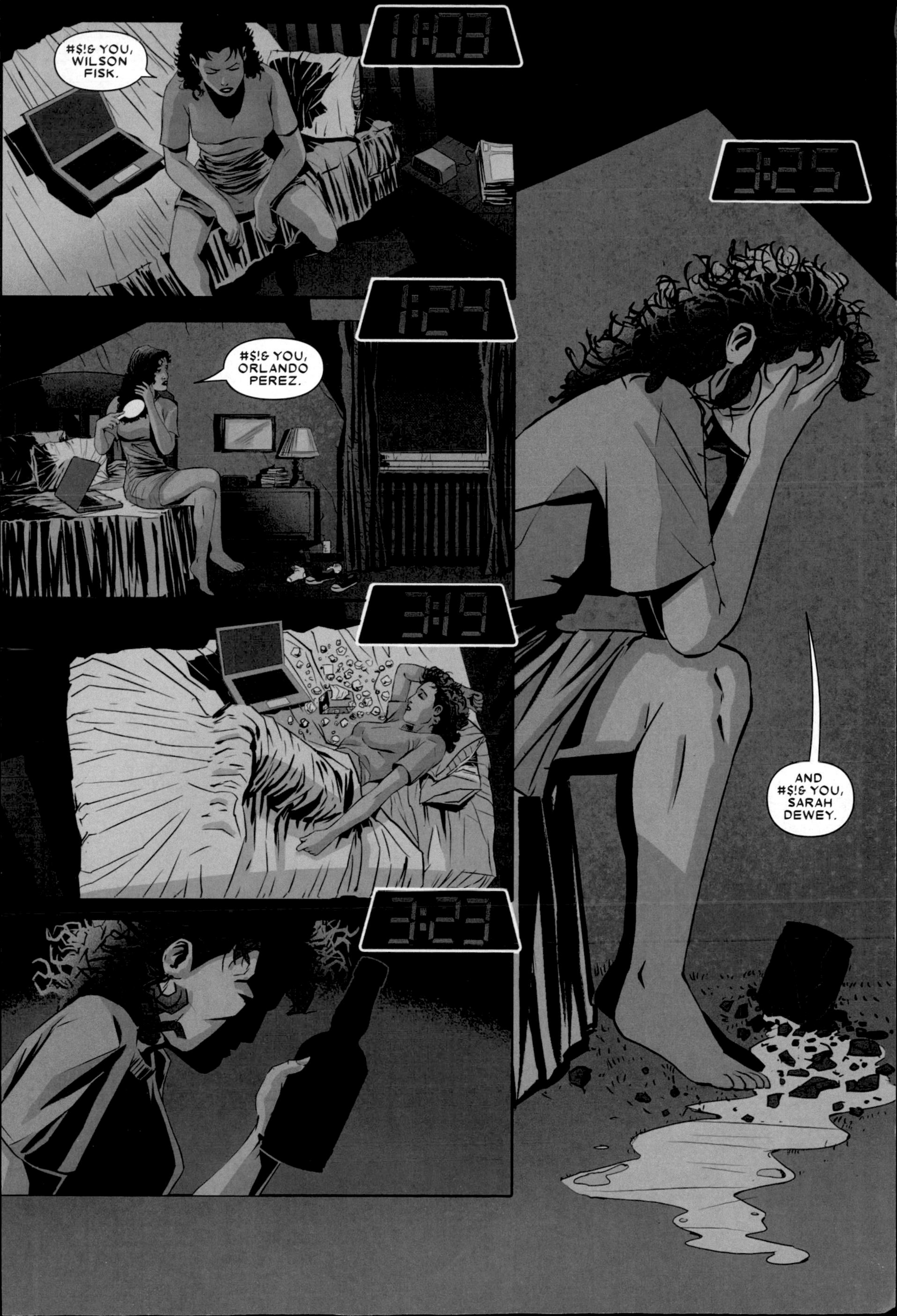

11:03
#$!& YOU, WILSON FISK.
1:24
#$!& YOU, ORLANDO PEREZ.
3:19
3:23
3:25
AND #$!& YOU, SARAH DEWEY.

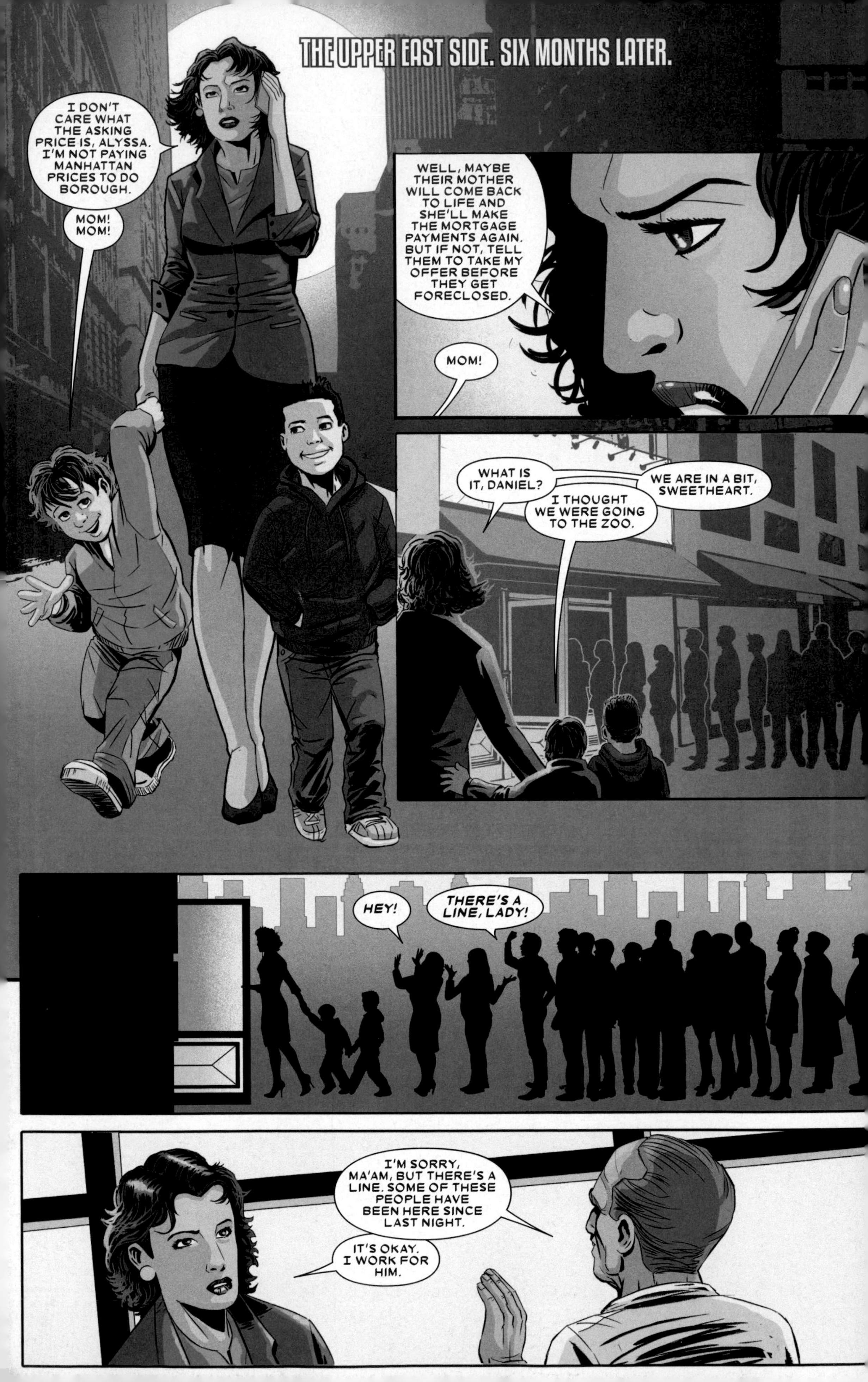
THE UPPER EAST SIDE. SIX MONTHS LATER.
I DON'T CARE WHAT THE ASKING PRICE IS, ALYSSA. I'M NOT PAYING MANHATTAN PRICES TO DO BOROUGH.
MOM! MOM!
WELL, MAYBE THEIR MOTHER WILL COME BACK TO LIFE AND SHE'LL MAKE THE MORTGAGE PAYMENTS AGAIN. BUT IF NOT, TELL THEM TO TAKE MY OFFER BEFORE THEY GET FORECLOSED.
MOM!
WHAT IS IT, DANIEL?
I THOUGHT WE WERE GOING TO THE ZOO.
WE ARE IN A BIT, SWEETHEART.
HEY!
THERE'S A LINE, LADY!
I'M SORRY, MA'AM, BUT THERE'S A LINE. SOME OF THESE PEOPLE HAVE BEEN HERE SINCE LAST NIGHT.
IT'S OKAY. I WORK FOR HIM.

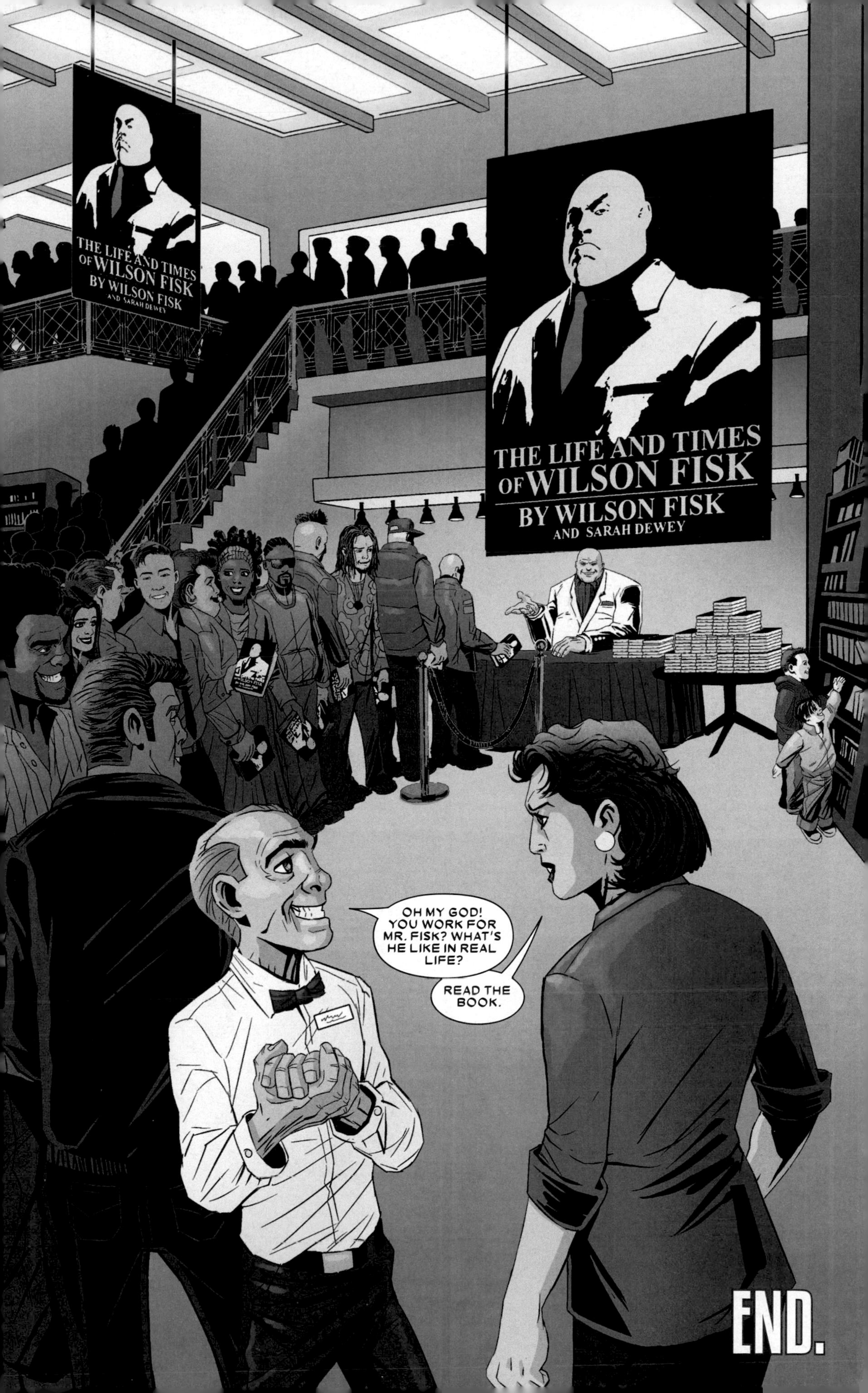
THE LIFE AND TIMES OF WILSON FISK
BY WILSON FISK
AND SARAH DEWEY
THE LIFE AND TIMES OF WILSON FISK
BY WILSON FISK
AND SARAH DEWEY
OH MY GOD! YOU WORK FOR MR. FISK? WHAT'S HE LIKE IN REAL LIFE?
READ THE BOOK.
END.

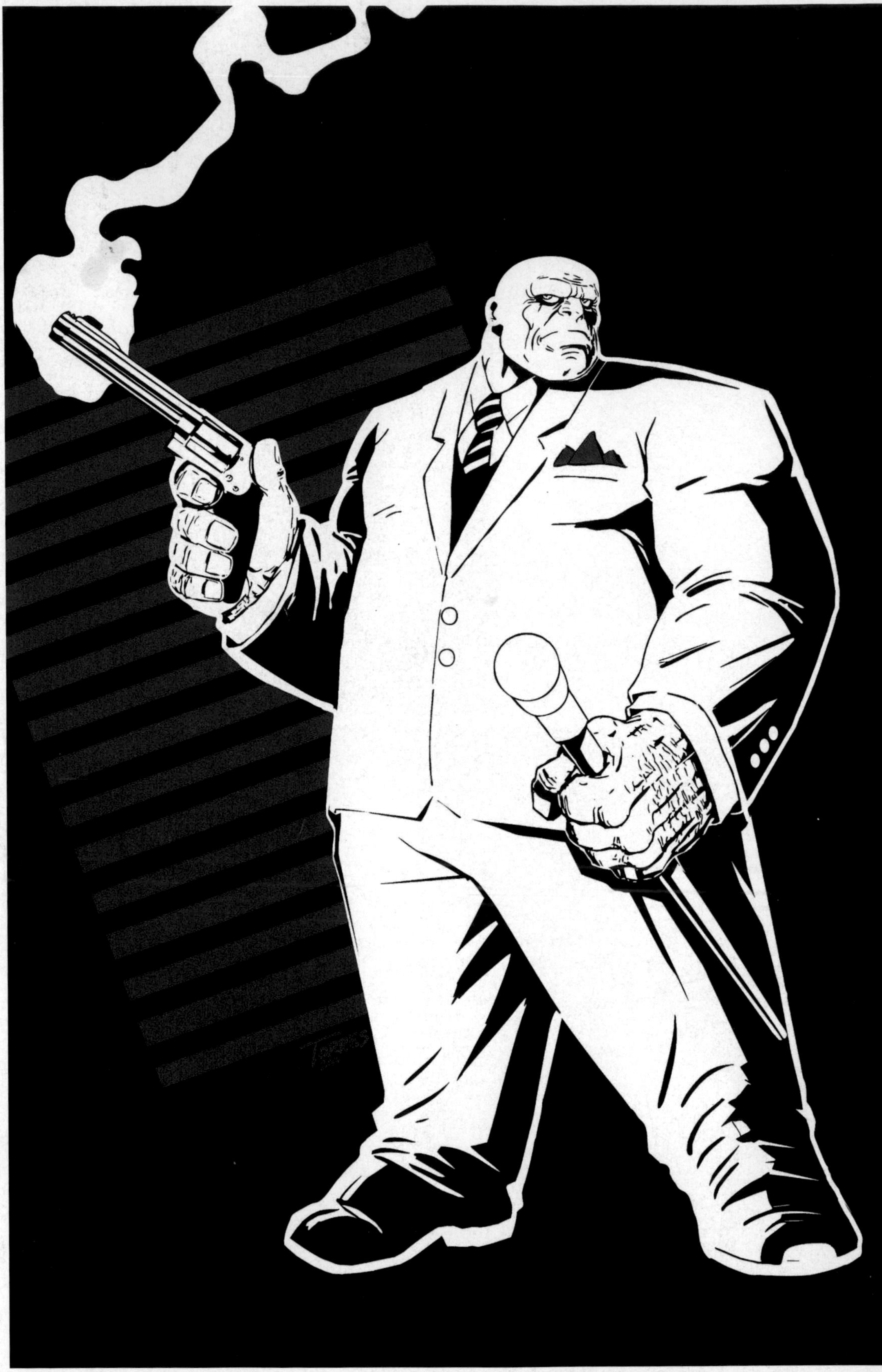

BEN TORRES

1 VARIANT

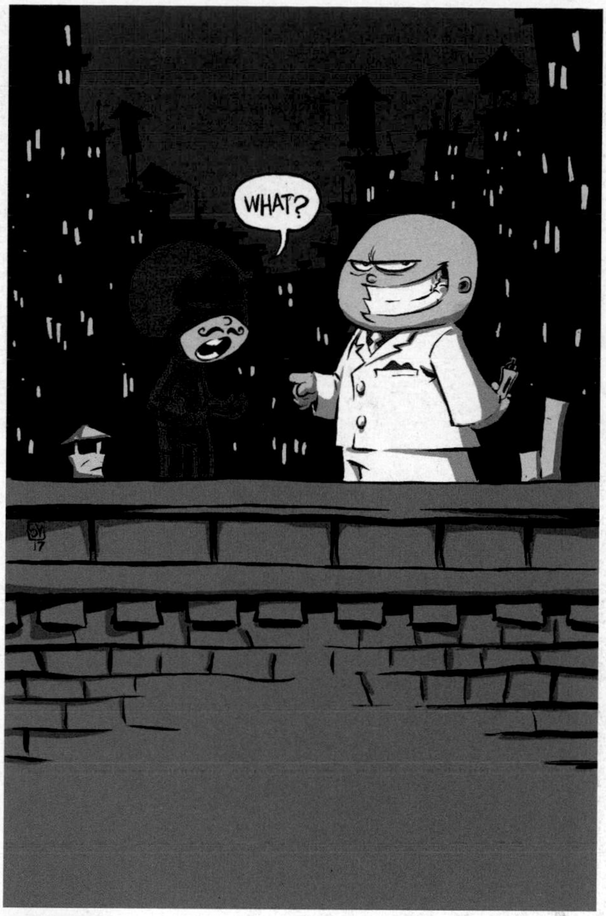
WHAT?

SKOTTIE YOUNG
1 VARIANT

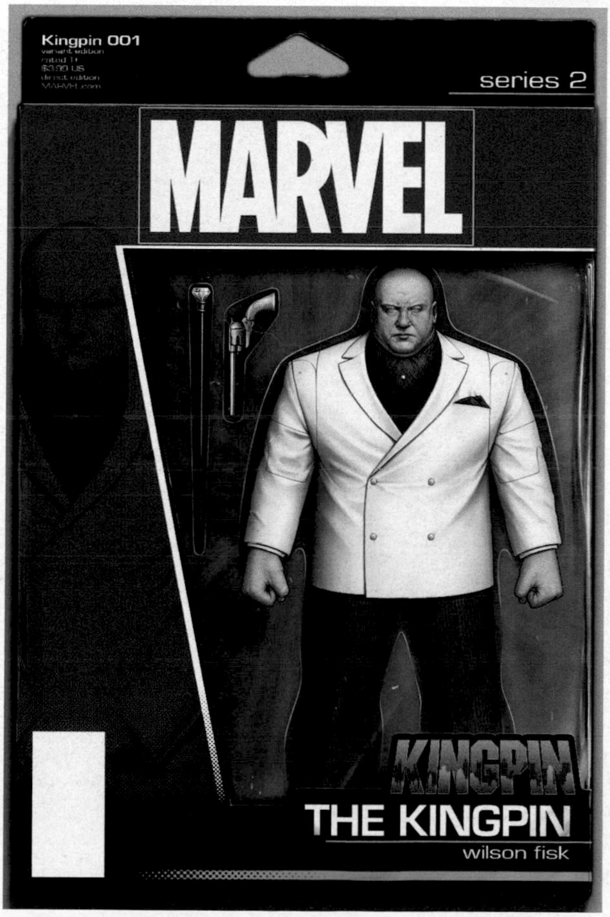
Kingpin 001
series 2
MARVEL
KINGPIN
THE KINGPIN
wilson fisk

JOHN TYLER CHRISTOPHER
1 ACTION FIGURE VARIANT

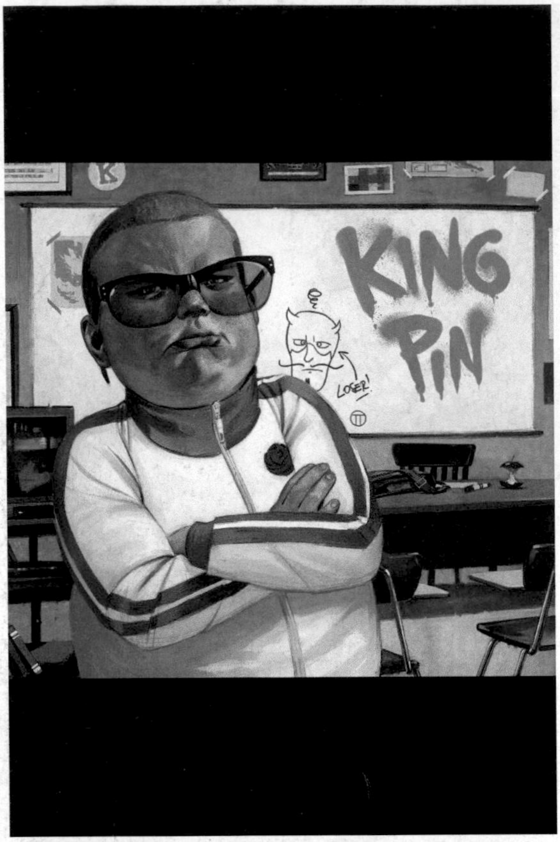
KING PIN
LOSER!

JULIAN TOTINO TEDESCO
1 HIP-HOP VARIANT

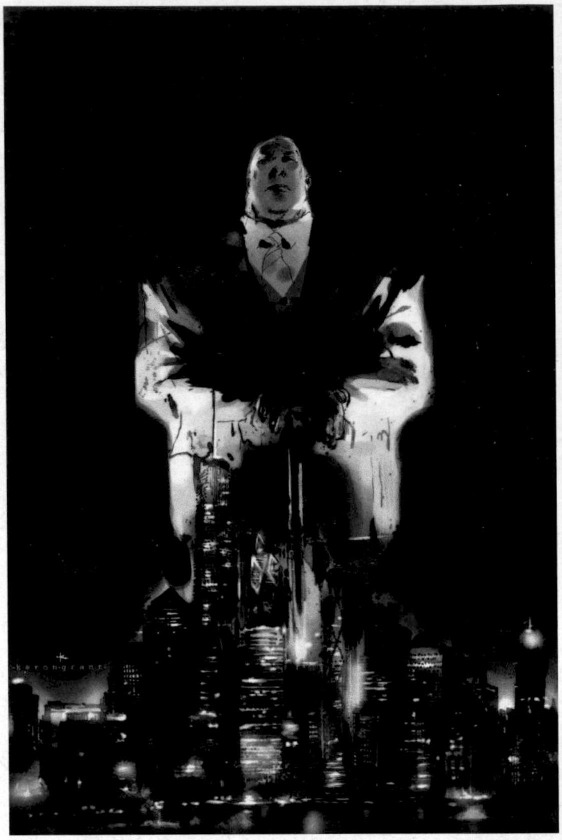

KERON GRANT
1 VARIANT

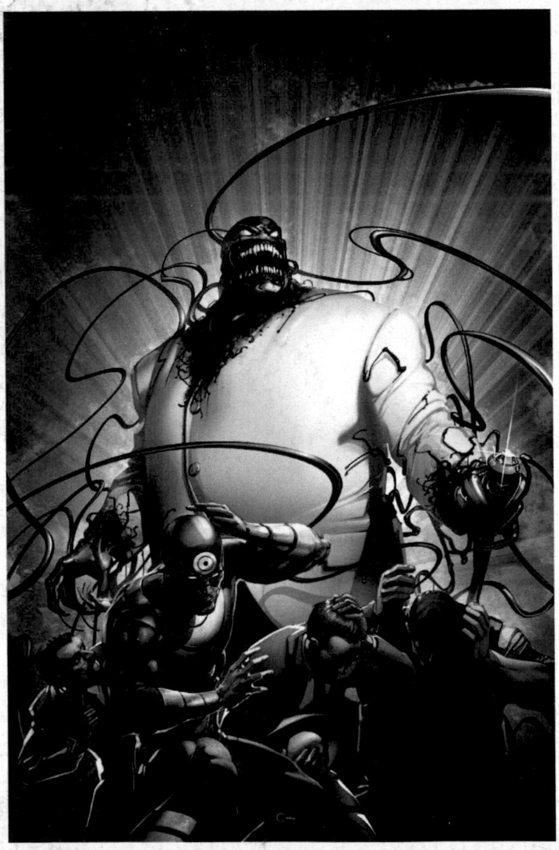

CLAYTON CRAIN
2 VENOMIZED VARIANT

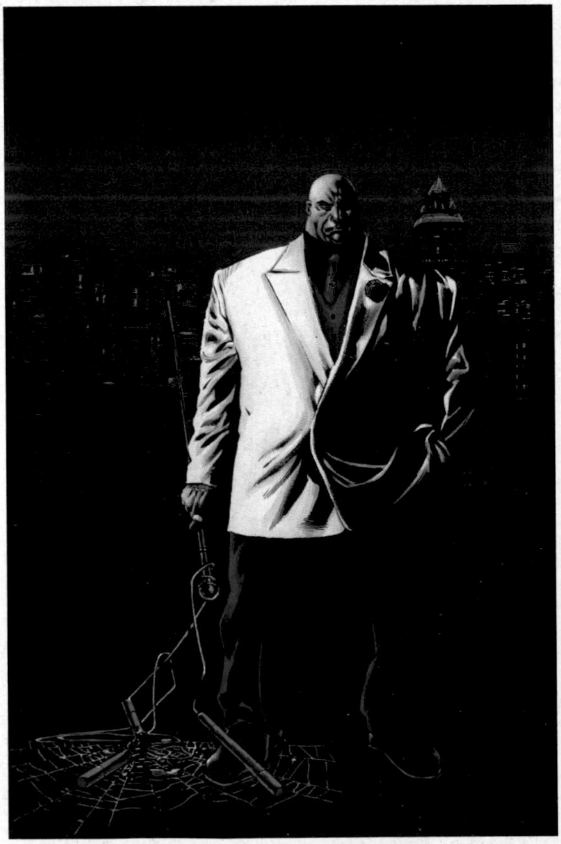

MIKE PERKINS & ANDY TROY
3 VARIANT